A SILENT CURE

TRANSFORMING PRE-VERBAL TRAUMA THROUGH MEDITATION

GINGER CLARKSON

A SILENT CURE
TRANSFORMING PRE-VERBAL TRAUMA
THROUGH MEDITATION

velvet spring press

Velvet Spring Press, Boulder, CO, USA

Copyright © 2007 Ginger Clarkson

ISBN: 978-0-9771232-2-3

Printed in the United States of America.

Design Coordinator: Leonel Del Angel.
Designed by Daniela Del Angel, Felipe Romano.

www.VelvetSpringPress.com

Proceeds from this book will be donated to
Spirit Rock Meditation Center.

DEDICATION

This book is dedicated to my six creative and resilient nieces and nephews, who are transmuting our family history and learning how to be of service in the world:

Laetia Livingston Kress
Whitney Leigh McGiffin Kress
Schuyler Alexander Laird
Elena Lomax Laird
Emily Elizabeth Clarkson
Matthew Austrian Clarkson

ACKNOWLEDGMENTS

This book would not have been possible without the support of my meditation teachers, Jack Kornfield, Julie Wester, and Robert Hall, who reviewed early drafts of the manuscript and made helpful suggestions for revisions. I am profoundly grateful to my husband, Mark B. Ryan, for his steady encouragement and meticulous editing, which inspired me to further refine my writing. Mark also deserves credit for the photograph of the author. I thank Leonel Del Angel for his sensitivity in designing the layout of the book. Doreen Schweizer kindly granted me permission to use her lovely photograph entitled "Sunrise" on the front cover. John Kadlecek had enough faith in me to publish my story. I bow to all the staff, teachers and fellow yogis at Spirit Rock Meditation Center. Thanks go to my sangha in Cholula, Mexico for supporting my regular dharma practice.

CONTENTS

PROLOGUE

I s it possible to rework the past? Do we have the capacity to recall long forgotten injuries and to reconstruct the foundation of our lives? Can we free ourselves from habitual chains? This is a story about the possibility of healing early childhood trauma — even wounds that occurred before the development of language — within the shelter of a prolonged, silent, Vipassana meditation retreat.

Vipassana (or "insight") is an advanced form of meditation that involves becoming aware of the processes of the mind through careful observation. Its practitioners believe that insight meditation helps them to go beyond knowing information and to reach wisdom through deeply understanding the true nature of phenomena. The discipline of Vipassana is associated with the Buddhist tradition called Theravada, which, in the Pali language of the Buddha's original discourses, means "Teachings of the Elders." Known as the "Small Vehicle," Theravada is practiced principally today in Sri Lanka, Thailand, and Burma, where conservative monks are dedicated to observing the rules and preserving the principles of the Buddha's oral teachings ("suttas" in Pali or "sutras" in Sanskrit) from the fifth century B.C.E. Theravada contrasts with the later, less orthodox school of Buddhism, Mahayana or "Great Vehicle," which is more inclusive of lay practitioners, and which spread through northern India to China, Tibet, Korea, Japan and Vietnam. Vajrayana (Sanskrit for "Diamond Vehicle") is a third, still later and more mystical school that involves intense visualization practices. Today His Holiness the Dalai Lama, exiled Tibetan leader, is one of the best-known adherents of the latter tradition.

In the 1960's and 70's, Buddhist masters from these three schools began teaching in the United States, where the atmosphere was more welcoming than in their war-torn homelands. In that era, a group of intellectually curious, predominantly Jewish Westerners who found mysticism inaccessible in their own religions were seeking direct contact with receptive teachers of wisdom in other spiritual traditions (Kamenetz, 1994, p. 148). My Vipassana teacher, Jack Kornfield, was drawn to Buddhist practice while he was working with the Peace Corps in Cambodia. Later he ordained as a Theravada Buddhist monk and for six years studied with various masters, including Ajahn Chaa and Ajahn Buddhasa in forest monasteries in Thailand and the venerable Mahasi Sayadaw in Burma. Jack returned to the United States and in the summer of 1974, with Joseph Goldstein and Sharon Salzberg, offered dharma teachings to Westerners at the Naropa Institute, in Boulder, Colorado. It was a remarkable gathering, presided over by Naropa's founder ChöghamTrungpa Rinpoche, a Tibetan master of "crazy wisdom," and attended by such illustrious teachers and authors as Reb Zalmon Schachter, a charismatic leader of the Jewish renewal movement; Ram Dass, an American Hindu guru; and the Beat poet Allen Ginsberg. Not long afterwards, in 1975, Jack, Joseph and Sharon joined with Jaqueline Schwartz, another "Jubu," to found the Insight Meditation Society in Barre, Massachusetts. Before his death in 1982, the dharma master, Mahasi Sayadaw, oversaw the dedication ceremony at IMS.

For independent seekers like myself, such centers as IMS offer the possibility of learning the practice of meditation without having to convert to the religion of Buddhism. Their teachers, however, are part of a continuous lineage of experienced guides who can lead practitioners progressively along a clearly mapped-out contemplative path. Jack and his colleagues are serving as a bridge between ordained, self-abnegating monks, who have been safeguarding esoteric Buddhist secrets in Asia, and egocentric American meditation students, who have jobs and families and who have opted for "temporary monasticism" in the form of periodic retreats (Kamenetz, 1994, p. 287). I am among the growing number of Western practitioners who try to balance the solitude and purity of meditative life with the distractions and temptations of secular society.

Like me, many Vipassana practitioners in the West combine meditation with some type of psychotherapy in order to enhance inner understanding. During and after my training as a music therapist, I have had numerous sessions of Jungian dream analysis, Gestalt therapy, Core Energetics bodywork, Authentic Movement, Stan and Christina Grof's Holotropic Breathwork, and the Bonny Method of Guided Imagery and Music (GIM). In different ways, each of these forms of psychotherapy has helped me integrate insights and cope with difficult psychodynamic material arising during intensive periods of meditation. On a month-long retreat in 2003, in spite of my long history of self-examination, I found myself inundated by early sensorial memories, reliving sensations and emotions from a two-month period when I was a year-and-a-half old. It was not until after I left the retreat that I learned about the concept of pre-verbal trauma and various forms of therapy that have evolved to treat it.

Pre-verbal trauma refers to injury or shock that is experienced before the development of language, so that it is impossible to articulate associated feelings. A number of treatment modalities have arisen to help people work through aftereffects of pre-verbal wounds, such as those stemming from physical or sexual abuse, neglect, abandonment, bodily injury, or invasive medical intervention.

In the 1960's, Arthur Janov founded the Primal Institute in Los Angeles to help patients suffering from early childhood trauma. He encouraged clients to regress and express their grief and pain through "primal screams" and extreme physical movements in order to release energy blockages in the body. Jules Roth was the original director of therapist training at the Institute. His wife Helen was one of the first patients and therapists at the Institute to recognize the value of re-experiencing birth and in-utero history, at a time when Janov himself did not believe that patients could truly relive birth trauma. Helen and Jules parted ways with Janov and started the Primal Therapy Center of Denver, which applies Janov's methods but emphasizes in-utero and birth trauma (Wareham, 2003).

Bill Swartley, a Canadian who invented in the 1970's a form of personal growth work called Primal Integration, is another therapist who believes that trauma that occurs before, during and soon after birth influences how people interpret and cope with all future experience. Unlike Primal therapists, who guide patients' work, Primary Integration facilitators encourage clients to direct the exploration of their own psyches and allow vocalizations and body movements to emerge naturally (Rowan, 1988).

One of today's leading authorities on healing trauma is Peter A. Levine, a former student of the acclaimed body-worker Ida Rolf, and the author of *Waking the Tiger*. According to Levine, trauma is a common experience that can be healed and can result in transformation. In his view, post-traumatic stress disorder (PTSD) is not a "pathology that needs to be managed, suppressed, or adjusted to, but the result of a natural process gone awry." He relates "developmental trauma" to "psychologically based issues that are usually a result of inadequate nurturing and guidance through critical developmental periods during childhood" (1997, pp. 2, 3, 6, 10).

Levine believes that trauma, developmental or otherwise, can never be fully healed without the patient's being aware of how the "body is experiencing emotions in the form of sensations and thoughts." He warns against using cathartic approaches such as primal therapies, fearing that they can "re-traumatize" and/or "create dependency on continuing catharsis and encourage the emergence of so-called 'false memories.'" His method, called *Somatic Experiencing*, helps patients use the "felt sense" of their own organism to find their innate capacity to heal (1997, pp. 7, 10, 12).

Levine reminds us that "the involuntary and instinctual portions of the human brain and nervous system are virtually identical to those of other mammals and even reptiles." Our "triune brain" consists of the instinctual reptilian brain; the limbic or mammalian brain, home to our emotions; and the neo-cortex or rational human brain. It is Levine's belief that all animals, including humans, have a repertoire of three primary responses to overwhelming threat: fight, flight, and freezing or immobility. By freezing, an animal of prey can "play dead" and fool its attacker, and it can enter into "an altered state in which no pain is experienced." If their pursuer becomes distracted, animals have the capacity to awaken from their frozen state and escape. Once free, the animal usually "literally shakes off the residual effects of the immobility response and gains full control of its body." Unfortunately, humans tend to be afraid of immobility and avoid it because it is considered a sign of weakness or cowardice, and "because it is a state very similar to death" (1997, pp. 16,17). Instead, they develop a state of hyper-arousal in an unconscious attempt to defend themselves from reliving panic or anxiety related to shock.

The irony is that re-enactments of trauma occur no matter how well we try to protect ourselves. Levine states,

> *The drive to complete and heal trauma is as powerful and tenacious as the symptoms it creates. The urge to resolve trauma through re-enactment can be severe and compulsive. We are inextricably drawn into situations that replicate the original trauma in both obvious and unobvious ways* (1997, p. 173).

By making a distinction between unconscious re-enactment (associated with the reptilian brain), and conscious renegotiation (associated with the neo-cortex), therapists trained in Somatic Experiencing emphasize the crucial importance of consciousness in the healing process. Unlike animals, humans are capable of being *consciously* aware of inner experience. If we can slow down and follow the felt sense of all the sensations and feelings that accompany traumatic patterns, allowing them to complete themselves, "we begin to access and transform the drives and motivations that otherwise compel us to re-enact traumatic events" (1997, p. 187).

Levine's method entails trusting the "inner healer" in clients and encouraging them to talk about details, no matter how vaguely recalled, related to a traumatic event. As clients are recounting a scary experience, they often become agitated and start sweating, with more rapid breathing and heart rate. At this point, the therapist asks the client to stop talking and to focus on body sensations, which frequently include shaking and trembling. Levine assures his clients that this type of response is a natural way for the body to discharge energy related to trauma. He helps clients become conscious of and slowly explore any reactions and spontaneous body movements that arise. After about an hour's work, the client's breathing usually becomes easier, the heart rate is steadier, and the extremities are warmer. In this state of energetic discharge, most people report a feeling of relief. Sometimes the Somatic therapist will schedule an additional session or sessions to bring a client back to the traumatic scene, until the trauma has been fully discharged from the neurological system (1997, pp. 237-240). Levine's Somatic Experiencing and offshoots, such as William Redpath's

"Trauma Energetics" and Linda Edwards' "Somatic Hypnotherapy," allow traumatized people to express nonverbal feelings and to release excess neurochemical energy (Redpath, 1995 and Edwards, 2002).

In the following pages, I report my own experience of regression, disintegration, healing, and re-integration during a Vipassana retreat. Very like Levine's Somatic Experiencing, Vipassana focuses on consciously tracking body sensations, feelings and thoughts as they are surfacing. With the skillful support of male and female teachers whom I trusted to act in the role of good parents, and in the protected container of the retreat, I was able to work through feelings of fear and abandonment. I emerged with a sense of renewal, forgiveness and gratitude for the blessings in my life. In retrospect, I recognize that I had been preparing subconsciously for this radical form of recovery since my pre-teen years.

My mother honored my eleventh birthday by giving me my first diary, a small, leather-bound, golden-hued journal with a key to guard its secret contents. I recall my delight in carefully penning the initial entry, the start of forty-five years of filling a series of journals of various colors and sizes. In my mid-fifties, I still have a journal at bedside to record dreams, memories and reflections. My husband has become accustomed to awakening to the sound of scribbling at dawn. As far back as I can remember I have been drawn to spiritual and esoteric concerns, and I have written about my inner life. The early diaries contain reflections about homesickness, adolescent longings, and new friendships formed at Miss Porter's School, an elite New England boarding school for girls of high school age. More than once, "house mothers" in the dormitories scolded me for writing in my diary after the 9:30 p.m. curfew.

I have an ongoing impulse to understand the workings of my mind and to examine my purpose in life. Over time, my spiritual life has diverged increasingly from traditional religious frameworks. Raised as an Episcopalian, I questioned the words of the Creed soon after memorizing them for my confirmation ceremony. I began to verbally edit prayers and to recite only the words I believed. By the time I attended Wheaton College in Massachusetts, I had virtually stopped attending church. Yet I longed for spiritual community. In my search for a more compatible religious refuge, I visited Catholic churches, Quaker meetinghouses, and Jewish synagogues. While I was completing a Master's degree in music therapy at New York University, I read about Buddhism and Sufism. Later on, I was married in a Unitarian church near Yale University, where my husband was a professor and residential college dean, and where I taught music therapy seminars. I appreciated the Unitarian lack of dogma and emphasis on tolerance towards all people regardless of spiritual background. However, despite feeling intellectually stimulated by the sermons and sensing common values with the congregation, I missed a mystical, more experiential element.

I found some of that missing ingredient in my work as a music therapist in New Haven, Connecticut. For twenty-five years my professional focus was autism. While improvising songs to communicate with nonverbal students, I felt connected with the essential beings underlying seemingly crazy behavior. When my husband and I moved to Puebla, Mexico to teach at the Universidad de las Américas (UDLA), I paid tribute to my remarkable former students with a book called *I Dreamed I Was Normal*. My work now centers on conducting a private music psychotherapy practice and leading international trainings in the Bonny Method of Guided Imagery and Music. In this transpersonal therapy technique, classical music selections evoke imagery, memories, emotions, and body sensations in a kind of waking dream. The music often awakens the unconscious wisdom of GIM "travelers," who gain insight into problems and dilemmas. It is the capacity that music has for transcending barriers within and among human beings that continues to inspire me as a music therapist.

Alongside my professional path, meditation has become an integral part of my life. While I was pursuing graduate studies in 1970, I began practicing Transcendental Meditation (TM), brought to the United States by an Indian master named Maharishi Mahesh Yogi. During my initiation ceremony in the basement of a building on New York University's downtown campus, I laid offerings of flowers and a clean white handkerchief in front of the statue of a Hindu deity. Then a white-clad TM teacher intoned two syllables in Sanskrit several times. With a solemn expression, he instructed me to memorize the sound and thenceforth to repeat it silently to myself as a mantra for meditating. I was warned that if I ever divulged the secret of my particular mantra, it would lose its energetic power to help my mind concentrate. Although I am notoriously bad at keeping secrets, nobody has yet learned my TM mantra. For several years, I sat with eyes closed for twenty minutes each morning and afternoon and attempted to keep my mind focused on the internal sound. The first time I tried Transcendental Meditation, I was astounded by the mental and sensorial clarity that resulted. I remember walking through Washington Square, where the sounds of birds seemed amplified and the colors of trees and flowers appeared radiant. I felt such a strong surge of energy in my body that I stayed awake that whole night to write a term paper and felt no fatigue the following day. It was as if all my senses had been cleansed. These dramatic effects did not recur, however, and gradually I neglected the discipline of meditating.

But my longing for a daily spiritual practice did not disappear. In 1988, I heard about the Insight Meditation Society in Massachusetts and signed up for my first Vipassana retreat. For nine days I did my best to apply instructions originally transmitted by the Buddha himself: concentrate on the breath rising and falling; make a note of distracting thoughts, feelings or physical sensations; and return repeatedly to the breath. In what the Buddha referred to as "Noble Silence," I found a spiritual home.

Almost every evening since that time, my husband and I have been sitting quietly for a half hour to help maintain our balance in a complex and rapidly changing world. I guide a weekly meditation class for students and professors at the Mexican university where we teach. Over the past few years, I studied Buddhist philosophy in the Community Dharma Leader training program at Spirit Rock Meditation Center in Woodacre, California, north of San Franciscio, and I have attended three of the month-long, silent retreats conducted there each March by Jack Kornfield and other Vipassana teachers.

This is my story of what transpired during the spring retreat of 2003, followed by a retrospective analysis. In the first ten chapters, I attempt to report the feelings, sensations, mental states, and relationships just as I experienced them on the retreat. Drawing from pages of extensive journaling during the month of meditation, I re-enter the inner journey that I took. Unlike precise transcripts or tape recordings, the journal notes capture my own interpretations rather than a literal account of what the dharma teachers said. The teachers' remarks are paraphrased rather than quoted. In these initial chapters, there is no pretense of objective distancing or hindsight. The subsequent chapters are more reflective: they provide my later assessment of the retreat experience, as well as a review of current psychological theories that support my thesis: meditation can benefit those who have suffered preverbal trauma. Finally, in an epilogue, I convey how my newfound calm and tranquility during the March retreat a year later was possible because of the stormy regression and integration that preceded it.

I now have a more objective perspective on my inner journey in March of 2003. With the passage of time, I am aware, for example, that I unconsciously projected aspects of myself onto teachers and other meditators, and that I transferred onto interactions with them elements from past relationships. Psychologically, transference occurs when a person replicates in a present relationship patterns learned in the past. When I abandoned my ego, I relied on two principle dharma teachers, Jack and Julie, as surrogate parents, to help contain my energy and limit my excesses. Unready to take responsibility for my own inner knowing, I gave my teachers credit for any wisdom that guided me.

After integrating the retreat experiences in therapy sessions, journal entries, and discussions with my husband and close friends, I recognize that I had cast Jack and Julie in the roles of idealized parents. As part of my healing journey, I idolized them and accepted their counsel uncritically. It was only after the retreat that I could begin the process of establishing a more realistic relationship and mature friendship with my teachers. In my professional life as a music psychotherapist, I have been on the receiving end of both positive and negative projections from my clients. I know that it can feel just as uncomfortable to be praised and adored as it does to be unjustly criticized. The capacity of the Spirit Rock teachers to support me lovingly and to allow a period of idolization as part of my personal development serves as a model for how I treat the patients who turn to me for guidance.

What occurred at Spirit Rock in the spring of 2003 has enabled me to feel a measure of equilibrium in my daily life that I had not experienced beforehand. Meditation has been a path to cleanse wounds from the past and to find contentment in my present life. This book is written with the hope that others might benefit in similar ways. ✻

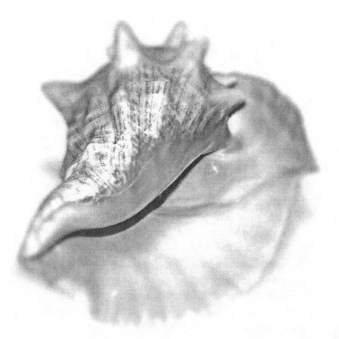

CHAPTER ONE
THRESHOLD

N oble Silence beckons me once again. Months before the annual March retreat at Spirit Rock, my dream life begins to fill with preparatory imagery. On August 30, 2002, I dream about reading aloud a poem by Jack Kornfield. The subject of the poetry is an ephemeral butterfly, and I recognize that Jack's perception is exquisitely refined by the amount of meditation that he has done over the years. I resolve to keep fine-tuning the connection between my words and my senses. I know that meditation facilitates that process.

The following dream comes to me on the morning of September 11, 2002, the first anniversary of the fall of the Twin Towers in New York City:

> *A Mexican friend and I attend a Vipassana retreat led by Jack Kornfield at Spirit Rock. Jorge and I sit on beige pillows in the first row of a series of rooms that are full of experienced meditators. Jack sits in the center of this first room, and he gives us instructions for practicing mindfulness. I feel happy to be with my spiritual teacher once again and to share the experience with Jorge, who is in his first meditation retreat in the United States. After the opening "sit," Jack walks to another building. To my dismay, Jorge and a fiery-haired Russian woman start talking. I notice other meditators chatting. I had assumed that we were on a silent retreat, but I realize that Jack made no mention of "Noble Silence" in his instructions. Seeking a quiet place, I move my pillows to the opposite side of the room. But I am now right next to a coat rack, where meditators are fetching their jackets. Again I pick up my pillows and search for a silent spot. The other rooms are so full of meditators that I decide to walk to an outdoor site that overlooks the hills and valleys of Spirit Rock. The view is stunningly beautiful. I wonder if Jack still appreciates the beauty of the meditation center that he founded. After meditating in peace, I jump down from the platform where I have been sitting. I leave behind a book about meditation and climb back up to retrieve it. On my way down to the dining hall, I pass some familiar "yogis," who have accompanied me on other retreats. Spontaneously we greet each other: "Hi." I resist the temptation to speak further. It has been such a challenge to find silence and stillness, even at Spirit Rock.*

On December 17, 2002, another pertinent dream attracts my attention:

> *I arrive at the Insight Meditation Society and find my teacher Jack sitting outside on the grass. I have just discovered that I am one of two people on the waiting list who were not accepted for the retreat that begins today. I feel disappointed, and when I speak to Jack, he says that he checked to see if I had made it into the retreat at the last moment.*

He is sad that I have not. I realize that half the appeal of being on retreat is to have personal time with Jack, and I am enjoying our talk in this present moment. This thought consoles me. Later, on, I arrive early enough at another retreat to sit in the front row of the meditation hall, close to Jack's "zafu" (meditation pillow). He tells me and a few other seasoned meditators that he was recently in the middle of a counseling session with a yogi, when her husband barged in to question Jack's interventions. Even as I empathize with my teacher about this infringement of boundaries, I realize that I have stretched out my feet in a relaxed manner, so that they are lying across Jack's zafu. I withdraw my feet, which are invading his personal space. In a silent way, Jack helps me become conscious that although I notice when other people fail to respect boundaries, I cross some boundaries myself. I feel humbled and grateful for my teacher's lesson. I become aware that many meditators have arrived, so that the hall is crowded now.

Closer to my departure time, on February 19, 2003, I have another dream about my meditation teacher:

I meet Jack, who is sitting comfortably outside on a low stool in a forest clearing. There is a seat available for me, facing him. I tell him that I am preparing to attend the March retreat at the end of next week. He smiles and says that he is pleased that we will be meditating together again. I mention that I enjoyed being with his colleague Joseph Goldstein at the community Dharma Leader training in January. Jack asks if I have heard that Joseph has arthritis. I reply that I am not surprised because I had noticed Joseph's slow, stiff body movements when I saw him. I say, "His mind is still flexible and agile." Jack and I smile at each other as we acknowledge, in concert, "We are all getting older."

The week before leaving for the retreat, I am scurrying around the campus of the Universidad de las Américas, where my husband and I live in faculty housing. I tend to last minute e-mail messages and phone calls to loved ones. I refer my music psychotherapy patients to trusted colleagues for a month of weekly sessions. My psychology and music students need reassurance that I plan to teach a course in the fall term. I buy provisions: vitamins, an alarm clock for rising before the break of day, and thermal rub for muscles that become sore from hours of sitting in meditation. I spend extra time with my husband, Mark, reassuring him that my month-long absence does not mean any diminishment in my love for him. I thank him for being so understanding about my recurring urge to embark on spiritual quests.

When departure day arrives, I feel a pang of doubt. I am leaving behind so many friends, students, and colleagues I love. I wonder if I have covered all of my professional responsibilities for the time that I will be away. As I board a bus for the two-hour ride to the Mexico City airport, I attempt to memorize the features on my husband's face. On the direct four-hour flight to San Francisco, I read articles about meditation in the fall issue of *Insight Journal*, which I have not had time to open in the rush to prepare for the retreat. After clearing customs in San Francisco, I catch the airport shuttle bus to Larkspur Landing, where two "dharma buddies," who share my dedication to meditation, kindly host me for the night. The next day Brian and his wife Betsy arrange a "farewell massage" for me before we drive at slow speed to Spirit Rock. In the car we listen to a recording by Paul Simon, the last music I will be hearing for a month.

I feel excited and nervous as we glimpse the familiar horses that graze in a paddock at the entrance to the retreat center. We all laugh appreciatively at the road sign that announces: "Yield to the present moment." We pass the small round Katiññata (Gratitude) building that commemorates Spirit Rock donors as well as Burmese, Thai, and Indian dharma masters of teachers who founded Buddhist retreat centers in the West. Further on, at a graceful wooden gate, a notice reads, "Retreatants Only Beyond This Point. Retreat Area—Retreatants Only—Silence Please." We unload my luggage and, while Brian and Betsy park their car, I spin the prayer wheel next to the gate. The Tibetan-style wheel is painted with rows of inscriptions and pictures of creatures on land, sea, and air. The top row entreats, "May all beings be well, safe from danger, held in compassion," and depicts two peaceful cows beneath a pair of doves perched on spreading tree branches. Below I read the invocation, "May all beings be liberated, safe, peaceful, happy," which accompanies colorful paintings of fish playing in the ocean. Inscribed around the wheel's base are words from the Buddha's Noble Eightfold Path, leading to enlightenment and liberation: "wise concentration," "wise attention," "wise livelihood," "wise action," "wise speech," "wise intention," "wise understanding," and "wise effort." With a burst of energy, I spin the prayer wheel and watch to see where it stops. My maxim for initiating this retreat turns out to be "wise understanding."

Brian and Betsy decide to break the rules and accompany me beyond the "point of no return" into territory reserved for retreatants. We arrive at the Council House on the dot of 3:00, just in time for registration of incoming "yogis," who are being assigned to either single or double rooms in one of four dormitories. Leaving my two companions to fend for themselves, I join a line of people waiting to choose from a list of daily tasks for "working meditation." I enlist to be on a team of three "veggie choppers" each evening for the whole month. In addition, I volunteer for an extra job as one of the bell-ringers who summon fellow meditators to forty-five minute sitting periods that mark the day between six a.m. and ten p.m. My time slot is right after lunch period, for the two o'clock "sit." The musician in me enjoys striking the tall iron gong outside the meditation hall and sensing its strong vibrations rippling through my body and echoing across the valley below.

One of the volunteer registrars mentions that my requisite Meditation Retreat Questionnaire is missing, probably lost in the Mexican mail system. I find a spot to sit and write answers to a series of questions, first listing a relative, doctor, and psychotherapist to contact in case of emergency. As I note down the dates and teachers of my previous Vipassana retreats, I recognize how often I have sought the spiritual guidance of Jack Kornfield. Regarding my motivation for doing a retreat at this time, I write about the need to integrate numerous professional activities and interpersonal events from my intense life.

Although I respond "No" to the question, "Do you have any condition or history of physical illness or physical limitations that might interfere with or might be aggravated by sitting and walking practice?" I take time answering the query, "Have you ever had or been treated for a psychological condition such as depression, eating disorder, drug/alcohol addiction, anxiety disorder, psychosis, schizophrenia, mania or any other psychological condition?" According to the instructions, I specify dates when I experienced hypo-manic episodes: once, just before my thirtieth birthday, in the aftermath of divorcing my first husband, and a second time in 1995, when my current husband and I took a semester's leave of absence from Yale University to teach in Mexico, as a rehearsal for moving South of the Border. It is a relief to be able to respond negatively to the question: "Are you currently taking medication for any physical or psychological conditions? "See above" answers the next item on the questionnaire: "Have you experienced any significant emotional, psychological or spiritual difficulty in your life (*that affected your ability to function*)?"

At this point, even though I feel irritated about having to respond to so many detailed personal queries, I appreciate the responsibility and care implied by interviewing each retreatant, so that we can receive necessary support services from the teachers. I quickly check off "No" to questions about whether I have ever attempted to take my life, and whether I have suffered from childhood physical and/or sexual abuse. Asked how the practice of meditation, silence and retreat affect all of the above conditions, I respond, "by calming me down and slowing my pace." The final question is "Are there present conditions in your life which may be placing you under stress, or which might make meditation difficult for you at this time (e.g. fasting, recent loss of a loved one, substance abuse/withdrawal, relationship ending)?" Without adequate reflection, because I feel impatient to finish, I scrawl, "No," and hand in the form to the registrar.

Feeling liberated from preliminary bureaucratic tasks, I walk outside and find that Brian and Betsy are still hanging around the registration area. As we exchange farewell hugs, I sense Brian's regret that he will not be accompanying me on this particular retreat. He and his wife descend the hill to the parking lot in slow motion, postponing their departure, because they share my love for this serene sanctuary.

Spirit Rock Meditation Center (SRMC) sits amidst four hundred acres of rolling hills and woods, traversed by a brook, on the outskirts of the tranquil community of Woodacre in Marin county. It carries the energy of prior inhabitants, a Native American tribe of Miwoks, who used to hunt ancestors of the wild deer and turkey that still roam there freely. With the leadership of Jack Kornfield and other Vipassana teachers, and with the support of generous donors, some of whom had been meditating together since 1974, the land was purchased from the Nature Conservancy in 1987. It took about a decade to raise money for the construction of a meditation hall, a kitchen and communal dining room, and dormitories. The residential meditation center opened in July of 1998, for retreats ranging in length from two nights to two months. SRMC is filled year-round with meditators, or "yogis," who come from all parts of the United States, Canada, and Europe to develop mindfulness, wisdom, and compassion. Although in past retreats I have met a few yogis from as far away as South Africa, I am the only one this time to travel from Mexico. I feel lucky to be among the seventy-odd meditators who have won a lottery for available space in this retreat. We newcomers exchange nods or smiles with meditators who are leaving Spirit Rock after practicing throughout the month of February. About half of those who started at the beginning of February will be continuing their silent practice with me until the end of March.

I follow instructions written on my registration sheet and roll my suitcase uphill to the farthest residence hall, an attractive two-story wooden building equipped with handicap access ramps. Over the years I have been assigned to each of the dormitories, which are named for the four "Divine Abodes" or, in both Sanskrit and related Pali languages, the "Brahma-Viharas," concentrated meditation practices directed towards opening the heart. I pass "Metta" (translated as "loving kindness," from the ancient language of Pali, in which the Buddha's teachings were first recorded), "Karuna" (compassion), and "Mudita" (sympathetic joy). As I enter "Upekkha" (equanimity), I lose any semblance of equanimity upon realizing that I have been assigned to a double room.

My entire nervous system rebels at the thought of spending twenty-seven nights in close proximity to a stranger. Thirty years of meditation practice, two years of Jungian analysis, and twenty years of Core Energetics and Gestalt psychotherapy have been for naught! I have instantly regressed to the age of an egocentric kindergarten child who does not want to share toys with her classmates. I face with aversion the Japanese-style screen that separates two single beds with their bedside tables and lamps in the small, spare, clean room that is my dreadful destiny to inhabit. Before my unknown roommate arrives, I have time to choose the bed nearest the sink and to arrange my belongings on one of two sets of shelves and hangers. Following the honor system, I leave money in an envelope when I fetch rental sheets and towels in the upstairs linen closet. Then I make up the bed with a pillow and two neatly folded woolen blankets that have been left atop the mattress. Sliding my empty suitcase under the bed, I wait for the anticipated invasion.

To calm my nerves, I read signs posted on the door of my room and in the nearby communal bathroom:

> *Please extend mindfulness of silence in residence halls.*
> *Walk quietly on stairs and hallways (especially early a.m. and late p.m.).*
> *Gently open and close doors.*
> *Close toilet lids with care. Please flush only when necessary at night.*
> *No showers 10 p.m. to 5 a.m.*

On the entrance door I read, "Door is tight. Please close securely and quietly." Another petition states, "Please check to make sure this door latches closed when you shut it." The bulletins remind me how hypersensitive my hearing becomes during weeks of silence. I resolve to be considerate of residents who have been meditating for a month.

Near the stairway a schedule is posted for the March retreat:

*5:00 wake up bell	*2:00 sitting
5:30 Qigong in upper	2:45 walking meditation or Qigong
walking hall	*3:30 sitting
6:00 sitting meditation	4:15 walking
6:45 breakfast	*5:00 sitting/Brahma Vihara
7:30 work meditation	instructions
*8:30 sitting meditation and	5:30 evening meal
instructions	*6:45 sitting
9:30 walking meditation	7:25 stretch break
*10:15 sitting	*7:35 dharma talk
11:00 walking	8:30 walking
*11:30 sitting	*9:00 sitting/evening chanting
12:15 lunch	9:40 sleep or further practice

Recalling that asterisks indicate when bells are rung, I feel grateful that the retreat manager Andrea has taken care to post signs that make it possible for yogis to live harmoniously in community without the need for speech.

It feels like an anti-climax when my roommate Alison arrives, lugging her bags and greeting me with a friendly smile. She is tall and athletically built, with closely cropped graying hair. She turns out to be a sensitive and considerate woman close to my own menopausal age. During our brief exchange before taking vows of silence, she confides that this is her first long silent retreat, and she asks for my counsel as a more experienced meditator. I like her instantly and feel ridiculous about my initial reaction of horror about her presence in My Room.

Alison accompanies me on a silent walk, past a line of teacher interview rooms, to the large central building, which houses an octagonal, wooden meditation hall. In the lobby we each choose a cubby to store our coats and shoes. Then we check the bulletin board with its announcements and neatly arranged signs, including "notes for yogis," "notes for manager," and "notes for teachers." I stop a moment in front of a "thangka" that depicts the compassionate goddess Green Tara, overlooking a small table that holds statuettes of male and female personifications of the Buddha, a vase of lovely fresh cut flowers, boxes of tissues for emotional yogis, and song sheets for evening chanting. As Alison and I walk in stocking feet across the lobby's thick red, blue, and beige rug with its intricate hummingbird pattern, I feel excited about approaching the double set of red doors that lead to the inner sanctum, the hall where we will be practicing for so many hours. I read a familiar sign hanging between the doors: "To care for our beautiful floor, please no tea, no food, no water bottles. Remove shoes before entering. Thanks."

We cross the threshold and pause to survey the spacious room lit by large windows on six of its eight sides and by skylights in a cupola at the peak of the high ceiling. On my right side is a community altar displaying photos and memorabilia of spiritual teachers, beloved friends and family members, alive and deceased. These precious items are guarded by female figurines of graceful Kwan Yin and dignified Pajma Paramita (a lay teacher known as "the Perfection of Wisdom"). To my left are two signs: "Zafus (cushions) here" and "Zabutons (mats) here." Because I did not carry my own meditation pillow from Mexico, I search through the pile and select a plump, firm zafu, embroidered with the prayer "May you be happy," and a matching maroon-colored zabuton. Staking out my claim for the site where I will be sitting for the next month, I choose a free spot at the far left side near the front of the hall, so that I can easily see and hear the six teachers, whose cushions are spread in a horizontal line on a raised platform near the main altar. I incline my head towards the altar, graced, as usual, with fresh flowers, glowing candles, and two statues that represent the Buddha and his female counterpart.

Lagging behind Alison, I leave the building by the rear exit to look at the Tibetan prayer flags fluttering from the eaves above the back patio. I visit a stone statue of Kwan Yin, in a dignified dancing posture, guarding the central path to woods and a stream behind the meditation hall. It pleases me to see how many offerings of acorns, feathers, oak leaves, and crystals have been left in the lap of the goddess. Slowly I meander downhill, passing the Smoker's Hut, partially hidden behind a large stone statue of a peacefully sitting Buddha. It is rare to glimpse occasional "sinners" sneaking back there to smoke.

At the entrance to the dining hall stands an iron gong amidst a lovely land-scaped garden dedicated to Gina Thompson, a supporter of Spirit Rock. A signpost states, "The heart is our garden." As I enter the dining room, I read familiar announcements: "Shoes are required at all times in this building," and "chairs needing bottom floor pads replaced" next to "chairs ready to go." Beside a large metal container for hot water, notices say "hot cups," "cold cups," "clean spoons," and "dirty spoons." Tightly lidded glass jars contain many varieties of organic, herbal, green, and black teas, beneath the label "tea."

The large open dining room is lit by skylights and windows on three sides. On the swinging door to the kitchen is an announcement, "Please do not enter kitchen except for yogi jobs." Peeking inside the open door, where busy volunteer chefs are removing enormous salads from a huge walk-in refrigerator, I see, hanging above the immense industrial stove, a cheerfully painted wooden sign that reads, "Cook's walk: Let the cooks perform their dance." On multitudinous shelves, all the storage spaces for utensils, bowls, pitchers, pots and pans are carefully categorized and labeled. One tag proclaims, "oddball useful containers with lids." It reminds me of the poet Donald Hall's description of a label on a box in his grandparents' attic: "string too short to be saved."

In the midst of scrutinizing the details of my environment, I look around the room and recognize about a dozen familiar faces from previous retreats. We grin at each other and join two long lines to wait for the dinner bell. With the kitchen crew witnessing, the head cook for that evening bows three times to a golden Buddha statue that stands by the kitchen door. The jewel-encrusted figure is the same height as the person paying homage. It overlooks two long buffet tables laden with serving dishes of fresh aromatic food. The cook solemnly rings thrice a small bell held in the hands of the statue and then bows to the hungrily waiting yogis. At this signal, we start to take turns serving ourselves. Each dish is labeled with its ingredients, and I find lactose-free options at the "special needs" counter.

I sit at one of the rectangular tables and make no attempt to meet the eyes of those who are eating mindfully next to me. During other prolonged periods of silence, I have learned how invasive direct eye contact can feel. Instead, I gaze at a pale green and salmon-colored mandala hanging on the wall opposite me. Inscribed within the spiraling design are the names of many of Spirit Rock's founding donors. It makes me happy to find most of my favorite dharma teachers listed there, as well as organizations like the San Francisco Zen Center and internationally respected spiritual leaders such as Thich Nhat Hanh. The mandala serves to connect me to dharma practitioners of various disciplines around the globe. After finishing a tasty, light, vegetarian dinner, I receive patient instructions from the SRMC kitchen crew for the job I will be sharing with Ida from Switzerland and Toby, a local yogi. On our way out of the dining room, we check the bulletin board for "notes to yogis," next to "notes to cooks" and "notes to housekeeping."

Under a bright starry night, I climb the hill to the meditation hall, whose soft lights beam from its cupola. I take my seat in the hall with about seventy fellow yogis, who appear as quietly expectant as I am. As I gaze at the dharma teachers, my eyes fill with tears of gratitude to be entering the container of Noble Silence once more. I recognize Julie Wester, John Travis,

Robert Hall, Anna Douglas, and Eugene Cash, all flanking my teacher Jack Kornfield, who welcomes us newcomers. I soak up the familiar sound of his kind, resonant voice that has nourished me on retreats since 1988. Jack asks us to respect the stillness generated by those who have been practicing meditation throughout February. He announces that the wake-up bell will ring a half-hour later than usual tomorrow morning so that travelers from far away can rest.

We follow the classic Buddhist ritual for beginning a retreat: repeating the Three Refuges and the Five Precepts that provide safety for yogis. With my companions, I invoke the support of the Buddha (both the model of the historical figure as well as the potential within each human being to become enlightened), the dharma (the teachings of the Buddha and other sages), and the sangha (the community of fellow meditators present here and around the globe). Then we take vows to adhere to five ethical rules that are intended to guide our conduct: I promise to refrain from taking the life of any sentient being (including pesky ants crawling around dormitory sinks); and to adhere to what the Buddha called "Right Speech," speaking only the truth (a relatively effortless task since we will be honoring Noble Silence, except during fifteen-minute teacher interviews scheduled every other day). As a group, we continue reciting traditional vows to abstain from taking anything that is not freely given, to avoid ingesting any intoxicants that can cloud the mind, and to refrain from misusing our sexual energy (a seemingly simple matter on a retreat that not only requires celibacy but also discourages even eye contact). I appreciate the protection of knowing that I can leave my belongings in an unlocked bedroom and in an open cubbyhole near the meditation hall lobby, with no fear of theft. It is reassuring to trust that nobody will be high on alcohol or recreational drugs while I might be feeling emotionally vulnerable.

Despite feeling tired from jetlag and multiple adjustments to the retreat setting, I find it hard to settle into sleep. I can hear Alison's soft, even breathing, and I am thankful that my roommate does not snore. My mind is busy reviewing the day with its smooth and rocky transitions. It is hard to believe that two days ago I was in Mexico with my husband. Visualizing Mark in our campus home, I send him loving energy. In a calmer state, I doze off and on until the wake-up bell at 5:30 a.m. ❧

CHAPTER TWO

ENTRY INTO NOBLE SILENCE

I have set out my towel and toiletries so that I can rush to the communal bathroom on our floor for a quick hot shower before the first sit of the day. To my dismay, both showers are already occupied when I arrive. I resolve to set my alarm tomorrow a few minutes before the wake-up bell, so that I can beat the bathroom rush hour. Today I barely have time to rinse off my body and dry my hair before throwing on layers of loose cotton clothing and a fleece vest and parka. The stars are still out as I run to the meditation hall.

I land on my zafu on the dot of 6:00 and tune into my husband at our agreed-upon time for five minutes of focusing on one another. Imagining Mark sitting in our meditation room, on Central time, two hours ahead of me, I wish him a happy and fulfilling and safe day. Then I begin Metta practice, visualizing in turn the members of my family, friends around the world, teachers and therapists who have guided me over the years, my music and psychology students, and psychotherapy patients under my care. I pray for each person: "May you be peaceful and happy. May you be safe from inner and outer harm. May you be healthy in body and mind. And may you be free from fear and suffering." I include special prayers for the healing of friends and family members who are ill or in crisis. Finally, I close the session by radiating Metta outward towards all sentient beings. By the end of the forty-five minute sitting period, I feel connected to a big circle of loved ones.

I am happy to be able to relish a hearty breakfast of steaming oatmeal and fresh fruit at a slow pace. Because my yogi job is not until evening, I can relax and concentrate on tasting food that I usually swallow unconsciously. As I leave the dining hall, I remember my morning routine from previous retreats, and I turn right, towards the entrance gate to the retreat area. There I spin the prayer wheel that holds slips of paper that meditators have inscribed with good wishes, hopes, and prayers. I wait for the wheel to slow to a stop so that I can see which of the Buddha's words land directly in front of me. This time I read "Right Concentration." I feel like a gambler watching a rotating roulette wheel, and winning the message I am meant to receive for that day. Each morning I have eight options, and sometimes I can guess in advance which one will face me as the wheel spins to a halt.

On my way uphill, I observe a large, white-breasted bird perched atop the tallest in a line of pine trees. He seems to be surveying the progress of the yogis below. I wonder how he is assessing me. In the "regular world" outside of SRMC, friends who are unfamiliar with the rigors of meditation practice question how I can tolerate being in the "boredom" of silence for such long stretches of time. Little do they know the fun mental games I create in between scheduled meditation periods.

I head for an empty space at the far end of a long, narrow room to perform my daily yoga routine. I am careful not to disturb a small group of people who are concentrating on walking meditation; with downcast eyes, they are attentively lifting, moving and placing each foot in turn. Each yogi has a unique style of walking in slow motion. I visualize the concentrated brain waves of my companions as they note distractions and bring their attention back repeatedly to sensing the subtle movements of their feet. Turning to my own yoga discipline, I coordinate inhalations and exhalations with unhurried stretches of each body part, holding some postures or "asanas" for longer than others, depending on the degree of muscle tension. By the time the bell rings to announce the eight-thirty a.m. sit, I feel relaxed and energized.

This particular morning sitting period is guided by the teachers, who take turns each day giving us increasingly complex instructions for Vipassana meditation practice. No matter how often I hear directions to notice whenever the mind is not focused on the sensation of incoming or outgoing breath, I appreciate being reminded of such a deceptively simple goal. The mind is like a monkey that leaps from branch to branch, tempted to explore every new sight, sound, and sensation. Over and over, I catch myself planning for the future or remembering past events instead of staying with the present moment and attending to the beginning, the middle, and the ending of each breath. After fifteen years of practicing Vipassana, I have learned to be patient with the vagaries of my mind, and to stop judging with so much impatience my restlessness, sleepiness, doubt, desire, and aversion. I know by now that the impediments that block me from inner tranquility have afflicted all meditators since the Buddha's epoch in the fifth century B.C.

At the end of the sit, the teachers answer questions about the practice. I like being in a group of experienced meditators who pose thought-provoking queries that benefit the entire sangha. To participate in long retreats of one or two months, applicants are required to have practiced meditation for at least one nine or ten-day period. The only exception in this retreat seems to be an awkward-looking man sitting in the back of the hall. His questions are almost shouted and reflect both cognitive intelligence and confusion about the entire process of internal reflection. He does not appear to understand emotional nuances. After so many years of doing music therapy with verbal and nonverbal people who suffer from autism, I immediately suspect that "Edgar" has a high functioning type of autism called Asperger's syndrome. I watch his clumsy body movements and his socially inappropriate use of words and physical space. In the dining hall I notice his ritual of fetching a tray and piling on several glasses of milk and plates laden with extra food. He is noisy in all of his activities. My heart feels drawn to this brave soul, who is undertaking two months of silent meditation with so many obstacles in his path. But the reality is that not one of us is free from obstacles along the route towards inner peace.

Our day is punctuated by alternating forty-five minute periods of sitting and walking meditation. I prefer to walk outside, back and forth for the distance of twelve steps, in a wooded area beside a stream in back of the meditation hall. Once I slow down and center myself, I am amazed by how much is happening around this small patch of forest. I catch a glimpse of a deer grazing under the spreading boughs of a venerable oak tree. A gaggle of raucous wild turkeys strut in a disorganized line on the hillside above me. I stoop to pick up a hawk feather near the path, and then I narrow my focus to concentrate on the motion of my feet, ankles, knees, and legs. Although my activities have been limited to bathing, eating, stretching, sitting, and walking, all in silence, the morning passes quickly.

At ten minutes to 2:00, I start walking briskly from dormitory to dormitory, ringing a small, pagoda-shaped peace gong that is formed from melted armaments. The clear reverberations rouse yogis who are taking a post-lunch nap. Just before 2:00, I strike the grand gong by the meditation hall ten times with the sturdy mallet that hangs from one of its supporting posts, and, with my body still vibrating from the resonance, I follow other yogis entering the meditation hall to sit. Rona, a yoga teacher who has led classes in various SRMC retreats, announces that she will be offering beginning and intermediate sessions this afternoon. A new teacher named Teja stands up to introduce himself and to inform us that he will be conducting a half-hour Qigong classes every morning at 5:30, before the first sit of the day. He explains that Qigong is an ancient Eastern martial art that awakens and moves subtle energy. I am instantly drawn to Teja's manner of quiet authority. He is tall and wears his hair back in a small ponytail. I resolve to set my alarm clock early enough to practice Qigong.

After dinner, I write pertinent points in my journal while Anna Douglas gives a dharma talk on the theme of awakening wisdom and compassion. She sits tall and straight, with clear, intelligent eyes that seem to perceive all that is occurring around her. Everyone laughs at her joke about Spirit Rock being a "CNN-free zone," where we can escape the daily bombardment of news about whether or not President George W. Bush will declare war on Saddam Hussein in Iraq. Anna declares, "Here we are seeking a way to make peace in a world determined to make war." She reminds us to wake fully to the present moment and to try to find equanimity with whatever presents itself, without imposing comments or judgments on what we encounter. Anna asks, "Can we experience suffering without evaluating it?" I resonate with her words: "The heart opens only when it feels safe. Nonjudgmental, kind attention allows the heart to unfold."

I like Anna's precise manner as she states, "The breath is a changing flow of sensory experience—not a solid entity. We enter into a stream of being and awaken to a wise view." She quotes the sixth Zen patriarch: "Awareness itself is the substance of wisdom, the function of awareness. Meditation and wisdom are the same. Compassion is the other wing of the bird—the quivering of the heart in response to suffering. Awareness itself is the substance of kindness, the function of awareness. Meditation and kindness are the same." Anna points out that two of the kindest spiritual leaders of our times, the Dalai Lama and Thich Nhat Hanh, have developed compassion through suffering and fleeing from violence in their respective homelands, Tibet and Vietnam. Then she quotes Robert Thurman, scholar of Tibetan Buddhism and director of Tibet House in New York City: "The human hand is an indication, a symbol of our compassion. Our hands are not weapons of war, but instruments of compassion."

Anna recalls that after the devastating aerial attacks on the Twin Towers in New York and the Pentagon in Washington D.C. on September 11, 2001, survivors connected naturally with strangers; sharing this national tragedy opened peoples' habitually numb hearts. She finishes the dharma talk by encouraging us to dedicate ourselves wholeheartedly to the practice of meditation: "We use the simplest of objects for attention, the breath and the body. The more we look, the more we see. We keep looking, and we learn a way of being with life. We become intimate with our own minds. Cultivating wisdom and compassion gives us wings that allow us to fly. We need both wings."

While I head downhill to join my team in the kitchen, I feel how lucky I am to receive guidance from such experienced dharma teachers. Ida, Toby and I read our "yogi job list" posted on the industrial refrigerator and follow instructions for scrubbing squash, potatoes, and turnips and then storing them underneath clean towels in rubberized tubs for the cooks to use in the morning. The hour passes quickly amidst fun nonverbal interactions. By the time I reach my bedroom at 9:30 p.m., Alison is already tucked into bed on her side of the partition. As quietly as possible, I change into my nightgown, brush my teeth, and set out my clothes for rising before dawn. I set the alarm clock for 5:00 a.m. and slip into bed. It seems strange not to say "good night" to my roommate, and I sleep fitfully, sensing her presence.

I awake before the alarm is set to ring and tiptoe down the hall to wash up and dress. This third day of March is cold and windy. I remember the old saying, "March comes in like a lion, and goes out like a lamb." Today is definitely a lion-like day. Clouds obscure the stars, and I shiver on my brisk hike to the walking meditation room, where Teja is starting to demonstrate the opening Qigong exercises. I am surprised to find the room filled with eager-looking yogis. I stand at the back of the room and follow the simple movements, surrendering to the flow of light, liquid motions punctuated by periods of stillness. Almost as one unit, thirty people perform "Whole Body

Breathing," gently moving the palms of the hands down the right and left energy channels alongside the torso, and upwards along "centerline." The only exercise that gives me trouble is "Golden Dragon Moves its Head in Four Ways." My neck is so stiff that I cannot bend it towards the right ear or pull my chin down to the chest. At the end of the class, Teja encourages us to write him notes with any questions about Qigong practice. Before the 6:00 a.m. sit, I jot a note requesting suggestions to alleviate neck pain, and I tack the slip of paper below the label "Teja" in the row of teachers' names on the bulletin board in the lobby. I wonder if he will respond today. Then my attention shifts to other concerns.

During today's walking meditation in the woods behind the meditation hall, I watch a bee traveling from flower to flower, and, almost effortlessly, the following poem takes shape in my mind:

A promiscuous bumblebee
Alights upon a fragile blue blossom
Atop tiers of delicate azure flowers.
The pale green stem bows graciously,
Honored that he chose her array
Over so many rivals,
Displaying their own tempting wares.

But the bee samples only
Two or three dainty blooms
Before he zooms across the path
To a neighbor's floral show.
The receptive hostess nods,
Pleased by the visitor's attention
To her blushing blossoms.

Now the bee is off again
To taste another delicacy.
He never looks back at the
Trail of abandoned flowers.
Their petals droop wanly.

Don Juan zigzags onward,
Blithely breaking hearts,
Flaunting his plump, pollen-coated body.
Eagerly awaiting their turn,
His new conquests enjoy the present moment,
Because that is all there is.

Before the bell rings for the next sit, I visit my bedroom to inscribe the poem in my journal, so that I do not forget the words. To prepare in case I have another burst of inspiration, I stick a pen and piece of paper in my jacket pocket. I feel so excited by this surprising, creative outpouring from my subconscious mind that I arrive slightly breathless at the meditation hall. During the next walking meditation period, I select a secluded forest path with determination to focus on each careful step. But I notice a slug inching along nearby, and before I can control the impulse, another poem emerges in my mind:

> Slowing down my steps,
> Attending to lifting, moving, placing
> Each foot in turn
> On the dirt trail to the woods,
> I note when my attention wanders.
>
> Pleased with my process,
> Mindful at rubato tempo,
> I spy a long slimy slug,
> Oozing his way across
> A patch of parched brown leaves.
>
> His barely perceptible movements
> Undulate silently.
> Black-horned antennae
> Scan the forest floor ahead.
> Sliding effortlessly,
> He appears almost stationary.
>
> Like a languidly licking tan tongue,
> The slug mocks my meditative march,
> Trumping me in the race
> To master the slowest pace.

I convince myself that it is important to chronicle this original opus before the walking period ends. Although I reach my zafu on time for the sit, thoughts about possible revisions to the latest verses pop into my head and distract me from following the sensation of my breath. I notice that inhaling is easier for me than exhaling. My exhalations are like the trail behind a jet plane: they are smooth and clearly defined at the start, and they become progressively hesitant and fuzzy.

During today's lunch I resolve to do an "eating meditation." I place my fork down between each bite, and I relish tasting each succulent morsel of vegetarian chili. To my surprise, I realize that I tend to chew only on the right side of my mouth. In the rest period after lunch, I recall last night's dream and record it in my dream journal:

> *Mom tells me that she wants to give me a birthday present. My brother Bayard is driving us in his car. When he parks, he notices that he has lost his antique watch. He is upset that he has nothing to keep time. I go on a job interview to work as a teacher. I take my time. I am in no rush for the interview. I meet with Mom and my sister Lindsay, who are discussing plans for a family reunion. Mom asks, "How can we make this trip work smoothly?" I say, "Mom, our family dynamic is changing." Lindsay smiles and nods, and Mom relaxes.*

My associations with the dream have to do with letting go of keeping track of time as measured by the world outside the retreat setting. Here at Spirit Rock, I feel less rushed and pressured than I do in normal workdays. In the months preceding the retreat, I worked in a therapeutic group process called Family Constellations, developed by the German psychotherapist Bert Hellinger. As a result, I feel as if I am outgrowing old patterns of relating to my parents and my three younger siblings.

Right after I ring the bell for the first meditation sit of the afternoon, I join five other yogis for a group interview with Jack Kornfield. His penetrating dark eyes are softened by a gentle, welcoming smile. His thin, slightly stooped body, receding hairline and prominent ears give him a vulnerable look that diminishes any feelings of intimidation I might feel around such an internationally renowned meditation teacher and author.

I first met Jack when he was leading the IMS New Year retreat of 1988, a year after he helped buy land to develop Spirit Rock on the West coast. We had an instant connection, as if recognizing one another. In my first interview with him I recall wearing, wrapped around my arm, a mala of sandalwood beads that had been blessed in an audience with His Holiness the Dalai Lama in Dharamsala, India the previous year. Intuiting my attachment to the prayer beads, Jack asked about their origin. He reminisced about his own dialogues with the exiled Tibetan spiritual leader and was pleased to hear that my husband had invited His Holiness to address students and professors at Yale University, where Mark was then a dean of students. It was the first time since my trip to India that I had encountered someone who understood the profundity of being in the presence of a soul as kind and joyous as the Dalai Lama. By the end of that initial interview with Jack, I knew that I had found the spiritual mentor I had been seeking. Despite being only a few years my senior, he has seemed like a positive father figure, especially since I learned that his birthday is the day after my actual father's July 15th birth date.

Today Jack gives us a chance to learn each other's first names and to speak briefly about issues and intentions that we bring to this month of silence. Sensing their interest in me, I am curious to hear about my Swiss veggie-washing buddy Ida; Laurence from South Africa; Gina, a Jamaican woman who lives in New York state; Dina from Washington D.C.; and Cornelia, a local artist and retired professor. As Jack points out, all of us are experienced meditators who have attended numerous retreats. I sense a high level of collective consciousness in the room. After listening to my colleagues' stories of family births, deaths, and illnesses that have occurred over the past year, I speak about Guided Imagery and Music trainings faltering in Mexico because my co-directors are going through a painful marital separation. In addition, the ex-president of the UDLA recently tried to oust his unpopular successor, so that the university where I live and teach is in turmoil. I am worried about the U.S. threatening to wage war on Iraq. "The only part of my life that makes sense these days," I say, "is meditation."

Jack asks me to close my eyes and sense in my heart how it feels to be here on retreat. I acknowledge feelings of relief at slowing down and connecting with nature's rhythms. I grow tearful about how close a beloved adolescent godchild came to killing herself last fall, and how much grieving and self-examination I have been doing since her suicide attempt. Jack proposes that I dedicate this retreat to Ashley, and that my increased consciousness shine a light of hope in her life. I appreciate how Jack helps me deepen from reporting life events to sharing emotions. With his dual training as clinical psychologist and former monk, he projects authority and compassion.

Robert Hall's dharma talk is honest, witty, and full of his characteristically exuberant life force. His plump, balding, jovial figure evokes images of the laughing Buddha. I record his words in my journal, as he describes El Dharma, his newly founded retreat center in Baja California Sur, and he contrasts its warm sunny ambience with the cold, rainy, dismal site of the first meditation retreat he attended in 1975, in an old abandoned high school. Although Robert has moved from northern California to a part of Mexico far from the central highlands where I live, his presence in Todos Santos makes me feel less isolated from the Spirit Rock community.

Robert recounts how his Tibetan Buddhist teacher Trungpa Rinpoche taught him how to "befriend fear" and transform upsetting ideas by staying with the body's sensations. I like listening to Robert's vibrant voice reciting from a poem by T.S. Eliot:

> I said to my soul, 'Be still'...
> The darkness shall be the light...
> What you do not know is what you know.

Robert reminds us that difficult mind states are part of the spiritual path, a doorway to deeper understanding. He explains how "judging mind" distinguishes between what is pleasant and what is unpleasant. We use "projecting mind" to compare ourselves with others. "Lamenting mind" despairs and loses a sense of connection to self and others. "Racing mind" is hard to contain, while "rambling mind" free associates. "Desperate mind" seeks addictions, and "sinking mind" falls into sloth and torpor. "Angry mind" results in "lonely mind," and "obsessing mind" catches us in thought loops. "Lusting mind" can be combined with "obsessing mind," and "rationalizing mind" analyzes everything. "Doubting mind" can lead to the worst condition of all, "despairing mind." I laugh out loud at Robert's quip, "Difficult mind states have no pride!" He quotes the author Barbara Kingsolver: "Attending carefully to one thing, I learn to love my life again. I have taught myself joy over and over again."

Robert points out how the body reflects every mind state, and self-obsessed thinking contracts the body. He suggests that we turn our attention away from the content of thoughts to the accompanying body sensation: "Bare attention has no agenda, no expectation, but accepts reality just as it is. We are practicing self-acceptance. With concentration comes relaxation, letting go of the heart and opening to life as it is." I feel so uplifted by Robert's concluding words that I nearly float down the hill to wash vegetables.

In the pitch-black dark of pre-dawn on March 4, I have no trouble waking up. At Qigong class, I delight in following with fluid arm movements what Teja calls the Eight Actions of Qi (or Chi): gathering, lifting, expanding, contracting, flowing in, flowing out, falling, and dispersing energy.

Today feels full of magical moments: As I walk across the planks of a platform on a hill overlooking the meditation hall, I spot a lizard watching me intently. I decide that he is my "guardian lizard" for this particular walking meditation. On the way down to the next sit, I am surprised by three white-bottomed deer, almost near enough to touch. Unperturbed by my proximity, the deer continue munching grass. Under the eaves of my dormitory, I hear a pair of doves cooing affectionately.

Eugene Cash, the meditation teacher I think of as a "spiritual warrior," guides us with detailed instructions for "eating meditation." His short, wiry body is fit from long morning bike rides, and his piercing eyes peer through thick-lensed spectacles. He represents "tough love" and seems to expect that his meditation students follow as rigorous a discipline as he models for them. I respect his high standards, and I have seen evidence of the sweet "mensch" heart beneath his rather severe facade. Eugene recommends taking one bite at a time with eyes closed, and laying down the fork to note the sequence of "tasting, chomping, sloshing, chewing, sucking, swishing," and what he calls "mopping up," before picking up the fork again to stab the next morsel. I practice, noticing more frustration than anything else. How hard it is to slow down and be aware of each element in eating! I have moments of gratitude for succulent soy loaf (a vegetarian substitute for meatloaf), green beans and bright orange carrots, mashed potatoes, multi-colored salad with mouth-watering dressing, and clear, clean, filtered water. This is a long meal, full of impatience. I try to give equal chewing time on the left side of my mouth.

When I return to my bedroom, the furniture arrangement does not feel right to me. I do not want my bed to face the back wall. On impulse, I strip the bed and remake it, reversing the direction of the head, so that when I prop myself up to read or write, I can look outside at the hills where the deer graze. Alison enters the room to brush her teeth, and I wonder how my quiet, independent roommate is reacting to my eccentricities. With the "feng shui" established to my liking, I feel better about having to share the room.

I check the message board and find a note from Teja arranging to meet me in one of the teacher interview rooms after the first afternoon sit. I have mixed reactions. Even though I want advice about my chronically stiff neck, I feel ambivalent about consulting him because I do not want to break silence. I am nervous as I enter the small room where Teja awaits me. He is so tall that he seems to fill the entire space. I receive far more instruction than anticipated. Teja shows me how to stand with flexed knees, placing my weight on the outer edge of the feet to allow the energy to flow along the "yang" outer side of the legs, opening the backs of the knees instead of pressuring the kneecaps. He guides me to hold my arms gently away from my sides to open up the armpits and permit the inner connective tissues to strengthen. He demonstrates how forming an "arm circle," with the palms of the hands triangulating with the "third eye," also fortifies the armpit region.

Teja asks me to sense the difference between energizing myself by standing on the balls of the feet versus grounding myself with more weight on the heels. At one point he touches the sensitive nape of my neck to guide my posture. I sense an electric shock passing through my body. Teaching for the first time on an extended retreat, where nobody usually touches one another, Teja seems unaware of the galvanizing effect of this physical contact. He counsels me to use only seventy percent of my energy and extension for daily Qigong exercises. I agree with him that in modern society we tend to over-use our bodies. I resolve to follow Teja's advice to expend less physical effort and instead employ more visualization, so that my auric field extends and my movements flow without strain.

I leave the interview room with a feeling of excitement and synchronicity. Back in Mexico, I have just enrolled in a two-year course called "Sanación Energética" (Energy Healing), which is training me to work with subtle energy of chakras and auras and to heal with my hands. After attending years of modern dance classes and Feldenkrais body work courses, I am happy to meet Teja, who furthers my understanding about themes I am dedicated to mastering. We speak the same language. I even found out that Teja lives in the same town where my dear friend Andy has his medical practice in northern California. What an amazingly small world.

With a burst of energy, I set off to walk in the hills. As I observe the clouds, the words to a poem coalesce in my mind, and I jot down the phrases on one of the slips of paper in the pocket of my down vest:

A barrel-chested cloud
Muscles its way above
The grassy hill before me.
Shimmering in the morning sunshine,
A silver jet plane
Marks its path with
A clear white blaze
Across the deep blue sky.

Like a glowing meteor,
The jet slices through
The cloud's brawny chest
And disappears from view
For a slow count of ten.

It pops out of the
Cloud's flexed bicep
And draws a ruler-straight chalky line
To prove its passage into One Mind.
Deflated, the cloud's bulk dissolves,
Losing half its body weight.
Nebulous steamy wisps
Stream away in the wind.

As the jet plane disappears
Over the far hills,
Its trail blurs fuzzily
Like the end of an exhalation,
Erased by the breeze.
The white line whispers away,
As impermanent as the cloud.

I return to my bedroom to polish my latest poetic creation and to copy it into my journal. Then I run downhill for dinner.

Eugene gives tonight's dharma talk on the topic of Mindfulness of Breathing, based on the Anapanasati Sutta in "The Middle Length Discourses of the Buddha." I notice how each of the teachers brings a unique perspective and flavor to their teachings about Buddhist philosophy. Eugene explains how the Buddha's four Satipatanas focus on keeping the mind with the breath and refining our mindfulness. To improve attentiveness, we can pretend that each breath is either the first or the very last respiration in our lifetime. Eugene reminds us that on the night of enlightenment, the Buddha was practicing the same mindfulness of breathing that he later recommended to his followers. Today, 2600 years later, we can still benefit from accepting each breath as it is, without trying to control it. Eugene transmits the Buddha's message that by training "chita," or the "heart-mind," we can cultivate non-judgment and kindness towards ourselves, restrain the mind from indulging itself, develop a noble presence, and build the foundation for "right effort." I sit up straighter, remembering that this morning, when I spun the prayer wheel, it had stopped at the words "Right Effort."

Eugene continues, "We don't have to be an idea of how we are supposed to be. The habits of life fall away with the intimacy of breath.... The in-breath is inspiration, breathing in life. The out-breath is expiration, breathing out waste." He suggests that at the beginning of each sit, we first sense the body by scanning or sweeping attentively from head to toe. A formal intention might help: "May mindfulness of breath arrive now." We can practice noting each in-breath and out-breath, and their length, texture, beginning, and ending. Before concluding his remarks, Eugene advises us to relax the body and to let the breath come to us, feeling its sensuality.

Even though he has said nothing radically new about Vipassana practice, Eugene's words inspire me to renew my attention to breathing, a process so basic and yet so elusive. I recognize that I tend to focus on the beginnings of breaths and to lose the endings. That pattern is a metaphor for the way I live my life. As a fiery Aries woman, I am great at starting new creative projects, but I tend to become bored with maintenance and follow-up efforts. Silently, before retiring for the night, I recite a prayer that I say daily: "May I be thankful for the miracle of breath and life."

I awake on March 5, Ash Wednesday, with the following dream:

> *I meet one of my former music therapy and meditation students on the campus of the Universidad de las Américas. We are happy to see one another. She tells me that she has a class which conflicts with the time of my weekly meditation group. I ask if she is meditating on her own, and she smiles, assuring me that she maintains a regular daily practice. I am pleased that she has incorporated my teachings into her life.*

In an upbeat mood, I record this positive dream before rushing to Qigong class. At the first meditation sit, Eugene announces that yoga exercises have just been prohibited in the upper walking meditation room in the hour after breakfast. People who do walking meditation there at that hour have been complaining about feeling distracted by the movements of yoga practitioners like me. I notice my instant inner reaction of irritation and rebelliousness to this prohibition. Instead of attending to in-breaths and out-breaths, I find myself ruminating on this problem. I wonder if the Council House is vacant at that time of day. There is no space in my double bedroom for yoga exercises.

Right after breakfast, I spin the prayer wheel and see that "Right Livelihood" is my guiding message for the day. I start to free associate. How can I be present enough at the Universidad de las Américas to teach music, psychology, and meditation, plus take time for a month-long annual retreat at a time that meshes with Jack Kornfield's schedule? March falls directly in the middle of the spring term at the University, and I have to sacrifice teaching a course and find a substitute to lead the UDLA sangha during my absence. How can I tend to my marriage enough if I go on long annual retreats? I console myself with the idea of going for just two weeks of retreat next March, and postponing another month-long retreat until the following year. I could teach a course and invite a colleague to cover two weeks of classes. Suddenly I catch myself "planning, planning." In my thoughts, I have jumped ahead two years and switched to another country! I reel in my mind to focus on the sensation of my feet climbing the hill.

I feel a bit nervous before my scheduled teacher interview with Julie Wester. We have had little contact, except in her capacity as a guest lecturer in Community Dharma Leader training sessions. Immediately dispelling my anxiety, she sets me at ease with a warm, friendly smile. I like her short rounded form and broad, open face crowned by hair that seems to shift from ash blond to white in color. The sight of her bare feet evokes a casual atmosphere that helps me relax even more. For decades she has devoted herself to practicing meditation in the tradition of the Burmese master U Ba Khin, who guided her teacher Ruth Denison. Because she has incorporated intensive spiritual discipline into her counseling practice, Julie's senses are awake to subtle nonverbal clues while she listens.

I recount today's dream and speak about how challenging it is for me to integrate long retreats into my marriage and my busy music therapy schedule. Julie asks me to close my eyes and contact my "heart's longing to do the soul's journey well." I sense tears welling up in my eyes and feel relieved to cry and alleviate the heavy pressure on my chest. As I recall that tomorrow is my twenty-first wedding anniversary, and I am aware of Mark's loving presence with me. Reflecting upon how generous he is to support my meditation practice, I sob. He has given me the best present I could ask for: a month of silence that ends on March 28, my fifty-fifth birthday.

Julie interrupts my tearful musing to advise me to connect fully with the sensations of my body and the emotions of my heart. That way I can integrate the larger panorama of my life into the present moment of this retreat. By entering completely into whatever the silence has to teach me, I will gain insight about how to blend my meditation practice into daily life even more completely than I already have. At this moment I am aware of my positive transference towards Julie as the "good mother."

As she counsels me, I acknowledge the many blessings in my life, the love of my family and friends, the career that meshes so well with mindfulness practice, and the financial abundance that enables me to take time for retreats. I tell her that since attending the CDL training, I have witnessed the manifestation of a meditation sangha that includes over fifty professors and students at the Universidad de las Américas. Before I made the commitment to study Buddhist philosophy and to learn how to give dharma talks in my home community, only five people attended the weekly sits. Now the group is so big that Mark and I have had to relocate the site from our campus home to the auditorium of the residential college where he is the "Regente," or administrative director. Julie confirms my intuition that, in the words of the famous "Desiderata" prayer of 1692 (from Old Saint Paul's Church in Baltimore), "no doubt the universe is unfolding as it should."

I leave the interview with a feeling of gratitude for Julie's ability to help me affirm my deepest values. But for some reason I neglect to mention how much I have been breaking the rules about not reading or writing during retreats. My right forearm is beginning to feel the strain of penning poems, dreams, and reflections on dharma talks.

After lunch, I encounter a doe and two fawns grazing right by the side of the road. One young deer trots across the road directly in front of me. I stop abruptly and realize that I am standing in between the fawn and her sibling, who is still close by their mother. As I witness the deer's family drama unfolding, I start to compose the following poem:

> *Trudging up the steep hill,*
> *Lunch heavy in my belly,*
> *I surprise a doe and twin fawns,*
> *Grazing close to the asphalt path.*
>
> *All three stop simultaneously*
> *To check me out*
> *With serious, dark, round eyes.*
> *Their long, sensitive ears lift*
> *Like emphatic exclamation points.*
>
> *I pause and hold my breath.*
> *Will I pass inspection?*
> *One fawn judges me harmless.*
> *She dashes across the pavement*
> *Right in front of me,*
> *Hard hooves tapping a*
> *Syncopated staccato beat.*
> *She bows and chews a*
> *Tuft of coarse grass*
> *To celebrate her safe passage.*

Her sister watches jealously
From the other side
And glances at me,
As if to ask,
"Is the grass greener over there?"

She too trots across the asphalt,
Clip-clopping on spindly legs.
Side by side, the twins feed,
Content for a moment.

Suddenly both fawns
Lift their heads and
Peer anxiously at their mother,
Gazing at them calmly,
Still munching, but not budging
From her chosen spot.

The twins exchange looks
And bound back over
To join their feasting mother.
Relaxing in synchrony,
The threesome performs the
Downward dog yoga posture,
White rumps raised high,
Noses deep in clover.

The lesson is clear.
Mother knows best
Where the sweetest grass grows.

Julie gives tonight's dharma talk, and I feel pleased to have a second opportunity to learn from her today. She starts off by quipping: "I was not a dharma bum in Asia like many of the other Spirit Rock teachers. I stayed behind to meditate with Ruth Denison. Thirty years ago, when I was twenty-three years old, I was awash with emotions during retreats." Julie has an intimate style of conversing with her audience. She continues, "This practice is possible with generosity of spirit and acceptance. We can learn how to hold ourselves."

Julie comments that the Buddha's first two Foundations of Mindfulness help us to be present in this very moment, noting the elemental energies of sensation: "Our bodies are made of energy. We are not separate from air, fire, water, and earth. We are not alone." She asks us to participate actively in meditating upon relaxing our hands. (I have to put down my pen in order to follow her instructions.) While relaxing my hand muscles, I try to be aware of the effect on the rest of the body, as well as sensing the body's energetic field: "earthy solidity, fiery warmth, airy movement and vibration, and watery fluidity." Once again, I am struck by the synchronicity of being asked to practice subtle energy exercises similar to those I have been learning in the Sanación Energética course in Mexico. Julie coaches us to sense how the earth holds us: "Our hands go with us wherever we are. Our experience of continuity includes times of both remembering and forgetting the body."

She cites the Buddha's advice to his son Rahula: "Be like the elements. Whatever happens, the earth is unmoved, undisturbed, with equanimity." Julie's statement resonates with my own experience that suffering comes when we forget our elemental connection to all life. After reminiscing about elemental moments in her own childhood, when she watched fireflies glimmering on her grandmother's farm in Georgia, Julie exhorts us to explore the four hundred acres at Spirit Rock: "Try wading in the creek!" I like the idea and consider how right she is that we are not used to relaxing the body. She suggests that we notice our relaxation on a cellular level: "Directly sensing our aliveness in the present moment is mystical. Feel the pulsation and the vibration. It is not easy to stay with the body from moment to moment. We have vulnerable cellular memories. We must bow to every bit of numbness, freezing, armoring that we needed to protect ourselves in the past, that helped us arrive at this retreat now, and that we may no longer need." I am moved to tears by Julie's sensitivity and gentleness. She asks if we can try staying with our tender sensations or emotions one more moment than we did previously.

Julie explains that the energy field of the retreat helps to hold us and to allow us to connect to our true nature: "We can trust the process of unfolding, knowing that our direct experience will lead to more and more freedom. We can trust our growing capacity to hold ourselves." By the end of the dharma talk, Julie has reinforced my belief that "Vipassana practice works."

On March 6, my wedding anniversary, I awake at 4:20 a.m. with the following dream:

> *Mark and I are at an official event in Mexico City. He accompanies me to the parking lot to send me off in our car to Puebla, where I have to pay back a loan to a professor at the UDLA.*

A lady asks Mark for help with car problems. As he tends to her, I keep hoping that he will see me departing and that he will give me a farewell hug. Just as I enter the traffic on the busy street outside the parking lot, Mark approaches me. He looks handsome in his tan Italian-cut suit, but it is too late for me to turn back. My car is already in the stream of traffic. Too late, I realize that I forgot to ask him for directions to Puebla. I feel lost in Mexico City. An adolescent boy materializes in the car, blocking my view of the road. I tell him firmly to change seats so that I can drive safely. He follows my instructions. I worry that if I am lost for too long, I will not reach Puebla by nightfall. I don't want to drive in the dark. I feel pressure to repay my loan on time.

With an effort not to disturb Alison, I leave our room to write down my dream in the bathroom. I feel as if I am back at boarding school, writing after "lights out" time. I remember Jack Kornfield saying, "Get curious about what is difficult for you." I have to admit that the prospect of weeks of sneaking to the bathroom to record dreams is not appealing. My dream reminds me of how much I miss my husband, and makes me wonder what adolescent tendencies are obstructing my vision.

Today at 7:30 a.m. I start stretching in the Council House, because I am now forbidden to do yoga in the upper walking room. Just as I begin to feel comfortable in my new surroundings, a yogi enters to vacuum the room. She performs her usual working meditation task around my body, while I lie on the floor and block my ears from the roaring sound of the vacuum cleaner. After she leaves, I start to cry. I feel forlorn and homeless. Other meditators enter the room, and one begins doing T'ai Chi.

During the question and answer period at the end of the 8:30 a.m. sit, I resolve to speak up for "yoga rights." In my mind I rehearse so that I will be able to speak simply, clearly, and humorously. As Jack fields questions, I decide to wait, and I am rewarded for my restraint. He announces the teachers' decision to open up the lower walking room for yoga, except on rainy days. What an inner drama I have gone through unnecessarily! I return to my bedroom to find a lovely red leaf lying on my pillow—a surprise gift from my roommate. My mood picks up considerably.

Today I volunteer for an extra yogi job, to ring the big, bowl-like gong, signaling the end of four different sitting meditation periods, while teachers are busy conducting interviews. I decide to dedicate these sessions to Mark as a tribute to our twenty-one years of marriage.

During a morning walk in the woods, I flash back to memories of walking barefoot on the gravely driveway of my family's home on Long Island. I recall trying to toughen the soles of my feet for running around without shoes during summer vacations on Lake Sunapee in New Hampshire. I can still remember the placement of each rock on the steep path between the "Big House," where my parents stayed, and the "Little House," which my sister Lindsay and I shared. Memories flow through me of stubbed toes, skinned knees, scary ghost stories about "Crazy Annie," playing with jacks and a small red rubber ball, spinning three large plastic hula-hoops around my body at once, and arranging my collection of foreign dolls and coins from distant lands.

Suddenly I am jolted back to the present moment. As I look down at my rainbow-colored socks, I am pleased to see that my sense of play is still intact. I realize that this chain of remembrances has been set off by a tiny leaf that is spinning like a top from a twig dangling in the breeze. With a sense of "tripping" on hallucinogenic drugs, I gaze at countless plants in myriad shades of green, with their multi-formed leaves shivering in the breeze. Everything is vibrating with energy.

Today at dinnertime, Margot sits across from me and creates an open-face sandwich of peanut butter and kiwi slices atop rice cakes. I follow her example, and I find the combination surprisingly delicious. We share conspiratorial smiles. What weird Vipassana humor!

Tonight's dharma talk is given by John Travis, whose beaming face, kind eyes, and casual attire make him seem instantly accessible. Unlike Julie, he is a "dharma bum," who lived in Asia for eight years and studied with various teachers of the Tibetan and Vipassana traditions. While maintaining close ties with the Spirit Rock community, he is the lead teacher at Mountain Stream Meditation Center in Auburn, California. John's theme is how to let go of what impedes enlightenment. He warns us, "Don't grasp at anything. Attachment is tied to the power of death." He reminisces about his transition in the 1960's from the tranquility of a Himalayan monastery to the noisy chaos of Benares, India, where the teacher S.N. Goenka was leading a retreat near the sacred Ganges River, on whose banks members of the untouchable caste burn bodies of the deceased. As he recalls his adverse reactions to his new surroundings, John says, "We stir up and muddy the pool with our wants and aversion. Stilling, stopping, and quieting settle the clear water." I like his metaphor of the psyche as a pool that we can either cleanse or pollute with our reactions. He goes on to explain how it is

A SILENT CURE

possible to develop stability of mind and concentration during the purification process of retreats, but only if we become conscious of our likes and dislikes and our judgmental tendencies.

I resonate with the words, "The truth of suffering binds us to the wheel of rebirth. We try to stop the river of changing experience to find comfort by holding on to what we like. Anything that lasts long enough turns into its opposite. Even eating [too much of] our favorite food can become aversive." While taking notes, I consider how often I repeat patterns that keep me stuck. John reminds me that on retreat "we have a chance to transform our suffering and learn what it has to teach. We can be thankful to our suffering for pointing us towards freedom." How paradoxical it is to consider pain as a friendly ally that helps me grow. I laugh at the comment, "Spirit Rock provides a tight, quiet container for meditation, and yet it is like a garbage dump for our troubles." John points out that by noticing our exhalations, we learn that it is impossible to hold onto anything. We are being born and dying with every cycle of inhaling and exhaling. He continues, "Freedom is not found by changing our circumstances, but by accepting them." As I write down this nugget of wisdom, I consider how challenging it is for me to accept aversive situations. I determine to note my positive and negative reactions as I scrub vegetables before bedtime.

On March 7 I wake with this dream:

> *Mark and I enter a fancy boutique where I see an elegant dress that looks totally different in the back than the front. Mark encourages me to try on the dress, which has a sheer, sexy blouse over a low-cut neckline. When I model for him, I feel taller than usual, like a queen. We both like the look of the pretty new dress on me. Mark goes to the cash register to pay for the dress. Both of us are shocked by the high price—thousands of dollars. But we agree that the beautiful dress is worth the cost. Mark reminds me that it is my birthday dress. As we walk down the street after buying my "birthday suit," I sense the intimacy of our steps matching perfectly. I lean over to kiss Mark and say, "I love you." He smiles at me, pleased by my spontaneous display of affection.*

Missing my husband, I tiptoe to the bathroom to record my dream and to wait for the 5:00 a.m. bell that signals permission to start showering. I dress carefully for today's morning interview with Jack. As my family constellation shifts, I sense my relationship with him changing. Aware that I no longer feel awed by his presence, I prepare to confront my mentor about neglecting to give me feedback about the draft of an article he had promised to review before I submitted it for publication.

When I am actually sitting face-to-face with Jack, I have to summon courage to remind him about my missing manuscript. Explaining that he is a terrible correspondent, he apologizes sincerely and admits that he forgot my request in the midst of his many responsibilities. My heart is touched by my teacher's simple honesty about his limitations, and I have no trouble forgiving him. I ask Jack if he has developed psychic abilities after so many years of practicing meditation. Smiling, he replies, "All good therapists develop psychic and intuitive powers. They are ordinary when we are open and aware. The trick is to use these abilities wisely and not be hooked by them, noting what is happening without being attached to the perception. Vipassana is about ordinary moments with awareness." Whenever I am with Jack, each instant is full of life lessons.

As I exit the small interview room, lyrics to a Beatle's song run through my mind: "Blackbird singing in the dead of night. Take these lonely wings and learn to fly. All your life, you have only waited for this moment to arrive." Music therapists like me are curious about the significance of melodies and lyrics that surface spontaneously. I wonder what particular "moment" is arriving today.

Tonight's dharma talk is by Jack, who starts off with a startling quotation by the Swiss psychologist Carl Jung: "The attainment of wholeness requires one to stake one's entire being. There can be no compromise." Jack asks us, "What is the sacred intention that brings you to this retreat?" As I doubt if my goal of achieving peace of mind is a sacred enough intent, he recounts the story about Mara (the manifestation of greed, hatred, and delusion) calling the Buddha "a slacker" on his spiritual quest. Just before reaching enlightenment, the Blessed One responded with the so-called Lion's Roar: "I have done all the ascetic practices. Now I have stopped. I declare freedom and compassion will be my unshakable stance." Jack follows up with a list of what modern Westerners do to alleviate the existential angst that is another aspect of Mara: "We have tried workshops, therapy, meditation, money, sex, travel, the 'California guru of the week,' overwork, and speed. None of it works. We are frightened to let go of the Body of Fear—the small sense of self."

As usual, Jack peppers his dharma talk with humorous comments that relieve the serious message he is conveying. We all laugh when he remarks, "Hollywood couldn't beat the scenes in our heads during meditation sits!"

Most meditators catch themselves fantasizing at one time or another, "I am going to reach enlightenment in this sitting." With a more solemn tone, he reminds us that the dharma is not about getting something but about letting go: "People seek the quicksand of something, when they need the firm ground of emptiness." I feel uncomfortable with Jack's statement that there is no way to escape death, because it "lies within us," but my mind eases as I hear, "Sitting with fear requires courage and compassion." Sometimes pursuing this spiritual path feels daunting to me. As I make an effort to record my teacher's words, my right hand feels tense and sore, but I do not let myself relax and simply listen.

Jack advises us to note subtle energies like "calm, calm, peace, peace, serenity, serenity" that arise in the "space of nothingness." I pay attention carefully as he continues, "Note the energy of thoughts like a bubble in the stream of consciousness. Be present for whatever arises, not only the big, dramatic moments." How often I react melodramatically with tears or excitement to both internal and external events! Jack observes that while some people are afraid of pleasure, others are scared of pain: "Some fear touching life and others fear leaving life. Whatever we have hidden from will find us if we wait long enough." I wonder why there is so much emphasis on fear in this dharma talk. So far my meditation sits have been free of fear.

Jack tells about his visit to a Cambodian refugee camp after Pol Pot's reign of terror. At the end of a row of huts, he saw a long line of survivors waiting to fetch a bucket of water from a well so that they could tend to the tiny gardens each person had planted. Despite so much deprivation, these Buddhist practitioners had enough faith to stay open to life's beauty and to trust that they would survive like the plants they were nurturing. Yes, Jack is right: "What we most long for—freedom, hope and compassion—is already here. We can open to life's mystery, trusting that the psyche knows how to open naturally." As the talk ends, I feel grateful to receive transmissions from this teacher, who seems to channel the dharma like a wizard.

On March 8, I awaken with a memory of my father saying, "Hurry or you'll be left behind." In a competitive race with three younger siblings, I began the life-long pattern of rushing that requires so much mindfulness to stop. Even on retreat, my tempo speeds up unless I monitor it consciously. Qigong class helps temper my accelerated rhythm. This morning Teja closes with the words, "Thank you dear ones," in such a kind tone of voice that my heart melts, and I cry throughout Metta prayers.

"Yawning, yawning," seems to be what I am noting more than anything else this morning. The more I yawn, the more my chronic jaw tension releases. "Right intention" is today's maxim. I wonder how much time I should devote to writing poetry during walking meditation periods. Suddenly Edgar jolts me out of these preoccupations as he runs unsteadily past, wearing shoes with untied laces. He lets the door to Upekkha slam in my face. My initial reaction of irritation dissolves when I enter the residential hall and see him sitting on the floor in the hallway and trying to figure out how to fix the vacuum cleaner. I feel compassion for how challenging it must be to overcome awkward motor coordination to carry out his daily yoga job.

Little by little, my senses are awakening. My nose opens to the scent of sweet grass. My taste buds are stimulated to the point of ecstasy by today's lunch, an Indian meal of chutney, raita and curry. I eat at one of the picnic tables outside the dining hall, so that I can listen to the gurgling of the stream and watch the glitter of sunlight on the water's surface. The murmuring sound and fluid motion are hypnotic. Amidst dizzy sensations like "tripping," I recall how I followed Julie's suggestion and waded in a more secluded part of the creek before lunch. With a poem brewing in my mind, I head for my bedroom to record it:

> *Blinded by the hot noonday sun,*
> *As I leap across a shallow brook,*
> *I miss my step and nearly fall*
> *Backwards into the stream.*
> *Arms helicoptering,*
> *I balance myself and pause.*
> *Why not stop and wade?*
>
> *Peeling off shoes and socks,*
> *I perch on a warm rounded rock*
> *To dangle naked pink feet in*
> *Clear water so chilly*
> *I gasp in shock.*
>
> *Seven curious skate bugs*
> *Scoot over to investigate*
> *The wiggling intruders*
> *In their quiet, backwater pool.*
> *With jerking breast strokes*
> *The skaters flit forward and sideways*
> *In idiosyncratic rhythms.*
> *They congregate around my toes*
> *In disorganized confusion.*

As I pull bluish icy feet
From the brook's basin,
The bugs spin in a tizzy.
Their shadows are magnified
To look like alien space men
On the sunlit stones
Lining the streambed.

Drying dripping feet
On the sunny rock,
I watch the seven skaters
Return to equilibrium.

No longer riled up
By uninvited invaders,
They slow down and
Perform a random skater's waltz
On the calm surface of the water.

By the time I finish scribbling, rest period has finished, and I rush to fetch the bell to rouse my companions for the first sit of the afternoon. When I strike the big iron gong, my right wrist throbs in the aftermath of so much writing.

Tonight Eugene bases his dharma talk, "Passion, Compassion and Dispassion," on the Satipattana Sutta from the Buddha's discourse about the Four Foundations of Mindfulness. This was one of the suttas assigned for study in the Community Dharma Leader training. From memory, I review the Foundations:

The body is the first object of mindfulness, and we can practice observing the origination and dissolution of sensations as well as paying attention to each change in posture, including lying, sitting, and standing. Taking this practice to the extreme, Theravada monks attempt to dissolve their identification with the corporal form by naming each part and function of the body, noticing the repulsiveness of such elements as pus, phlegm, and blood. Part of the monastic mindfulness practice involves spending time in cemeteries or around corpses to contemplate the various stages of disintegration of the body, as a further means of letting go of physical attachment.

Feelings are the second object of mindfulness, and we can notice the origin and dissolution of pleasant, unpleasant and neutral reactions to whatever stimuli is perceived. I am learning how to guard my "sense doors" so that I can catch positive and negative reactions before they lead to a series of associated thoughts. I am increasingly aware of how often sounds that I consider unpleasant in one context can seem pleasant in another one. Sometimes I enjoy the racket of frogs singing to one another outside the meditation hall, and other times I find the din an annoying distraction from following the flow of my breath.

The mind is the third object of mindfulness, and practitioners can observe the origin and dissolution of mental states such as anger, lust, sadness, fear, and joy. How much easier it is for me to identify with what I deem positive mental states than with those I consider negative! So often I become lost in the morass of whatever mental state arises and forget that it is not "mine." No matter how frequently impatience surges inside the mind, it passes away, as do all mental states. None is permanent.

The fourth Foundation of Mindfulness consists of "mental objects" such as the numbered lists that the Buddha used to help his followers remember important principles and aspects of consciousness. For instance, recalling the Buddha's "Five Hindrances" helps practitioners identify when the mind is absorbed with desire, aversion, sleepiness, restlessness, or doubt. I found it easy to memorize another set of mental objects known as the Four Noble Truths:

1. *Dukkha* or suffering affects all human beings who cannot accept that everything is impermanent and prone to change.
2. *Samudaya* or craving and thirst are the origin of *dukkha*.
3. *Nirudha* or the cessation of *dukkha* entails the extinction of desire, hatred and delusion.
4. *Magga*, the way leading to the cessation of *dukkha*, is moderation or the Middle Path, referred to as the Noble Eightfold Path.

I am interested in Eugene's interpretation of the Four Foundations of Mindfulness. He calls Vipassana a path of "heartfulness" or "bodyfulness" and asks us all to consider, "What touched your heart and called you to practice?" I remember falling in love with the dharma during my first retreat at IMS. From the start, the Buddha's teachings made sense to me on a deep and intuitive level. Eugene says, "As we marry ourselves to the dharma, we encounter the depth of the relationship." He recites a passage from one of the Buddha's discourses: "Because we hold ourselves dear, we maintain careful self-regard both day and night." I like the idea of including oneself in caring for all sentient beings. So often I have higher expectations and stricter standards for myself than I do for others. Eugene reminds us that Vipassana practice not only wakens our passion for higher consciousness, but it also fosters humanity, wisdom and compassion. He mentions Kwan Yin, the Bodhisattva of Compassion, who instead of resting in Nirvana uses her thousand arms and hands to comfort all those who suffer. I feel inspired by hearing about the mystical Kwan Yin practice of developing wisdom and compassion by listening to the sorrows of the world. That is my mission as a music therapist.

Eugene suggests that dispassion cools the fires of our greed and aversion and helps us see things as they really are. Indeed, Nirvana signifies "extinguishing." He recounts the familiar story of the Buddha asking a grieving mother who had lost her child to bring him a mustard seed from a home where nobody has died; by the time the mother returns empty-handed, she has learned the truth that everyone must die. Eugene quotes Victor Frankl, the survivor of a concentration camp: "What is to give light must endure burning," reminding us that we practice Vipassana to burn away cherished self-concepts and misguided ideas in the light of awareness. Shedding the personality and character defenses leaves us with our basic nature that is kind, intelligent and open. I delight in the closing excerpt from a poem by Goethe:

> In the calm waters of the love nights,
> Insane for the light, you are the
> Butterfly and you are gone....
> If you have not experienced this,
> You are only a troubled guest
> On this dark earth.

On March 9, I sleep until the 5:00 a.m. wake-up bell and arise feeling groggy. During the first sit of the day, I find myself reminiscing about the late 1960's, when I lived as a hippy and shared a big beach house with my first husband and five male friends who were all attending Yale University. I recall our beloved dog Dinkum and her tragic death after a botched surgery. My thoughts are so caught up in the past that I dissolve in tears and mourn for my pet who died over thirty years ago. The resonant ring of the gong that signals the end of the meditation period startles me out of my reverie. On my way to breakfast, I resolve that as soon as this retreat ends, Mark and I must acquire a puppy. He still misses his childhood dog named Abraham and has expressed longing for another canine companion. In the twenty-one years of our childless marriage both of us have been too absorbed in our professional pursuits and close friendships to shoulder the responsibility of taking care of any dependents. I had forgotten how much joy a dog can bring to my life.

Jack fields questions from the sangha during the sit after breakfast. After a yogi asks how to handle the hindrance of sleepiness, Jack describes hot afternoons at Burmese monasteries where hundreds of monks and nuns sit in meditation, and scores of them are dozing and nodding drowsily. He reminds us that energies of restlessness and sleepiness arise naturally in everyone. We can make an effort to note these energies mindfully, noticing any aversion and related suffering. If, after a period of mindfulness, the somnolent or unquiet state persists, it is skillful to apply an antidote, such as sitting up straighter or standing with eyes open to bring higher energy to the body, or scanning the sensations in each body part to ground mental restlessness. I make a resolution to transmit Jack's advice to one of my Mexican meditation students, who sleeps through most sits.

Another yogi poses a question about what she calls "selfing" and her aversion to self-referential and self-absorbed thoughts. Jack suggests expanding the field of attention around the energy of "selfing," observing what mind state precedes it, and noting "insecurity" or "wanting," etc. He recommends that we allow "selfing" to come and go just like any other wave of energy that moves through the body or mind. Everything is born from certain conditions and is arising for a cause. We can trust the way that the cosmos is evolving. I leave this question and answer period feeling reassured and less judgmental about practicing mindfulness.❧

CHAPTER THREE

ADDICTED TO WRITING

With some amusement, I notice how bouncy I am. Hardly ever taking time to honor transitions between activities, I tend to leap up from my seat as soon as the bell rings, to zip through doors, and to plop down on my zafu for sits. I decide to practice paying attention to transitions instead of noting only arrival points. As if my body were approving of this decision, I sense whorls of tension spiraling off of the left side of my upper back, directly behind my heart. A passage from Shakespeare's *Merchant of Venice* emerges in my mind:

The quality of mercy is not strained.
It droppeth as the gentle rain from heaven
Upon the place beneath; it is twice blessed;
It blesses him that gives, and him that takes....

How seldom do I treat myself with mercy and compassion, taking time to rest and receive. I am so focused on accomplishing tasks and meeting goals that I rarely pause to integrate and digest the effects of my activities.

At lunch, I glance out the window and see a mother deer and two fawns with noses slick from lapping water in the brook. While her children munch tall grass, the mother stretches her neck up high to sample the leaves of a nearby tree. I grin at the unexpected pleasure of being so near to deer.

I am shocked by how quickly I feel fear at the first sign of flu symptoms. Everyone around me has been coughing, including my roommate. Somehow I thought that I would be exempt from contamination. I visit the manager's office to purchase some homeopathic remedies on the honor system, placing the designated amount of money into an envelope that is bulging with similar contributions. How easily I lose my equilibrium! During the next walking period, I hike up the hill beyond Upekkha residence hall to a wooden platform, where I pace slowly back and forth, trying to regain my inner balance. With the steady rhythm of my steps, a poem forms, and I stop to write down the words:

My sturdy shoes resound
On the three wooden steps to
Worn, unvarnished boards,
Forming an octagonal platform.
It overlooks softly rounded hills,
Sprinkled with long dry grass
And yellow wild flowers.

Rough-hewn banisters
Lead up to a spare
But solidly built balustrade,
Safely containing the space.
Flanking both sides of
A central walkway,
Sixteen planks of gradated length
Terminate with triangular-cut
Wedges of wood at all eight points.

A SILENT CURE

I sit on the top step
To shed shoes and socks.
Bare feet spring free,
Liberating cramped toes,
Easing calloused heels.
My tender soles
Sense the warmth of
Sun-baked planks.
A blustery March breeze
Cools the tops of my feet.

Pacing slowly clockwise,
Hearing each foot slap the wood,
I am five years old again,
Running barefoot
On the boathouse dock
To skinny dip in Lake Sunapee.
In my mind I am
Three thousand miles away,
Fifty years in the past.

Tides of memory recede.
I feel my feet, high and dry,
Pattering on the planks.
Each board portrays
An aging diva's face,
Stripped of make-up,
With its own pattern of
Cracks, creases, wrinkles,
Scars, nicks and knots.

Splinters surround
Hardy metal screws,
Bolting the octagon together.
The balls of my feet
Absorb warm energy
On sunny patches,
And resist chilly boards
Shaded by nearby trees.
Gradually their shadows
Overtake the deck.

I don my sensible shoes.
Poised to descend the steps,
I hesitate and see
A small bronze bell
Standing in matching saucer,
Left by a meditator
Atop the balustrade.
Ritualistically ringing thrice
The high-pitched bell,
I honor the sacred octagonal space.

Even though my wrist feels strained, the act of writing calms me down, and I return to the meditation hall feeling more centered. Lunchtime feels peaceful; I sit on a bench near the stream and eat in close proximity to three foraging deer.

Tonight Jack, Anna and John lead a question and answer period. Throughout the day, yogis have written doubts and queries about Buddhist practice and have placed their slips of paper inside the big bowl-like gong near the teacher's zafus. The three teachers take turns reading out loud and responding to selected questions. I am intrigued by a question about the difference between U Pandita's microscopic style of concentration practice and the more expansive approach to mindfulness that is taught at Spirit Rock. Jack answers that although he has chosen to teach a "middle path way," there are great benefits from adhering to U Pandita's slow form of developing concentration. I laugh at Jack's quip, "There's no is-ness like slow is-ness!" Anna responds to a related question, "Isn't concentration impermanent? How can we cultivate it?" It is true that because a concentrated state of mind is dependent on quiet, still conditions, it can be interrupted when those conditions change. By returning over and over to the sensation of breathing, I can develop concentration, but I cannot hold onto it indefinitely.

Anna answers the question, "If we have no self, why do some yogis bow to the altar and Buddha images?" She reminds us that Japanese temples have low portals so that all must bow their heads to enter sacred space. She recalls that when the Dalai Lama and the venerable monk Gosanda, known as the "Gandhi of Cambodia," met at a Buddhist conference at Spirit Rock, each attempted to honor the other by bowing lower until their two bald heads nearly grazed the ground. On her first trip to Nepal, Anna met travelers from many countries, and everyone inclined their heads with the internationally familiar greeting, "Namaste," meaning, "I bow to your divine nature." A bow can represent awe and gratitude for the sacred mystery of life, and statues of the Buddha are symbols for our inner quest for liberation from suffering. While some yogis love ritual, others resist it. After Anna assures us that for those uncomfortable with bowing, it is fine to omit the ritual, I feel relieved. Although I admire Tibetan Buddhists for performing a hundred thousand full body prostrations throughout their lifetime, I prefer an understated manner of praying or meditating.

We all laugh at a question about how to handle "Vipassana romances." As sensitivity increases in the silence, it is common for yogis to sense a resonance with kindred spirits. From past retreats I know how it is to have intense feelings of longing for a person I have never met and with whom I cannot speak. At this moment I admit to myself that I am developing a crush on Teja. Every morning I show up in the front row for his Qigong classes and admire the grace of his movements and the deep resonance of his voice as he announces exotic names of exercises such as "Balancing Heaven and Earth." I enjoy the slow flowing motions of each exercise and sense heightened energy at the end of the half-hour sessions. Since our appointment when he touched my neck, I have written Teja several notes to clarify instructions about postural alignment and foundational practices. He responds promptly to each note and seems to like my enthusiastic interest in what he is teaching. One day I signed my note "Gingerita la Mariposita," and Teja answered with a witty note in Spanish signed "El Leopardo de la Nieve." Thus I learned that his totem animal is the snow leopard, just as he knows that mine is the Monarch butterfly. I recognize that we have been flirting in spite of the silence. In our most recent exchange of notes, we arranged for him to give me a private lesson about "Ming-men," or the "Gate of Life" around the kidneys. I wonder if Teja could give me a ride to Petaluma at the end of the retreat.

With a jolt, I force my attention back to Anna's voice, which is advising us to note "fantasizing, fantasizing," to observe feelings of loneliness underlying lust, and to avoid following "loved ones" around during walking meditations. She recalls that at a three month retreat at the Insight Meditation Society, one woman placed a love note in the Berkenstock sandal of the wrong yogi and had to discourage the flattered recipient at the retreat's end. Vipassana practice helps us stop believing and identifying with our thoughts. The silent reminder "Not now" can help us let go of obsessive thoughts. At this point in the question and answer period my pen runs out of ink, and I shake my right wrist to relieve the tension of trying to write down so many helpful words of advice.

As I wash vegetables alongside Ida tonight, I am still stimulated by the question and answer period, and I playfully toss some freshly scrubbed squash to my co-worker. When she responds with a look of irritation, I give her a friendly nudge with my hip. She surprises me by breaking silence to complain: "You are too quick for me." Ida turns away, and when I try to follow her, she repeats emphatically, with her Swiss accent, "You are too quick for me." I bow to her and back off to finish piling squash into a rubber tub for those who will be preparing tomorrow's lunch. I feel deflated and remorseful. My thoughts keep returning to Ida's comment, as I consider how speedy I have been throughout my life. I recall the series of bicycle and car accidents that I have survived, with broken collarbones, sprained ankles, and assorted bruises. My personal history is full of cuts and burns and risky trips to far-off and sometimes dangerous third world countries. A couple of hypo-manic episodes left a trail of disconcerted colleagues. I have been blessed with loyal and understanding friends and family members, who have accepted belated apologies for my impulsive and overly enthusiastic behavior. Still ruminating after my yogi job, I write a note of apology to Ida, promising her to slow down in future work periods, and I tack the note onto the bulletin board in the lobby of the meditation hall.

Back in the semi-refuge of my shared room, I reflect upon how much writing I have been doing on this retreat. My family name, "Clarkson," means "son of a clerk." Maybe that contributes to why I am such a scribe. Am I too compulsive? I have been waking up around 4:00 a.m. to write down dreams, noting spontaneous poems that arise during walking periods, journaling about my feelings, and taking notes during dharma talks and question-answer periods. Is it possible that I am writing to filter my onrushing experiences so that I will not feel overwhelmed? An insight arises that writing poetry helps me feel connected to my mother, a published poet. The nurturing I feel from my poems may be a link to maternal love. I decide to place the photo of me and my mom on the community altar in the meditation hall tomorrow.

On March 10, I wake up, eagerly anticipating an interview with Jack, only to discover that I am on Julie's list for this afternoon instead. As Anna says, "We have no idea what will happen today. We take what we get." Can I follow her counsel and let each moment unfold with curiosity and awareness? I notice emotional states rising and falling like weather changes and try not to identify with the positive and negative stories connected to my thoughts.

Julie proves to be the perfect counselor for my dilemma about writing to cope with the rapid flow of sensory and emotional impressions. My tears start in response to her reassuring words, "You deserve to enjoy beautiful sensations unfolding in the present moment. You can channel the words back into the sensations. You do not need to write for your mother or for people reading about this retreat. Simply soak up the direct experiences." I review my family history of emotional instability and depression, my maternal grandfather's suicide, and my own hypo-manic episodes. Julie advises me to "titrate" my journaling, using it wisely to self-medicate and maintain my balance, cutting back so that I do not miss the actual retreat experiences. I recognize that I do not need to protect myself as much as I did twenty years ago. Meditation, yoga, and silent walks in nature are all my allies for staying grounded and safe. Attending to transitions and endings, slowing my pace, and flowing more gracefully with life are all helpful practices. At the interview's end, Julie reminds me that whenever I feel pressured or hurried, the anchor of bodily sensations and the breath can sustain me.

Although I attend Rona's yoga class, I feel distracted and on the verge of crying. I decide to skip the next meditation sit and to take a "Metta nap" in my room. As soon as I lie down on the bed, waves of tears pour through me. After many years of pressure and rushing and striving to be good enough, I surrender. Like a small child, I rock and soothe myself. Suddenly the door opens and Alison interrupts my sobbing. Although she tries to be quiet and exits quickly, I feel invaded and exposed. On the way to dinner, I write Julie a note asking to speak with her before the next scheduled interview.

In a secluded corner of the dining hall, I am swept away by bouts of crying, unable to taste the food. When Ida approaches to sit nearby, I avoid meeting her eyes. If anyone looks at me sympathetically, I will dissolve again. Before a line gathers, I bus my plates and flee from the dining room. On a rational level I think that the psychiatrist Stan Grof would refer to my emotional turmoil as a "COEX;" I am confronting "systems of condensed experience" and a consistent pattern of response that affects various levels of consciousness (Grof, 193, p. 240). I have tapped into a lifelong theme of perfectionism that has plagued me and my family for generations. Beneath the surface of so much frenzied activity lie pools of grief and fatigue. In my present sensitive state, I perceive my deceased grandfather, my mother, my siblings and their children sharing my pain. When will we realize that we are lovable just as we are, with no need to prove anything?

On the way up the hill, I stop to watch my deer friends on their evening forage and notice a cigar-like slug oozing across the asphalt next to my feet. It calms me down to connect to animals. A blond woman with gentle eyes stops to admire the deer with me. I feel a friendly nonverbal rapport with her. Noble silence protects us from diminishing the experience by chatting about it.

During the 6:30 sit, song fragments from "Bridge Over Troubled Waters" and "Cry Me a River" flit through my mind. My chronically tight right shoulder begins to let go of the burden of so many years of taking course notes and copying music therapy manuscripts. I sense my stiff neck muscles loosening. Behind my heart, the upper back is starting to release. Alongside these physical sensations comes a feeling of gratitude for Vipassana practice, which helps me heal on such deep levels.

Robert gives tonight's dharma talk on the topic of why "anatta," the Buddhist concept of "no self," is so hard for us to understand. I cannot resist the temptation to record his opening words in my journal: "We are beings immersed in self. Egocentrism is hard-wired into our cells. Almost all thought is self-referential." My hand keeps penning in rhythm with his voice, which intones the Buddha's teachings about the five "aggregates" that prevent us from freeing the conditioned mind: "Whatever is not yours, abandon it. Material form, perception, feelings, and consciousness are not yours." Robert quotes Albert Einstein: "Humans live with an optical delusion of consciousness," then suggests that we need to expand our hearts to encompass the whole universe of which we are an inseparable part. He mentions the ego or "small self" that fears for its existence and seeks safety: "The small self cares for its family and wants to be good and even seeks a spiritual practice. It creates art, institutions, and longs to be free, especially as death approaches. The ego self seeks pleasurable experiences and recreates painful childhood experiences as a way of healing." After today's immersion in my own small self, I wonder if this dharma talk is being aimed directly at me.

Robert goes on to elucidate the aggregates, commencing with "form." Even though modern physics has shown that all that appears solid fluctuates between a particles and waves of energy, we tend to identify with the physical body. Thousands of years ago the Buddha mentioned the elements of earth, air, water, and fire that give us the illusion of solidity, and he taught that the true self is the "deathless" or "unborn." I ask myself what self I am trying to protect.

The second aggregate entails feelings about what is pleasant, unpleasant, or neutral around us. Roberts recalls that each of his three children had different responses to sensations. The oldest one was born smiling, the second was angry from birth, and the youngest was born with equanimity. These traits have persisted into adulthood. Because I tend to be an optimist who focuses on what is pleasant, it is challenging for me to understand people with aversive personality types or to fully accept my own negative reactions.

Perception is the third aggregate, with the tongue responding to taste, the nose to scents, the ears to sounds, the eyes to sights, and the skin to touch. As infants start to notice a division between themselves and the outer world, they experience the beginning of separateness, a split between inner and outer realms. In neurosis, the perception of distance is often distorted, so that boundaries with others are unclear. On retreat, I have experienced moments of returning to an infant-like state of pure receptivity, without perceiving myself as apart from my sensations.

Robert mentions, as the fourth aggregate, "mental formations" and "comparing mind," which stem from the developmental stage of a two-year-old child, who experiments with brief, independent forays away from the mother. When the child tries to control the surrounding environment, awareness of duality develops, and, under the influence of elders, belief systems start to form. The Buddha listed eleven "good" mental states, including faith, discipline, courage, equanimity, humility, and energy, as well as "evil" states such as ignorance, lust, anger, pride, doubt, and dogmatism. Sloth, remorse, intellectual speculation and knowing are viewed as "neutral" states of mind. As I remember my recent interaction with Ida, remorse does not seem at all neutral. I pay close attention when Robert states that insanity is a distortion in mental formations. Am I distorting personal history, or am I uncovering truths that will serve me and those I love?

Conditioned consciousness is the fifth and last aggregate: it involves the ego's intelligence, as well as our instincts and fears of our shadow, our darker selves. The bare attention of meditation helps us cut through polarities and open directly to sensations as they are, prior to making comparisons with other stimuli or to categorizing them as pleasant or unpleasant. Robert says that as we re-train our habits and develop an "addiction to mindfulness," we wean ourselves from "me-ing" and heal our dualistic neurosis. Then there is no more need to ask, "Who am I?" Whereas Western psychology studies the ego as is grows and strengthens, Buddhist practice studies the ego as it disintegrates. Robert's conclusion is that compassion is the healing balm, breaking our attachment to the aggregates, so that we operate from a heart beyond categories and conditions. I copy down some memorable lines from the closing poem: "Only love survives. Love is the destination and the answer. I worship love. That is all there is." What a delight to have a dharma teacher who is a poet and a psychiatrist knowledgeable about theories of child development.

At this moment, I feel free of my own personal concerns and reconnected to my heart. I recognize that Metta practice calms me down when I accelerate in tempo. Anna reminded us this morning that at any given time around the world someone is doing Metta prayers, chants, and rituals. Whenever I practice Metta, I am entering the stream of lovingkindness circling the globe. I carry warm feelings inside until bedtime.

I awaken on March 11 in the midst of a dream about a puppy interrupting my household chores and encouraging me to play outdoors by pulling my wrist towards the door. Is the message that I need to tend to my instinctual needs? Looking at the star-covered, dark blue cover of my dream journal, I am reminded of Vincent Van Gogh's painting "Starry Night," created while he was in an insane asylum. Since my hypo-manic episode twenty-five years ago, I have had an underlying fear of going crazy. Many of my daily routines keep me grounded. Writing has been a lifesaver. (At this moment my pen runs out of ink for the second time on this retreat. Is this a sign that I am writing too much?)

After scrambling to find another pen, I wonder if I can let go of being scared of insanity. Paul Simon's song "Still Crazy After all These Years" floats into my mind. Everyone has a zany part. When John Travis told us about his struggles with dyslexia, I found his vulnerability endearing. Edgar's autistic bumbling touches my heart. Our wounds can help us become healers in the world. I bear the scars of an appendectomy, sterilization, hysterectomy, and surgery to repair broken facial bones after a bicycle accident. Yet I feel whole—a survivor with compassion for others' injuries.

My serious mood lasts until Robert speaks after the morning sit. He remarks that "this is a room full of egocentric egos observing and studying themselves, sometimes in wholesome ways, sometimes in unwholesome ways," and the sangha erupts in laughter. Robert then switches to a more solemn tone: "Occasionally we have moments of grace when we transcend the ego and reach the bliss of freedom from self-centeredness. Even those who never have a spiritual practice deserve glimpses of grace. We do not know very much about divine grace. Life is a mystery, and we are not in charge." How right he is. I am feeling less and less in charge as this retreat progresses.

When I read Julie's note scheduling an extra interview for me at noon, I am gratified that I was able to ask for help and overcome my pride about being self-sufficient. After walking in the hills, I arrive at the Council House a bit late for the interview, and, in my rush, I forget the custom of removing my shoes at the door. To protect my face from the bright sun I am wearing a baseball cap, which makes me look far younger than my years. As I head for an empty chair facing Julie, I notice Diana Winston sitting in the corner. Since she and I already know each other from the Community Dharma Leader training, I readily grant her permission to witness the interview as part of her Vipassana teacher-in-training experience. Then I burst into tears. Julie offers to sit closer to me. Sobbing like a little child, I let her hold my hands. Even though I long for a hug, I am too timid to ask for one. In my physically undemonstrative, WASP family, I was seldom hugged or kissed, and I never considered requesting more affectionate touching. Julie tells me how beautiful I look, in my fragile vulnerability. After more than fifty years of being tightly wound, the top has blown off the pressure cooker. I recall the nicknames I have been given over the years: "wire woman," "fire woman," and in Mexico, "la flaquita" (skinny one). When I tell her about my "Metta nap," Julie congratulates me for taking good care of myself and reminds me that she and Jack are here for me, like surrogate parents. In response to worries about my compulsion to write, she suggests that I give thanks for the writing ability that is a gift from my ancestors, the original clerks who earned the name "Clarkson," and that has been my refuge and support for so long. Now I have an opportunity to learn to choose freely when and how I use this gift.

Julie notes that by liberating myself from driven, compulsive, and rigid defenses, I am freeing not only myself but also my perfectionist family. I divulge that my mom's name is Virginia, as is mine, and that my maternal grandmother Deedee used to call me "Little Virginia." As I face how strongly I am connected to my mother, Julie asks if I would like a hug. I accept her offer gratefully and feel thin and small in her arms, even though I stand taller. Surrendering to another onslaught of tears, I confess how hard it is for me to be falling apart while sharing a double room, no matter how considerate my roommate is. Immediately Julie empathizes with my predicament and promises to lobby for my switching to a single room as soon as one is vacated. There will be a turnover of yogis coming and going this Saturday, as some people who have been meditating for six weeks leave, and newcomers arrive for the final two weeks of the retreat. What a relief to know that a reprieve is possible.

After Julie and Diana depart from the Council House, I stay and cry. It is only when hunger pangs enter my awareness that I wash my swollen eyes and run down to fetch a late lunch. There, as I eat and weep at an isolated bench behind the dining hall, I hear the voices of the teachers singing "Happy Birthday" in the yurt where they have their meals. Today feels like a birthing day for me, with new possibilities for freedom and relaxation and happiness in my life. Decades after the Easter Sunday of my birth, the egg-shell of my defenses is cracking open. I notice multi-colored butterflies fluttering around me: some are white and silky, others have speckled orange wings, and still others are tiny yellow specimens. My totem "mariposas" seem to be protecting me today.

I feel safe at Spirit Rock under the care of Jack and Julie. Somehow when I met Jack, I knew that he had the key to my healing. I have followed him loyally from coast to coast, on progressively longer retreats. Now I understand why.

Vipassana practice has helped me trust myself enough to let go of layers of protective armor. My chest feels raw and exposed, and I am so dizzy and tired that I nearly fainted during Qigong exercises this morning. It is clear that I need to move slowly and treat my emerging child-self with tenderness. Julie has the wisdom to encourage me to write whenever I need to catch up with the flow of emotions during this crisis period.

More tears flow during the post-lunch sit. My maternal great-grandmother, Deedee's mother, comes to my mind. I reflect upon how she died giving birth to my uncle Jack. There was nobody to cuddle my grandmother and her baby brother. Deedee grew up too proper and lady-like to cuddle my mom as an infant. Perhaps one of the reasons my mother has not been physically affectionate with me is that she was traumatized by her dad's sudden early death. On Dad's side of the family, his mom's brother Earl was killed as a boy in a shotgun accident. While she accompanied my paternal grandfather, "Pappy," on business trips around the world, my grandmother, "Gram," left Dad and his two brothers with a variety of governesses, who treated the three boys severely. My father received no cuddling. As an eighteen-year-old military medical aide, he was emotionally overwhelmed by helping to evacuate Bergen Belsen concentration camp at the end of World War II, and by witnessing the death of his younger brother Peter, who developed polio of the brain soon after my birth. Dad did not cuddle me either. We are a "touch-free" family that is not inclined to hug or kiss one another. I recall an aunt visiting us when I was a child. She would bend down to present her cool, immaculately made-up cheek for a brief peck of a kiss and then pull back quickly to adjust her perfectly sprayed hairdo. On the spectrum of hot to cold, my aunt was the chilliest of my relatives, but nobody else was particularly steamy.

By nature I am a snuggler and a hand-holder. I used to wonder if I had been adopted by my puritanical New England family, which had no such inclinations. My hands and feet are usually icy cold, as if they are seeking the warmth of physical contact. When Mark and I fell in love in his home state of Texas, I was so happy to have found a man who hugs me regularly and holds my hand on walks. Like me, he gravitates towards the warmth of southern climes and prefers the climate of our present home in Mexico to the snowy winters of New England. However, we both have the tendency to become caught up in academic work and to forget the sensual side of life. As soon as this retreat ends, I want to ask Mark to join me in making cuddling time a priority in our marriage.

Waves of fear surge through me during dinner, as I remember how crazy I have been in the past. I recall the story of the Buddha touching the earth when Mara was trying to confuse and distract him from the goal of becoming enlightened. I place my hand on the solid wood of the dining table to ground myself in the present moment and return to tasting my food. What a blessing that the Spirit Rock cooks are experienced meditators who give loving attention to preparing each meal. The colors, textures, and tastes are all presented exquisitely, and they merit appreciation and mindfulness: "pleasant, pleasant."

By the time I walk up the hill, I feel better and sense my feet on the hard asphalt. Still tearful, I miss Mark and the comfort of family. Throughout the evening sit, I note "fear, fear, sadness, sadness" until I hear the woman beside me crying in harmony with me. Suddenly I am smiling at the thought of how many tears we yogis have shed collectively in this meditation hall. The ego's sense of humor comes to my rescue.

Anna gives tonight's dharma talk and tells us that in 1980 she attended her first Vipassana retreat, after years of Zen and Tibetan Buddhist practice, and after earning a doctorate in clinical psychology. By then she had benefited from many sessions of psychotherapy. At a three-month retreat at the Insight Meditation Society, Anna was shocked to encounter fear. Because of all her inner preparation, she had considered herself immune to feeling scared. Once the shock subsided, she used simple attentiveness to relate to the fear until her relationship to it transformed. At this instant I feel as if Anna is addressing me: "Fear is part of the process of mindfulness. Mindfulness is like a light to illuminate where we resist and cling."

Because her personal story has caught my attention, I follow as Anna speaks on a more abstract level about the characteristic, function and manifestation of mindfulness. The characteristic is "penetrating deeply beneath the appearance of solidity" of pain in the body or fear in the mind, and noticing how the energy field changes continuously. The function of mindfulness is "non-disappearance." With practice, we learn to recognize the truth honestly, without ignoring or pretending that pain or fear are not happening. Whatever we try to exclude will reveal itself eventually. The manifestation of mindfulness is "confrontation." We learn to meet whatever emerges with energy, directly.

When Anna states, "fear is a trance state," I am highly motivated to understand her meaning. She tells us that fear is accompanied by stories and unpleasant body sensations. It is impersonal and goes through changes. Fear does not have to lead to increased suffering. Seeing what is true in the moment is the salvation. Fear recurs to show us how much we need to learn about it. We can practice letting go of fear without imagining that it will return, or creating stories about it. Anna recommends that we avoid analyzing the reasons for our fear: it is not possible to make sense of an uncontrollable and unpredictable universe.

"Don't judge your experiences as if they shouldn't be happening," says Anna. Is she reading my mind? She recalls her journey as a meditator, starting practice in the mid-1970's with the image of going to extremes to rid herself of all unpleasant experiences. Her first teacher was a Tibetan monk who transmitted so much energy that Anna fell in love with him. After she left to study with an eighty-year-old Zen master in Japan, she found herself in "Zen boot camp," arising at 3:30 each morning to chant prayers in Japanese. She attended four daily interviews with Suzuki Roshi, who posed questions such as "What is your Buddha nature when you hear the sound of a bird?" Anna felt clueless. The Zen meditation posture was extremely precise, and monks with sticks would strike her back to remind her to sit up straighter. When a devoted Zen practitioner shouted, "Die on the pillow," she had a "Zen nervous breakdown" and dissolved in tears. It was Joseph Goldstein at IMS who gave Anna the first meditation instruction that she was able to follow successfully: "Pay attention to your breath."

Anna reminds us that the Buddha was an extreme seeker, who nearly starved to death as an ascetic monk, until he connected with a childhood memory of sitting contentedly beneath a rose apple tree. At that point, the Buddha let go of striving and arrived at "The Middle Way" of moment-to-moment mindfulness. He realized that everything is conditioned by a chain of dependent origination. With each moment of sensory contact, pleasant, unpleasant, or neutral feelings arise naturally. We can break the chain by noting our feelings. Otherwise we react with desire, aversion, or boredom. Simply seeing the moment of contact for what it is, without editing, liberates us from being enslaved by our desires.

Anna mentions the Buddhist psychological types: greedy, aversive, and deluded or confused. I identify myself as a greedy type thousands of years after the Buddha defined these categories. In the fifth century B.C., he recommended that aversive types find serene dwelling places, that greedy types live where they must confront noise and discomfort, and that deluded types dwell in simple and structured places. Anna comments that we all need a balance of pleasant, unpleasant, and neutral sensations in our lives. Instead of trying to transcend pain, we can use attention at the "sense doors" to balance our sensory intake. Whereas traumatized people must cultivate attention to what is pleasant in order to feel safe, those who tend to deny suffering need to face unpleasantness. (That is exactly what I am dealing with on this retreat.) How right Anna is that extremes of pleasure or pain lead to being caught in views about ourselves or opinions about others: "Treasures are found in the Middle Ground."

In conclusion, Anna says that the ground of being is always present. We can trust emptiness to hold us. Nothing is missing. Everything is as it should be. We do not need to add or omit anything. When seen in the right way, everything we strive for is already here. We must balance practice with opening to what is true. I could not ask for a dharma talk more tailored to my immediate needs.

On March 12, I am startled at 3:30 a.m. and sit up in bed, sensing the energetic presence of my sponsored Tibetan daughter, Tenchoe, and her baby, Tenyang, with me. I tiptoe down the hall to the bathroom to drink a soporific "Rescue Remedy cocktail" and to write without disturbing Alison. My bright red pashmina shawl and heavy socks keep me warm. A composite image comes to me of Anna praying at this hour when she was in the Zen monastery and of monks and nuns around the world chanting Metta prayers. It consoles me to recall words from recent dharma talks that relate to my own experience. As Robert said, the ego has remarkable creative powers of self-healing. In yesterday's interview, Julie pointed out that I know how to mother and comfort myself. I feel confident that all the inner resources that I have developed in years of psychotherapy and meditative practice are sufficient for me to move through this stage of growth.

In order to care for my aching right wrist, I vow to take a break from writing poetry on this retreat. John's mantra "Not now" comes to mind. It feels fine to postpone penning and polishing poetry until my equilibrium is re-established. I resolve to write only about moment-to-moment inner processes and healing insights. Instead of trying to catch every word during dharma talks, I can jot down summaries of essential points. It is time to wean myself from my addiction to writing.

Recalling the sense of presence that woke me up in the middle of the night, I feel grateful to be the spiritual mother of Tenchoe in Dharamsala, India and the godmother of Virginia Carolina in León, Nicaragua. Several of my Mexican music therapy students consider me their "good mother," and one even brings me roses every Mother's Day. To be without biological children has not deprived me of experiencing motherhood on a spiritual level. The universe provides me with a wealth of children in the form of nieces, nephews, godchildren, students, and therapy clients. I remember the sensation of Virginia Carolina's little hand holding mine during my last visit to Nicaragua. What a blessing to be the inspiration for her name. Now there is an "even littler Virginia" in my family. My sense of family has expanded far beyond blood relationships in the Clarkson clan.

Noting sensations as they unfold, I feel my stomach aching and the right side of my body releasing tension through the neck and shoulder. My feet are solidly planted on the tiles of the bathroom floor. My goal is to find my own balance. With consciousness of every step, I return to bed to warm up and do Metta practice. Suddenly I am acutely aware that love is all there is. Love is the only force that makes sense to pursue or receive. In the movie "A Beautiful Mind," love is what motivates the schizophrenic Princeton mathematics professor to master his inner demons. Gradually he is able to differentiate his essence from his hallucinations and to distance himself from the visions that have been ruling his behavior. Painfully, he learns to confront his insane parts without being identified with them. He is able to accept his imperfections and to receive the love and respect of his wife. When his colleagues pay him the honor of giving him their pens, they recognized his courage in mastering his own mind. May I be inspired by his example. Letting go of tight and limiting habits is my path to freedom.

On the way to Qigong class I think of my mother, always clutching her yellow legal pad to write whenever she has a free moment. I have been carrying on her compulsion to filter life by recording it. How can I balance the writing that connects me to Mom's brilliance and creativity, and that also connects me to her fear and need for control? Right now I am doing healing work that benefits both of us. Teja snaps me out of my musings with the words, "It is your birthright to be nourished by the earth and the universe." How can I learn to accept that birthright fully?

In the meditation hall, Julie initiates a guided meditation to help us sense the energy field of our bodies, within the larger energy field of mindfulness that we have been creating together, within the enormous energy field of the universe: "Fear, grief or anger can feel too big for one small body to hold, but not for the expanse of the universe to contain." She suggests that we each choose one obvious body sensation as a focus of attention and then notice elemental energy shifts occurring. I concentrate on the changing sensations in my chronically stiff, sore right shoulder, my "broken wing." Julie asks us to pay attention to any story line associated with the sensations and to follow the story's stream back to the actual sense of earthy solidity, watery fluidity, airy vibration, or fiery warmth. She reminds us that each sensation is unfolding in the present moment, and that, like the breath, body sensations are dependable and honest. We can send waves of emotion, connected to body sensations, down into the earth to ground them.

During this exercise, I am aware of how much I have "shouldered," especially with all the writing I do with my dominant right hand. I resolve to be kind and loving to my poor, abused right shoulder, rubbing it with the analgesic cream that the retreat manager Andrea purchased for me. The shoulder can serve as my ally, helping me to do less, and to diminish my "breakneck" speed of living. Right now I can attend to the message from my body instead of resisting the pain. The lyrics from one of Sting's songs play through my mind: "Every breath you take, every move you make, I'll be watching you." What a perfect Vipassana instruction.

Jack greets me for today's interview in an especially attentive manner. He says, "I'm pleased that you're here on retreat, even though it's hard for you and Mark to be apart for a month, because you travel so much." I reply, "What I'm learning here will benefit my marriage. If I'm less driven and addicted to compulsive writing, I'll have more time to devote to Mark." Jack grins appreciatively, "That's sweet." How lovely to talk to my teacher without feeling intimidated or having anything to prove.

We continue our openhearted and frank exchange. He is pleased to hear about my decision to give up writing poetry on this retreat, and he observes approvingly that I am deviating from my family's tradition of striving for achievement. Jack laughs as I present him with a paper napkin on which is printed a slogan chosen by Mom: "My family tree is full of nuts." Indeed, what family tree is not that way? In a more serious vein, I report using Metta practice to comfort myself before dawn each day and Vipassana practice to restore equilibrium. When I mention feeling compassion for Edgar, the yogi who appears to have Asperger's syndrome, Jack responds, "He is benefiting from practice in his own way." Of course. Rather than worrying about the experience of other yogis, I need to tend to my own emotional ups and downs. As I depart from the interview, I say spontaneously, straight from the heart, "I love you dearly." Jack smiles and answers, "I love you too."

My heart feels so full that I walk energetically to the forest altar to give thanks for such happiness. Unlike my father, who is so undemonstrative, Jack is warmly responsive to my genuine expressions of love. A wounded infantile place deep within me is beginning to relax, now that the loving words that I have been longing to hear are no longer being withheld. I am allowing Jack to re-parent me. Inside of me is a new sense of freedom, with none of the usual pressure to rush back to my room to record my emotions. It is a relief to know that I will have time to rest after lunch today, without any poems to transcribe.

After yoga class, I surrender to a "Metta nap," lying face down on my bed, with my heart wide open to receive the support of the pillow. I am able to sleep profoundly, soaking up the rest I have been denying myself for so long. I wake up crying gently, with my heart as tender as a baby's. A dream from my nap lingers:

> *I am standing next to a male friend, Alan, whose creativity and sensitivity I admire. A couple next to us begins to dance to very slow music. Alan reaches for my hand, and I move into his arms to dance. As our bodies sway gently together, I allow myself to lie fully against his chest. He draws me to his heart and murmurs, "Yes!"*

It is strange to sense that I have arrived "home." There is nowhere to go, no reason to rush. I am here now completely: fragile, open, and ready to weep. I feel bone-tired and so sluggish that I can barely move. It is time to nourish my exhausted body with some delicious Spirit Rock food.

What synchronicity. At dinner the man who sits opposite me is wearing a tee shirt that proclaims, "The wait is over." The scent of hot gingerbread brings memories of the "Reds and Blues," swimming teams that competed at the Lake Sunapee Yacht Club on Friday afternoons each summer of my childhood. Our reward for enduring countless laps of sidestroke and butterfly kicks in the chilly water was steamy slices of spicy gingerbread. Tonight those of us who are lactose intolerant enjoy the luxury of topping our helpings with "hot whip," a non-dairy whipped cream. Spirit Rock is like paradise; nothing is lacking. Our minds are what create problems.

I notice a man dissolving in tears as he waits to bus his dirty dishes. Because I was in the same plight last night, I reach out my hand for his plates. He surrenders them thankfully and scurries out of the dining hall. It is so easy to be compassionate when my heart is raw and tender. There is no interference to responding naturally to suffering. On the slow uphill walk I see the silhouettes of feeding deer at the summit of a distant ridge, highlighted by the sunset's rosy clouds. As darkness blurs the boundaries between earth and sky, a half moon emerges, outlined by a huge silvery circle, like a gong, and the Big Dipper and Orion's Belt are clear as bells in the quiet night sky. "Later and slower" bring rewards.❧

CHAPTER FOUR

PLUNGING INWARD

S ynchronicities abound as the second week of the retreat nears its end. John Travis gives tonight's dharma talk about the Buddha's "Wheel of Life," which illustrates the causation and cessation of suffering. Once again, the theme resonates with my present experience. He states, "There is suffering that leads to more suffering, and there is suffering that leads to the end of suffering. Vipassana is a skillful way to end it."

The original paintings of what the Buddha described in detail to his followers as the Wheel of Life were lost in the twelfth century during the Muslim invasions of India. Fortunately, precious copies were preserved in Tibet. On a wall of the meditation hall, John has hung a diagram of the wheel for us to follow while he explains the significance of each part. As a symbol of impermanence, "dependent origination" is depicted by four wheels, symbolizing the realms of existence that revolve around greed, hatred, and delusion. All these conditions for suffering are held in the mouth of the Lord of Death. This fearsome Lord wears five skull-shaped crowns that represent the five aggregates. At the wheel's center is a pig, the force of ignorance, covering its eyes in mud. Out of the pig's mouth comes a snake, the force of greed. Biting the pig's tail is a cock, the force of aversion. Comprising the second wheel are illustrations of karmic actions that cause suffering, juxtaposed with figures evolving to monkdom and Buddhahood. The third wheel holds six realms, starting with the animal realm, which stands for predictable habits and instinctual urges to eat and copulate. In this realm there is no speculation or understanding about the meaning of life. The next realm of "hungry ghosts" symbolizes addictions as well as endless insufficiency and neediness, without satisfaction. The third realm of thought entails opinions, ideas, and concentration or subtle mind states that are all impermanent. The jealous God realm is a place of war, the result of attachment to possessions and power and trying to hold onto what is impermanent. Contraction, hatred, and anger lead to the hell realm.

The human realm is the sixth one and involves narcissism, accompanied inevitably by arrogance and deflation. In this middle realm human beings become so lost in stories about themselves that they forget the principle of conditionality. According to Buddhist psychology, the forces of ignorance and craving are conditions for "rebirth consciousness," what Joseph Goldstein refers to as "the arising of consciousness at the moment of conception" (Goldstein, 2002, p. 143). From the Buddhist perspective, people continue to be born as long as they are still caught in the illusion of self. It is only if we wake up from our trance of ignorance that we become free of the wheel of rebirth.

Although many Buddhist monks take the idea of rebirth literally, the concept can be viewed metaphorically as well. In his book *One Dharma*, Goldstein elucidates how often we experience "psychological rebirth" throughout our day-to-day existence:

> *When we get lost in some pleasant fantasy, the "I" is born in a pleasure realm. If we are caught by some intense unfulfilled wanting, we take birth in a hungry ghost realm. If we are lost*

in a sea of hatred, it is rebirth in a hell realm. And when the
mind is suffused with love or compassion, we dwell in what
the Buddha called the "Divine Abodes." The "I" is taking
rebirth countless times a day, traversing the Wheel of Life.
Whenever there is birth of "I" and "mine," born from grasp-
ing, there is suffering (Goldstein, 2002, p. 144).

John points out that the fourth wheel contains the twelve links of dependent origination and interdependent co-arising. The links of causality,
which include four that occur in the past, five in the present and the rest
in the future, form the basis of the Four Noble Truths. In this wheel the
Buddha is pictured pointing to a symbol of the truth. The first link portrays an old person carrying a bag through a leafless forest. This image
represents the ignorance of the pig, which leads humans to poison their
own planet. The next four links arise simultaneously to make up the five
aggregates. The second link shows a potter molding bowls; some are in a
stack of cracked ones, and others are in a stack of perfect ones. This scene
is a representation of karmic unfolding towards bad or good results of various causes. Next, consciousness, which arises from karma, is depicted as a
monkey, restlessly picking and throwing fruit down from trees. The fourth
picture shows the mind steering a boat (body) to indicate that physical form
arises from consciousness. The fifth link consists of the five senses and the
mind, depicted as a house with five windows and a door.

When all these conditions are present, the sixth link, "contact," occurs,
represented by a drawing of a couple embracing. Contact leads to feelings arising as the seventh link, portrayed by two arrows in a man's eyes,
conveying physical and mental pain associated with reactions to pleasant,
unpleasant and neutral sensations. It is at this crucial juncture that Vipassana practice helps us learn to stop moving towards pleasant sensations
and away from unpleasant ones, so that we can break subsequent links in
the wheel of causation of suffering. If we miss this opportunity to make
mindful choices, we proceed to the eighth link, which is craving, portrayed
by a glutton stuffing himself at a banquet table. The ninth link, "clinging
and grasping," pictures a person grabbing fruit from a tree to place atop a
basket that is already overflowing. At this stage, attachment has solidified
in our consciousness. A pregnant woman represents the tenth link, known
as "becoming" or "action." Link number eleven is "birth," and the twelfth
link entails disease, death and decay.

This chain is not linear but occurs in cycles. Outside of the wheel of causation is an image of the Buddha pointing to the way to break cycles of greed,

ignorance, and delusion. In each moment, we have chances to choose freedom. John closes his explication of the Wheel of Life by reminding us that the third Noble Truth, the cessation of suffering, is happening on this retreat: we are practicing choosing freedom.

On Thursday, March 13, I wake up at 2:30 a.m., facing stark fear. As I carry my journal to the bathroom to write, the confidence that I felt last night during John's dharma talk evaporates. Now the universe seems vast and awesome, and my boundaries are dissolving. This is the first time in years of Vipassana practice that I have surrendered my sense of a separate self to what seems like an endless void. Shivering with cold, I reassure my panicking ego that among the teachers at this retreat are Robert, a respected doctor and psychiatrist; Jack and Anna, both with doctoral degrees in clinical psychology; Eugene, an experienced psychotherapist; Julie, a skillful and deeply intuitive counselor; and John, who, like his colleagues, has developed wisdom and insight from meditating since the 1960's. I am in good hands here. Each time I have requested an extra interview from Jack or Julie, my wish has been granted. No longer do I feel like a warrior woman who is fearlessly following her spiritual quest. Right now I am more like a scared child, wondering if decades of psychotherapy, psychology courses, self-improvement workshops, and spiritual readings have taught me enough to be able to relinquish a sense of self.

My borders are dissipating as if on a LSD trip. But unlike the 1960's, when my "hippy" college friends and I were experimenting with hallucinogens, now I have more psychological resources, greater self-knowledge, and a safer container. I trust myself and the universe more fully. Memories arise of a "bad trip" at a Grateful Dead concert, when I curled up in a fetal position, closing my eyes tightly and covering my ears, to protect myself from the overwhelming sounds of the music. My friends had to carry me out of the auditorium. In tears, I told them that I was afraid to open my eyes in case I had been struck blind. A companion jammed my eyeglasses onto my face and ordered me to open my eyes. I wept with relief and gratitude that I could still see. How frightened I was to look at myself back then.

During "good trips" on peyote or LSD, I enjoyed loving connections with friends and sensed myself merging blissfully with musical vibrations and the subtle energy of trees. I remember watching my body parts as they appeared to elongate like an El Greco painting, or to dissolve into particles. My response at the time was curiosity rather than fear. What a blessing that I was relatively unscathed by drug experiences similar to those that in some cases contributed to psychotic breaks. It was sobering to do my music therapy internship at a psychiatric hospital on Long Island, and to help treat young adults just my age who had not stopped hallucinating months after ingesting LSD.

Since the sixties, without the influence of drugs, I have entered non-ordinary states of consciousness, facing inner demons and discovering internal allies on numerous GIM journeys and several Holotropic Breathwork odysseys. I feel grateful to my teachers, beginning with Vera Moretti, who introduced me to the field of music therapy during my junior year at college. Her expert piano playing and her sensitive manner of relating to children with severe disabilities inspired me to apply to graduate school in the pioneering career that I love. In the early seventies, Helen Bonny guided my first group GIM session with remarkable dignity and authority, and two of her first apprentices, Carol Bush and Sierra Stokes, trained me expertly to become a GIM facilitator and primary trainer. Eleanor Powers led me through Bioenergetics and Gestalt exercises that woke up my body and mind, and Ray Walker mined the symbolism of my dreams so thoroughly that I was tempted to follow his path as a Jungian analyst. More recently in Mexico, Mirna Molina's Core Energetics and Gestalt training has given me invaluable tools to understand myself and my clients. At Spirit Rock, James Baraz and Ajahn Amaro have introduced me to Buddhist philosophy in different but equally convincing ways. Since 1988, Jack has beamed a steady light on my spiritual path, and now Julie has appeared to lend me her support. As a seeker, I have encountered guides who have gladly shared their wisdom and vision with me. How blessed I am.

Writing here in the bathroom, I feel calmer and safer. Once again I can sense my breath "receiving and releasing" as an anchor. Metta practice provides me with a trustworthy safety net. Teja's Qigong classes and Rona's yoga sessions bolster my own daily grounding practices. With Rescue Remedy drops soothing my nervous system, I feel ready to return to bed.

The 5:00 a.m. bell awakens me from the following dream:

> *I am at the president's office (la rectoría) at the Universidad de las Américas. I overhear the Rectora saying that she does not want to cash any bad checks. Then I ask her secretary for a paycheck that I have earned for giving a workshop at the university. Unlike the Rectora, I trust that the check is good and that I will be able to cash it at a local bank. I hope that she does not throw away good checks out of fear that they are forged. The secretary admits how exhausted she feels working for such a demanding university president.*

She asks why I am holding a pillow over my stomach.
I reply that it helps me feel safe and relaxed. The secretary
smiles as if she would like to be carrying a pillow too.

With the themes of trust and safety in the forefront of my awareness, I drag my weary body out of bed to attend Qigong class. No matter how fatigued I feel, I do not want to miss Teja's teachings. My mind starts racing with plans for projects that I want to accomplish after the retreat. It is amazing how quickly my mind enters hungry ghost realms right after moments of peace and contentment. Suddenly John's words run through my head: "Voluntary simplicity and renunciation protect us from sensory overload." When John said that he has no television in his home, I felt good that Mark and I keep our T.V. hidden in a closet and pull it out only to view videos or special programs. By exercising restraint, I can choose not to follow every impulse.

Wild, gusty March winds and blasts of rain surprise me today. Braving the elements, I climb up to the deck on the hillside to leave a peso offering in the saucer under the little meditation bell on the balustrade. Then I start "toning" with a series of vocal sounds that merge with wailing blasts of wind buffeting my body. As I concentrate on each of my seven chakras in sequence from root to crown, I visualize corresponding colors and vocalize on gradually rising pitches: "oh," "oo," "ah," "ay," "ee," "mmm-nn," and "ng." Whenever fellow yogis walk past, I maintain silence until they are out of sight. My private concert takes place just beyond the sign that reads, "Silence: Retreat Area," so I am not breaking any rules. While toning, I appreciate in turn the bright red color of my woolen cape, the orange embroidered flower on my shirt, the yellow wild flowers beside the deck, the bright green of the grass, the turquoise of my scarf, and the indigo blue patches of sky amidst scattering, violet-grey rain clouds. My environment reflects all the colors associated with the chakras. Feeling energized from auditory and visual resonance, I ring the tiny bell three times and bow. End of ritual.

Back in the meditation hall, the image of Ajahn Amaro, a model of diligent mindfulness, comes to mind and inspires me to pay attention to guarding the sense doors. By wrestling with the continuous distractions of my own mind, I have learned to respect the spiritual advancement of this forest monk, in much the same way that I learned to appreciate the immensity of Johann Sebastian Bach's musical genius by struggling, as a music major in college, to compose what resulted in a merely mediocre fugue. Lost in the past, I have forgotten to attend to the sense doors once again. Am I resisting feeling the blockage in my right ear that has lasted since early this morning?

At lunch, a friendly woman sits opposite me beside a window. Simultaneously we see a moth caught between the screen and the glass pane. Coordinating our rescue efforts, I slide open the window, and her hand guides the moth to open air. Both of us accomplices grin in triumph as the moth flies free, liberated from suffering. Noticing that the potted plant beside the window has dry, browning leaves, I sprinkle water from my glass on its roots. The heart of compassion is opening to all life. Suddenly Edgar shatters the silence with a loud yell, "Shit!" With everyone's stunned eyes on him, he sets down his tray to clean up spilled milk from a broken glass. Internally, I applaud Edgar for his honest expression of frustration. Unlike the rest of us who are trying so hard to be quiet and exemplary yogis, he is showing his true feelings without inhibition.

The wind howls around the meditation hall tonight while Jack speaks to us about the "Three Characteristics" from Buddhist psychology: *Anatta* (translated as no-self, selflessness, or emptiness), *Anicci* (impermanence), and *Dukkha* (suffering). He asks, "To whom does life happen? With what archetypes do we identify?" Are we expected to answer these "koans"?

As usual, I delight in Jack's manner of developing his theme by drawing from a pile of readings that he has spread around his zafu. He picks up a poem by Pablo Naruda and reads:

> *What we know is so little,*
> *What we presume is so much…*
> *Why does the scorpion have poison*
> *And why is the elephant benign?*

While I jot down these excerpts, Jack is already citing a quotation from the sage Krishnamurti: "When we become still, the truth emerges. It is the truth that liberates and not our efforts to be free." How challenging it is for me to be still. So much of my striving is unnecessary activity. Referring to *Anatta,* Jack states that thoughts think themselves, and moods come and go according to conditions: "They are not in our possession or control. They disappear into the void." Is my teacher telepathic? Does he know that I woke up this morning petrified by the sense of losing my self in the void? As I tune into the dharma talk again, the topic is death, an even scarier concept. Jack says, "A conscious death is still, like a falling star." A quotation from the Sufi poet Hafiz follows: "We are a feather on the breath of God, and then the breath stops." As I begin to feel overwhelmed, my teacher reminds us that we have two simple tasks in Vipassana practice: acknowledge what is present and note what happens to it: "In this way we see the molecular moments that make up the illusion of solidity." Because he makes it sound so easy, I calm down.

As Jack discusses *Anicci*, I find myself laughing along with the sangha at his quick juxtaposition of quotations: Suzuki Roshi's explanation of life, "Not always so," followed by Helen Keller's, "Security is mostly a superstition," and Ajahn Chah's, "Uncertain, isn't it?" Many deep thinkers have confirmed the Buddha's understanding that everything shifts and changes above a ground of stillness. I need to let go into being here now, without clinging to anything. Jack counsels us to let go as if into a deep sleep, allowing the waters of life to hold us as we float and swim. These images console me and give me a respite from my fears.

The next topic is *Dukkha*, which is all too familiar. Even though I know that aging, sickness and death are natural and inescapable, I tend to resist these changes when they touch my own circle of family and friends. Jack warns, "We get rope burn from holding onto the rope of life too tightly." I listen carefully to his following words: "To open up means to accept the truth of pain. If we see things as they are, we are free. The divine purpose of suffering is to connect us to one another in natural caring. Being nothing, we are everything. The Buddha of compassion is in each realm to remind us how to find freedom and the essence of the true interconnectedness of all life." I drink in the truth and solace of this dharma talk like nectar for my soul.

Before finishing his discourse, Jack refers to the movie "A Prayer for the Enemy." In this documentary, a group of fifteen-year-old Tibetan nuns, who have been imprisoned by Chinese soldiers for chanting, are filmed as they pray for their enemy: "May you awaken." As I image these brave and compassionate nuns, I pray that President George W. Bush will awaken enough to avert war with Saddam Hussein in Iraq. I have been so absorbed in my own inner drama that I have nearly forgotten the threat of war hovering around the safe container of the retreat. The reassuring sound of Jack's voice draws my attention to an aphorism by James Baldwin: "People hold onto to their hatred and ignorance so that they don't have to face their pain." Fully present now, I appreciate Jack's closing recitation of two lines from the Japanese poet Isa: "The dew drop is so dear, refreshing, fleeting. /What can we do but care for this earth?"

On Friday, March 14, I awaken with a sore writing arm. The words, "Your body knows what it needs," run through my mind. When I remove the earplugs I have been using to block the sound of the drainpipe dripping outside our open window, I hear the refreshing sound of steady rain. My dominant arm is pleading for me to slow down: it is literally aching to stop.

As a little girl who craved an audience, I developed the habit of "verbal diarrhea." My family used to tease me for taking longer to tell the plot of a movie than the duration of the movie itself. By now, I have learned to stop trying to be the center of attention, but I tend to channel the excessive energy of my fifth chakra at the throat into compulsive writing with my right hand. Can I cut back and find moderation in all things?

During Qigong class, energy ripples through my body and feels delicious. Afterwards, Metta practice flows naturally. At breakfast, I perceive the auras of my fellow meditators, radiating around their softly opening faces. With so much sitting and walking practice, everyone is cleansing their auric field. Today, the theme song that echoes in my mind is "Amazing Grace." The lyrics, " I was blind, but now I see," seem to relate to the opening of my sixth chakra, the clairvoyant potential of the third eye.

At the 8:30 a.m. sit, Jack instructs us to note thoughts coming and going like clouds, noticing the energy field after each thought passes. I have a bliss-fully peaceful, cloud-like sitting period, not resisting thoughts, but merely catching their entry and observing their departure, some more slowly than others. Each thought leaves a particular flavor in its wake, before I return to "receiving" and "releasing" the breath. When it is time for questions from the sangha, I ask, "What is a skillful way to handle several stimuli arising simultaneously?" Jack's response is, "Keep it simple. Just note what is pre-dominant. If it is not clear what is arising, merely note 'sensing.' If various sensory experiences are arising at once, expand the lens of perception into a broader energy field that can encompass 'sensing.'"

Another yogi makes everybody laugh with her question, "What is the origin of weird thoughts like 'How are socks made?'" I recall wondering at breakfast, "Why do humans have hair atop their heads?" Jack reassures us that such questions are part of the collective, archetypal consciousness. These are thoughts that seem to be free of conditioning, although the probability is that aborigines meditating in the wilderness probably would not tap into collective thoughts about socks. Jack jokes that thoughts are shipped to Spirit Rock from Hollywood for our entertainment.

When I arrive for this morning's interview with Jack, Diana is quietly observing in a corner. My mood is calmer than when she witnessed the tearful catharsis with Julie. I speak about letting go of familiar structures and enjoying more spacious sittings. Jack asks me to close my eyes and report whatever sensations occur: "peaceful tingling." He is encouraging when I describe how, instead of copying down every word of last night's dharma talk, I recorded only what touched me deeply. Because my body clock is still upset, I arise at 3:00 a.m. and need afternoon naps, so I ask about the possibility of switching to a single bedroom tomorrow. I know from this morning's announcements that six yogis are departing after being on retreat for six weeks. They will be having a quiet closing ritual in the Community Hall this afternoon, so as not to disrupt the stream of energy in Noble Silence. Jack responds that my name is on a waiting list for a room transfer, but there are no guarantees. "Compared to the plight of the imprisoned Tibetan nuns," I remark, "sharing a double room isn't the worst situation in the world."

At the interview's end, I feel strong and invigorated. As soon as the rain stops, I run up into the hills. A venerable tree that shades the deck draws me to touch its rough bark and to plunge my hands into the thick, moist rug of moss on its trunk. What sensory delight. More and more, I am conscious of continuity between sitting still and moving, sensing changes in air temperature and energy fields between outside and inside spaces, and between one room and another. As I return to the meditation hall, I am aware of the cool hardness of the door against my hand and the bristly texture of the carpet beneath my feet in their thick, blue cotton socks.

During this sit, I have the sensation of being pulled backwards and falling into nothingness—emptiness with no sensation, movement, emotion or breath. The effect is peacefulness beyond ordinary peace. Before I let myself tilt backwards, with my inner vision, I see a bright light shimmering around my third eye. By lunchtime, I am dizzy and "stoned." I write Jack a note to report what I have been experiencing. As I savor succulent Indian dal, curry, raita and plum chutney, I feel as if I am being breathed. With no sense of self, I am watching eating happening. A moment of fear passes. Then I close my eyes to taste what my teeth are chewing, and to sense my thighs contacting the chair and my feet touching the floor. My vision is opening up, so I can see beyond people's faces, behind their eyes, to their essence. I notice a yogi named Patrick waiting in line to bus his teacup. Walking past him, I hold out my hand, and he bows, giving me his cup to wash with my dishes. My perception is expanding to encompass what is happening in peripheral areas that are normally outside of my ambit of awareness.

Setting intentions is a skillful means in Buddhist practice. This morning's prayer wheel spin brought me "right effort." Tuning into how tired my body is, I sense that it is time for another Metta nap. Rain, rain, and more rain is pouring down. A strong wind is whistling and keening, asserting its power. After thirteen days of sunshine, the weather is changing, changing. Song lyrics lull me to drowsiness: "To everything (turn, turn, turn) there is a season (turn, turn, turn), And a time for every purpose under heaven."

Progress. I arrive for tonight's dharma talk without my journal. It is lying forgotten beside my bed. Eugene is giving a discourse on the topic "Relative and Absolute Truths," the Buddha's distinction between what is true in a conventional and personal sense versus what is true in an ultimate and universal sense. I listen carefully to absorb the main points: "Our identities lose their solidity on retreats. Things are not what they seem, nor are they otherwise. Paradox means that 'the mind doesn't get it,' but the heart can understand. Our refuge is the ordinary meshing with the sacredness of each present moment, the Middle Way between knowing and not knowing."

How uncanny that Eugene is describing what I have been experiencing today. He is right that the reality of a retreat is physical and mundane: "All we do is sit, walk, eat, sleep, and go to the bathroom." Yet our discriminating awareness tends to expand, so that forms, colors, time, and space seem to break into particles: "We learn to rest between partial truths and the sublime. Without intuiting the sublime, we cannot awaken. On retreat we study personal truths and reach the sublime. Vipassana practice clarifies relative truths and reveals absolute truths. The wave is part of the ocean, and yet...."

Eugene refers to the Japanese poet Isa, who transcended a childhood so miserable that he never went to bed without crying, and who could see the mystery of life despite the death of his children. Instead of bemoaning his tragic fate, Isa celebrated the wonder of simple things by penning lines such as, "The world of dew is just the world of dew, and yet...and yet...." Eugene mentions that we recognize things by their opposites. There is a mutual dependency between dark and light, happy and sad, etc. While phenomena exist, their essence is not apparent. I smile at the statement that even the emptiest person is there. How true that emptiness is impersonal. According to the Buddha, everything exists due to conditions: "This is because that is. This is not because that is not." Thich Nhat Hanh warns, "We should not let relative truth imprison us. Relative and absolute truths interpenetrate. A piece of paper contains the seed, tree, wood, logger, mill, trucker, store, money exchange, buyer, writer—the universe."

Eugene cautions us further that one pitfall of spiritual practice is grasping for absolute truth, trying to fix our experiences to fit numinous ideals. His wife is a dedicated Zen student who has discovered in her meditation the same distinction between relative and absolute truths that pertains to Eugene's Vipassana practice. Could it be that world religions, which appear so different in their outer manifestation, provide culturally and personally relevant containers for people to discover the same absolute truths?

It helps me to hear Eugene say, "Thoughts and stories are not our enemies. During the retreat, we try to notice the energy of an unfolding story and to detect the grasping that leads to suffering. Often our attachment to a personal story is unconscious. We don't need to avoid stories, which emerge naturally, but simply note what we learn as we stay present with unfolding sensations and emotions connected to each story. Being caught in stories is part of conventional reality." I wonder what stories are about to surface from my unconscious realms, and what lessons I will be able to learn from them.

The sangha seems to breathe as one unit as Eugene tells us to trust reality and to have faith that the dharma will reveal its goodness: "Accept moments when you don't feel peaceful and loving. Discover the mind of absolute trust. You are the dharma, and each yogi gives *darshan* (spiritual instruction) to us teachers during interviews. Don't seek the experience you think you are supposed to be having. Don't denigrate the conventional. Don't idealize the absolute. Live in the middle." I am struck by how many obstacles lie along the middle way.

Mercifully, Eugene closes his dharma talk with a funny story about two yogis driving on snow-covered roads from a retreat to the airport. When the car skids on a patch of ice, one yells, "Shit!" and the other, drawing on her Hindu faith, exclaims in the same tone of voice, "Ram!" The car pulls out of the skid, they miss the plane, and both sides of the paradox are reconciled. Despite my intention to listen tonight without taking any notes, I have not been able to resist the temptation to jot down key elements of Eugene's discourse on small pieces of paper that have been stashed in my vest pocket "in case of emergencies."

Before the break of dawn on March 15, the "Ides of March," I record the following dream:

> *I attend a student government meeting at Jonathan Edwards College, a residential college at Yale, and ask the female class officers what they think of the light pop music that is being piped into the courtyard. The students admit that they had not been aware of the music until I drew their attention to it. They say that they can take it or leave it. I recommend silence in its place.*

Because I ate too much yesterday, in an attempt to stay grounded, my stomach feels bloated and uncomfortable. My digestive system is upset, and I feel exhausted by trying to digest so much inner and outer information.

The difficulty I have with assimilating it all is causing insomnia and strange sleep patterns. My focus shifts from inner discomfort to the climate changes outside. There is "enough blue to make a Dutchman's britches," as my mother used to say. The storm is clearing away, leaving the streams rushing with new water.

As I do yoga in the lower walking room, I notice a silvery spider descend on an invisible thread from the ceiling to my eye level. When I change my position, I can see a long, glistening filament highlighted by the morning sun; but after I shift back to my original position, once again the spider appears to be performing a magic trick and floating miraculously in thin air. With a wave of my hand, I catch the eye of the woman who accompanies me each day with her own exercise routine. She approaches from her regular spot at the other end of the room to join me in quiet admiration of the tiny aerial artist, suspended in space. As if he senses the presence of an appreciative audience for his act, the clever spider stretches one of his eight legs like a graceful ballerina. We witnesses grin in delight and applaud silently, before climbing the stairs to the meditation hall.

A note from Andrea, the retreat manager, awaits me on the bulletin board, advising me about the availability of a single room, number 225 in Karuna dormitory. Although I had relinquished hope about switching rooms, I feel relieved that I can stop sneaking out in the middle of the night to write in the bathroom. Somehow it seems right to be transferring from "Equanimity" to "Compassion" at this moment. I pen a note to Alison, informing her that I will be moving out before lunchtime. When she reads my message, she bursts out crying and finds me for a tearful hug. With a flurried exchange of notes, we express our mutual respect and caring for each other. Reassured, Alison helps me carry hastily packed luggage to my new bedroom. On our way, I see the six departing yogis rolling their suitcases towards the parking lot. I will miss their energy. My CDL friend Dianita, who is limping on crutches, assumes that I am leaving the retreat, and she hands me a sweet farewell note. Shaking my head, I scribble a brief explanation on the back of her missive. Dianita smiles, conveying that she is as pleased as I am that we will be able to celebrate together at the retreat's end. How much we all sense in silence. Dianita instantly perceived my change of routine. I have yet to discover the nonverbal habits of my new floor-mates.

States of concentration are so fragile. Today my meditation sits are full of thoughts about the change of residence and about Teja's reply to my most recent note, which had requested suggestions for grounding my high energy level. He addressed his response to "Luminous Butterfly" and signed off as "Snow Leopard." It is time to deal with my Vipassana crush on this tall, calm

Qigong teacher. I must stop participating in our frequent exchange of notes about subtle energy. Just this morning Eugene recommended a "Vipassana push" in the heart of the retreat: "Do what long distance swimmers do; go slowly at the beginning and ending, but push in the middle. On prolonged retreats this means moving extra slowly and mindfully in whatever we do."

At lunch, I make an effort to slow down and pay close attention to each sensation. I notice my preference for forks with three prongs instead of four and for silverware with a simple pattern of tiny dots rather than utensils with more elaborate designs. The mounds of string beans that I washed so carefully last night are being served in big bowls. Examining my portion carefully, I see how every bean has a unique shape and form. With mindful chewing, I truly taste the freshness of each bean. On the walk to my new dormitory, I witness a gaggle of turkeys exploding with chatter in response to whatever is being communicated by a stray comrade hidden from view in the woods. What pompous and silly-looking characters they are.

At times I feel like Anaïs Nin, continuously writing "no matter what." The act of writing centers, balances, and grounds me, especially when I make changes or transitions. Fatigue hits me with the recognition that it is time for this "mariposa" to crawl into a cocoon to rest. I like my little "nun's cell." Arranging the room has taken considerable thought. As I lie propped up by pillows on the bed, the photo of Mark is on the small table to my left, and through the window on my right side I have a view of a stream winding into the woods, with distant hills in the background. Aside from a tiny sink, a few shelves, and hooks and hangers for my clothes, there is not much else in my new home. Wait! I am leaving out a lovely picture of Kwan Yin hanging on the wall. I have become so used to the bare walls of most Spirit Rock bedrooms that at first I screened out the rosy-hued Goddess of Compassion, whose image is smiling at me as I write. While I am scanning around me with closer attention, I notice a diminutive, Native American dream-catcher tacked onto the wall near the sink. This feels like the perfect room for a devoted dreamer who is committed to regular Metta practice.

Anna gives tonight's dharma talk on the theme of "thinking." She starts off with a question from Suzuki Roshi: "When you are sitting and thinking of your problem, which is more real, your problem or yourself—your presence?" Our original presence is the luminous essence that we veil in ordinary circumstances. Referring to the sage Buddhadasa, who described the world as "lost in thought," Anna states that the goal of practice is not to get rid of thoughts, but to understand the nature of thinking: "As long as you have a mind, you will have thoughts and emotions. Practice cultivates a relationship with thinking, without being identified with its content.

A SILENT CURE

Identifying with thoughts leads to suffering. Thoughts are impermanent and impersonal." Yet how personal my thoughts seem. Anna continues her discourse on thinking:

> *The breath breathes itself from birth, and nobody directs or controls the sense doors. But with thinking, we assume ownership. We think in the language that we were taught as children, with the vocabulary we understand and words that we have inherited from past generations. We think according to our background and cultural conditions. Not many of our thoughts are original. According to a study at Stanford University, 93% of our thoughts are repeated from yesterday.*

It is true that I have been ruminating about the very same preoccupations over the past few days. I like the sound of the word *papancha*, which Anna defines as the Pali term for "a tendency to get lost in thought." It indicates "mental proliferation," the kind of thinking that takes us away from direct experience, projecting onto reality positive or negative qualities—in other words, most of my thoughts.

Anna explains the four root causes of papancha: greed (*tanha*), aversion (*dosa*), opinions and views (*ditti*), and identity (*mana*). Vipassana practice helps us recognize our desires, the first root cause, instead of indulging them. Greed limits our vision. The sangha laughs at the adage, "When a pickpocket meets a saint, all he sees are the saint's pockets." I take seriously the Buddha's advice, "See everything in its suchness" and Suzuki Roshi's dictum, "Those who wish to awaken consume their desires joyfully." Anna says that the second root cause of *papancha* is aversion: thinking, "this should not be happening to me." In order to avoid what we dislike, we try to rearrange the world and make up rules for ourselves and others. The third root cause of mental proliferation is equally ineffectual. With our views and opinions, we avoid the experience of "not knowing." Dharma practice helps us cultivate and appreciate not knowing. As the Sufi poet Rumi wrote, "Out beyond all ideas of right and wrong, there is a field. I'll meet you there." The fourth root cause of losing ourselves in thought is "selfing," when everything is referenced to "me" and "mine." How can I understand life's unfolding without connecting experiences to myself? As I prepare for bed, hours after the dharma talk has ended, I am still pondering this conundrum.❧

A ROOM OF MY OWN

O n Sunday, March 16, I wake up at 3:15 a.m. with Mom's words, "It is done," in my mind. I remember her phone call years ago informing me that my beloved maternal grandmother had died after a stroke that robbed her of speech and strength. Lying here in bed and writing about Deedee's death, I feel calm and no longer worried about disturbing a roommate. For the first time, I am in touch with the enormity of Mom's task, as an only child, to deal with her mother's death and the aftermath of selling Deedee's houses in Florida and on Long Island.

While mourning, my mother must have experienced bittersweet memories as she sifted through old letters and photographs. I recall accompanying Mom on the long drive from New York City to South Hampton Hospital to visit Deedee during her last days of life. In the car, Mom and I shared recollections and cried together. At the hospital, I leaned over to speak loving words to my grandmother. Her sight had long since failed her, and then the stroke had cut off her last defense: charming, lady-like, sociable chatting. Deedee recognized me, her eldest grandchild, and mouthed the words, "I'm tired." Because I was expecting her to communicate something more dramatic, I almost did not understand her message. Now I realize that she was telling me the truth: after ninety years, she was tired of living—blind, single-breasted after surgery for cancer, and deprived of speech and movement. When she could still speak, Deedee had told me that she wanted to die with dignity and not be maintained by machines in a hospital. But she had never written a Living Will, so Mom and I had to fight with the doctors to release her from the life support system.

In the rush of related memories, I recall my last visit to Deedee's East Hampton home, when she was still strong enough to live there with her loyal attendant, Phyllis. My grandmother and I sat together next to the windows of the master bedroom and watched ivory-colored swans supervising their fluffy grey signets on an inlet from the Atlantic Ocean. We shared pleasurable moments of companionable tranquility. Breaking the silence, Deedee turned to me and said, "Don't ever forget me." My response was a solemn vow, "I will always remember you." Before giving her a farewell hug, I asked my grandmother, "How could I ever forget you?" Sensing that this might be our last time to declare our mutual love, we both started to cry. During my drive home, I sobbed so hard that I could barely follow the highway signs.

Now, over a decade later, writing alone in my single room, I pour out tears of grief for the loss of my "great mother." At one-and-a-half years old, I bonded with her during Mom and Dad's belated honeymoon in Spain. Deedee used to reminisce about my antics during the two months that I was with her in East Hampton, under the strict care of a briskly efficient nursemaid named Miss Jolly. This nurse did not live up to the promise of her appellation. Far from being jolly, she handled me roughly when adjusting my clothing or fixing my hair, and she was too rushed to demonstrate affection. Her tall, bony body was angular and hard-edged, and she smelled of disinfectant. Her starched white uniform was stiff and prickly to touch. At this preverbal stage of development, I conveyed my distaste for Miss Jolly by escaping from her surveillance whenever possible. If I could find my grandmother, I would crawl into her lap to sit amidst brightly colored balls of yarn. As she crafted cable knit sweaters for me and other family members, Deedee would talk to me in her soothing voice. Feeling comforted, I would nestle close to her ample bosom and inhale the pleasant fragrance of Chanel perfume. My grandmother's bright red fingernail polish and her pretty dresses, selected from a vast collection of frocks with pastel hues and floral prints, delighted my visual sense. In Deedee's lap, I felt safely at home. After fruitlessly searching the wing of the house where the nursery had been established, Miss Jolly would arrive breathlessly and apologize to my grandmother for losing me. If she did not have to prepare for a Garden Club meeting or for weekly card games with her Bridge group, Deedee would permit me to stay like a princess on her throne, and I would feel triumphant about thwarting Miss Jolly.

When I was visiting on vacation from boarding school many years later, Deedee described one of my "jailbreaks" as a toddler. Stark naked, I had crawled outside onto the extensive back lawn. From her bedroom upstairs, my grandmother had spied me dancing joyously, liberated from diapers and clothing, across the freshly-mowed grass. The vision was so entertaining for my grandmother that she had hesitated to inform my custodian about the escapade, for fear of cutting it short. Then she had watched Miss Jolly running outside with a diaper to corral the frolicking renegade.

As a 54-year-old yogi, I feel grateful to Deedee for having recounted this story about my exploits as a tot. Even though I have long since forgotten the sensory joy of dancing nude in public view, the knowledge that I did so pleases me. Underneath my somewhat rigid and controlled adult persona is an adventurous and resourceful child.

Memories surface of other childhood visits to East Hampton surface. When I was ten years old and my step-grandfather was still alive and strong, he chased a huge snapping turtle with a pitchfork, after it waddled ashore from the inland waterway. Doodles and I had watched the turtle diving off a rock to swim beneath an unsuspecting, floating family of swans. The predator had grabbed the feet of one of the signets and pulled it down under the water to devour it. The turtle was hoisting its heavy body onto my grandparents' lawn to digest its meal. With flapping outspread wings and furious hisses, a mother swan was pursuing the greedy turtle. I was an awed witness as Doodles bravely confronted both the snapping turtle and the irate swan. When he plunged the pitchfork prongs into the turtle's neck, he had to beat off the swan's attacking wings and avoid the gnashing jaws of her foe. As if satisfied that justice had been done, the swan waddled back to the water to tend to her surviving signets. Flailing unsuccessfully to dislodge the pitchfork, the snapping turtle weakened gradually and took hours to die in the hot sun. With a mixture of fascination and revulsion, I watched Doodles drag away the dead body to dispose of it at the end of the day. As a young girl, I considered my grandfather a heroic warrior for defending us from the mean, swan-killing turtle. In retrospect I reflect upon the cruelty of subjecting a living creature to such an excruciatingly slow form of death.

More pleasant memories involve saving breadcrumbs to feed mallard ducks in a pond near my grandparents' house. I recall savoring raspberry ice cream on crunchy sugar cones at the Maidstone Beach Club, where I liked to walk barefoot on the wooden slats of the boardwalk that protected my feet from the hot sand. Recollections emerge of cooling off in the club's wading pool, changing my wet bathing suit in the musty rented cabana, and sipping icy lemonade while Deedee served guests Bloody Mary cocktails and hors-d'oeuvres. On one scary occasion, a big ocean wave bowled me over, and I was sucked underwater by a powerful undertow. Unable to catch my breath, I saw images of my short life passing rapidly in my mind's eye. Sure that I was dying, I felt fear and then acceptance. In a sudden reprieve, the ocean spewed me out onto the hard, wet sand of the shore. Rubbed raw with sand, I lay gasping for air like a beached fish in the shallows of the receding tide.

One time I borrowed a rowboat from a neighbor to explore the inland waterway. Disoriented by heavy fog that rolled in while I was paddling around, I docked at the wrong house, on the opposite side of the inlet. Kind strangers let me use their phone to call Deedee, who drove around in her car to rescue me. We did not return the rowboat until the following day. On hot afternoons, I often volunteered to pick sprigs of mint from one of my grandmother's gardens to top off glasses of sugary iced tea. On my mission, I would daydream amidst stately purple irises, which won regular awards from the local Garden Club, and admire neat rows of delicate impatiens with blooms in gradated shades of pink. Silly-looking, droopy, white goosenecks added a comical note to the otherwise proper English garden. Carefully delivering Deedee's frosty glass of tea, I would walk barefoot on the cool cement floor of the porch, which was sheltered by an arcade with screened windows overlooking the lawn and inlet. We would sit together on pale blue striped pillows atop wrought iron porch chairs whose arm rests displayed a pattern of ivy leaves.

So many sensual memories are emerging. I feel grateful for these childhood experiences and tempted to pay tribute to them in the form of a poem. But I will keep the promise to myself: "Not now." Poetry writing is not the only temptation I am resisting. Opportunities for nonverbal communication abound in Noble Silence. During Qigong class, when we are imitating Teja and flapping our arms energetically from side to side, my hands slap against those of a handsome young yogi. He and I grin and bow to each other in apology. After class, I wave one foot at a woman who is wearing similar "cosmic" socks, decorated with glow-in-the-dark stars. She joins me in a spontaneous tap dance, which causes the yogis around us to laugh. I resolve to monitor my impulses more carefully, guarding the sense doors and refraining from writing notes. How can I best use this time in blessed silence?

My body is more and more sensitive to sensations. When I insert a pair of earrings, I can feel the holes in my pierced earlobes. At breakfast, my tongue savors the juice and pulp of fresh oranges. The tangy taste provokes an image of Martita, the plump "juice lady" in Cholula, Mexico. Every day for forty-three years she has opened her tiny, hole-in-the wall store at 5:00 a.m. to squeeze orange, papaya, mango, carrot, or grapefruit juice for thirsty customers. Squeezed into her workspace like a melon in a tight box, Martita is a magician, who can break open two eggs at once in her left hand and smoothly separate the whites from the unbroken yolks, which she adds to "power drinks." Suddenly I realize that my mind has traveled South of the Border, and I am no longer tasting the slice of orange in my mouth. The thought comes: "This is nothing to write home about." The task is simply to sense and experience what is unfolding now.

Atop the tallest pine tree near the dining hall, a kingly crow screeches "caw, caw," gloating over his peers, who are relegated to lower perches in the forest. On the way uphill to my new room, I pause to honor him. But I do not linger, because I must tend to the ants that have invaded my sink. Yesterday I courteously escorted dozens of them outside. But today scores of reinforcements have arrived to take their place. By keeping my room spotlessly clean and free from all food, I am hoping to discourage these little black creatures from taking up permanent residence. At the same time, I am trying to learn to live with them.

On a slow walk to the forest altar, all the edges that ordinarily separate objects appear blurred. Everything around me seems to be merging and vibrating. All is poetry in motion. Like the monarch butterfly, I fly thousands of miles each year to retreat in the same place. It feels reassuring to visit familiar landmarks like the altar. I like to hibernate in silence until spring erupts and my birthday initiates a new year of life. Bowing in front of the altar, I wonder where to lay my offering—a Mexican two-peso coin. I decide to "put my money where my mouth is" and place it on a flat rock near a cluster of coins from other foreign countries. This collection of money represents the international dissemination of the dharma.

Leaving the altar behind, I take myself for a walk, letting my feet lead me uphill, along a path through the woods. The sound of snapping twigs causes me to halt. I find myself staring directly into the startled eyes of a deer, which stands a few feet in front of me. Telepathically, I transmit: "Fear not." The vigilant doe relaxes her muscles and then shifts her gaze to look beyond my left shoulder. As I pivot deliberately, I meet the wide-eyed stare of a second deer. With my heart thumping, I realize that I am standing right between a mother deer and her fawn. The three of us stay transfixed until we hear someone's footsteps approaching. The frightened fawn rushes past me to join her mom, and the two of them bound away to find a more tranquil spot. Feeling awed, I nod at the yogi who arrives a second too late to witness my miraculous encounter; she passes by, ignorant of my bliss.

A light rain sprinkles droplets on my red cape, while the sun shines bravely amidst gathering clouds—rainbow potential. Wet and wild, miniature purple irises encircle a small, stone, Japanese-style lantern beside the path. Suddenly I discover a sturdy wooden platform with a spectacular view of distant, steep hills. There is even a yellow folding chair propped against one of the support posts. Is this heaven? Could I ask for anything more? From my throne atop the platform, I spy a seemingly bottomless hole that some rodent has bored into the moist, packed dirt of the path. Memories are triggered of "digging a hole to China" on the beach near Deedee's house in Ponte Vedra, Florida. As a little girl burrowing in the sand, I imagined popping out on the other side of the earth to surprise an Asian child. Surrendering to free association, I recall watching a family of four swans flying above me near the shore of Bayville, Long Island. The graceful, long-necked birds circled around and descended for a landing in the shallow coastal waters. Asserting his leadership role, the stately father landed masterfully like a seaplane balanced on pontoons. He was followed by the sleek mother, who glided in smoothly, leaving barely any wake behind her. But the two adolescent children crash-landed noisily with feet askew, splashing wildly. Their parents exchanged looks as if to say, "when will they ever learn?" And when will I ever learn to stay in the present moment? Yanking myself away from retrospection, I focus on uncomfortable bodily sensations.

Strange physical releases are starting to occur during my sitting periods in the meditation hall. I have moved to the far left of the front row, in a spot vacated by a departing yogi. My proximity to the teachers gives me hope that their high level of consciousness might rub off on me. As I meditate, I feel as if I am being pulled first backward and then forward, so that my torso is swaying subtly. In one of these cycles, I find myself in a yoga position, bent back, with each hand grabbing an ankle for support. My solar plexus begins to contract strongly and repeatedly, and my torso, neck and shoulders quiver. Whorls of energy continue to vibrate across the center of my back, behind the heart. I sense my chest opening and the front of my chronically stiff right shoulder releasing. Metaphorically, my body seems to be saying, "I am tired of bending over backwards to meet my family's expectations." Once I understand my body's message, the spontaneous movements cease.

As if reading my mind, Anna gives special instructions today: "Vipassana is not a practice of struggle. Rest in the flow of unfolding experiences. For strong energetic physical discharges, go with the energy, balancing the body, but not becoming obsessed with sensations or postures." Good advice, which I can apply immediately. A yogi at the back of the hall voices concerns about her strong desire to awaken and to open her heart. Anna responds that this is a healthy form of desire that does not cause suffering in the way that coveting power or material possessions does. She counsels us to use discernment as we let go of attachments. The first task is to learn detachment from suffering. Anna makes it sound so easy.

Lunch is a succulent Mexican meal that seems to take hours to consume. The colors of guacamole, chips, chili, corn salad, and kamut cornbread seem to swirl together. I feel dizzy from so many diverse tastes and visual stimuli. Dianita looks even more overwhelmed than I am, and after we eat, she gladly gives me her dishes to rinse with mine. It feels as if I am washing our cups, saucers, and plates forever. Time is stretching and contracting around me. Clock time seems meaningless now. How challenging to be mindful of my watch, so that I will not miss ringing the gong at 2:00. Today its resonance permeates my entire body. Watching my fellow yogis file into the meditation hall, I decide not to follow them, but to walk to my room for a "Metta nap" instead. Sensory overload hits me hard.

Lying on my belly, listening to the soothing sound of the stream outside my window, I sense my heart letting go, relaxing another notch, and trusting an inch more. I sleep profoundly, pulled out of my nap by the sound of the next bell. This retreat is so exquisitely structured and situated in such an idyllic place that it feels safe to let myself fall to pieces. In an altered state of mind, I head for the meditation hall, only to change my mind at the last moment. Right now I would rather take a walk in the warm sunshine than do guided Metta practice. I convince myself that I am a Metta expert. I feel tremendous love for my companions here. We are all losing our boundaries together.

As I climb a steep path, lyrics from the Broadway show "The Sound of Music" fill my mind: "I go to the hills when my heart is lonely. I know I will hear what I heard before. The hills are alive with the sound of music." My brain switches channels, and I hear "What a long, strange trip it's been" from a Grateful Dead song playing inside my head. My walk winds through a wooded copse, where I find a deer resting, with her long legs curled beneath her, in the shade of a tree. She perks up her ears, and we scrutinize each other. As I beam Metta at the doe, her ears relax and lower. A fawn approaches her and adds his stare to hers. The three of us calm down simultaneously. When I move to meander further along the path, the doe stands up and follows me a while. She seems as curious about me as I am about her. On both sides of the path, the tree trunks look as if they have patches of tender skin bandaged by thick, green moss. As I place my hand on a plump branch to check its pulse, I sense the cool calmness of the tree's spirit. At the bottom of the hill, I ford a stream to visit three horses grazing in a fenced-in pasture by the entrance to Spirit Rock. One sidles up and lets me pat his silky nose until he realizes that I have no treats to offer. Sulkily, he retreats to the far side of the paddock to munch grass with oversized teeth and rubbery lips. On the way back to my room, I pass the road sign, "Yield to the present." That is exactly what I am doing.

"Theresa-with-the-countless-shoes" lives across the hall from me. The floor outside her door is piled with high and low leather and rubber boots, sneakers with and without laces, open and closed-toed sandals, and other shoes, both fancy and sensible. She must have a different pair for each day of the retreat. Being an aficionado of zany socks, I am not one to make judgments about footwear. I am also fond of colorful umbrellas. When I was doing volunteer work in León, Nicaragua, friends used to tease me for using a red umbrella like a parasol to shield my face from the scorching sun. My nickname became Mary Poppins.

Where are these memories coming from? I can barely keep up with their pace. It is reassuring to look out the window at a fabulous, fat, full moon. Whereas gringos see a man in the moon, Mexican parents teach their children to look for the profile of a rabbit, "el conejo," on the lunar surface. As a New Yorker residing in Mexico, I see both possibilities.

On the bulletin board in the meditation hall lobby, Andrea has left me a typewritten note: "The essential needs item you requested has been picked up and is on the counter in the manager's office." With childlike excitement, I run to fetch the pre-paid Crayola crayons that I ordered this morning. Now that I have my own room, I am giving into my urge to sit on the floor and draw pictures. How thankful I am that Andrea did not question whether my request was truly "essential." Relinquishing my usually controlled way of following predictable daily routines, I am following my intuition about what is good for me.

Robert leads questions and answers this evening. I jot down some instances of the wit and wisdom that he shares with the sangha: "We use the self to study the self until our sense of a separate self falls away, and the heart opens to include all beings. To study the self is to forget the self. Therapy helps with this process but does not lead to the depth of insight that is possible with Vipassana practice." I appreciate the way Robert describes the ego self as "a tiny brush stroke in the painting of the sea of love, which contains the ego." He clarifies how love can lift us out of our preoccupation with ourselves. I wonder if I am too preoccupied with my own inner journey on this retreat. His next statement sets me at ease: "Relationship is a path to enlightenment. If you love yourself, you are capable of loving others." He equates love with life: "letting go into the mystery." It is through the process of knowing and befriending myself that I can prepare to practice selflessness in conscious relationships.

Everyone laughs at the next question, as Robert reads aloud: "What's interesting about boredom? Aren't sexual fantasies juicier?" He answers seriously, "Boredom stems from not looking deeply enough into the nature of things. Everything is new and fresh and constantly renewing itself. Boredom is a distraction from penetrating insight." Fritz Perls, Robert's first teacher, taught him that "boredom is not paying attention." I am surprised that any yogi could feel bored on this retreat, with so much happening inside and outside.

Another yogi asks, "Do you claim to be enlightened? If so, please describe the state." Robert's response is simple: "I have had moments free of suffering. This experience has come to be a guide for my life. Practice leads to unshakable faith." He remembers Trungpa Rinpoche's remark, "Enlightenment is the ultimate disappointment. There is no self to celebrate."

Robert informs us that the extra candles on the altar are part of a worldwide vigil for peace that is occurring today. Although the teachers have agreed to protect us from news broadcasts, I suspect that President Bush has decided to initiate war in Iraq. Can we beam enough Metta to all beings to change this fateful decision and prevent the suffering that would inevitably follow? I pray that George W. Bush awakens and learns to govern with wisdom and compassion.

On March 17, I jolt awake at 3:15 a.m., worrying about Mark and my parents and the world if the United States attacks Iraq. I resolve to wear green to honor Mark's Irish heritage on this day of Saint Patrick. An image comes to me of "Equus," the play about a disturbed boy whose passion for horses inspires an intellectual and emotionally arid psychiatrist to cry and recover his capacity to feel deeply. I sense the two extremes of emotionalism and rationalism healing and reconciling within myself. Underlying the silence and the multitudinous, soft sounds of nature outside my window, I hear the faint resonance of a bell. It is a beautiful, calming tone, full of harmonics. Am I detecting the harmony of the cosmos?

I fall back asleep until the 5:00 a.m. bell and take a long, luxurious shower to wake up fully. After delighting in the sensations of hot water on my scalp and body, I take time to massage my limbs with unscented hand cream. I like the body I have been given for this lifetime—small-boned, slender, and deer-like. Humming the tune to "I Feel Pretty" from the musical play "West Side Story," I dress for the day. Venus, the morning star, is glowing brightly, as the first blush of sunrise lights the sky.

My mood shifts abruptly, as soon as I see the world vigil candles still burning on the altar in the meditation hall. I have a tearful Metta sitting, grieving deeply for our war-torn world. At the end of the sit, I bow to life's mystery and surrender to divine wisdom. Is it the karma of those who die in wars to suffer so that others will awaken to the urgency for love and peace? I feel blessed to be in harmony with all beings at this moment. Nobody is excluded from my heart. When I spin the prayer wheel today it affirms my Metta practice: the words "right understanding" end up facing me.

Hooray! My dear friend Angie has arrived for the final fortnight of the retreat. She is unpacking in a single room right next to mine. We smile broadly with pleasure at seeing each other again after more than a year. I feel such a burst of joy and exuberant energy from reconnecting with such a beloved person that I hike way up to the summit of a hill. On the way, I crawl through underbrush, ford a stream, and rely on sturdy oak trees to shield me from gusty blast of wind. My reward is a spectacular aerial view of all the Spirit Rock buildings. From my perch on a sunny rock, the meditation center looks so small and fragile, nestled into protective trees. Spirit Rock seems vital for raising the level of human consciousness in these troubled times. I observe tiny figures pacing back and forth mindfully near the iron gong. Engrossed in thoughts, I barely hear the distant sound of the bell summoning us to the next sitting.

Help! I am so high up in the hills, so far away. Can I return on time? With my red cape flapping in the breeze, I half-run, half-slide, downhill. My white visor blows off, and recovering it slows down the descent. Racing onward, I skid and slither down long, dewy grass on my fanny, rudely interrupting three grazing deer. Startled, they bound away from my sprawled body. Dusting myself off, I continue hurtling downward without caring about Medusa-like, windswept hair, wet shoes, and damp pants. Under the wire, I land panting on my zafu. How grateful I am to my Mexican orthopedist for knee microsurgery that enabled such a Herculean expedition. For the duration of the sitting, I feel suffused with expansive happiness. At the end of the period, a yogi in front strikes the bowl gong with such a loud ring that I yelp in surprise, and the entire sangha erupts into laughter.

The apprenticing dharma teacher Mark Coleman observes my interview with Jack today. Although he is a newcomer to the retreat, he sets me at ease with his gentle manner. I speak about opening my heart wide enough to hold profound sorrow for the warring world and huge joy at reuniting with my dharma friend Angie. Jack asks how I am handling the sensations of blurring boundaries. My reply is, "by following my deepest intuition in each moment, choosing when to attend sittings, when to nap, when to go for a walk, and when to write for the purpose of integration. I have been using writing not as an escape or a filter, but rather to balance myself a couple of times each day." Jack is pleased about my inner process, and we bow to one another as I depart.

My feelings of wellbeing and confidence last only a short while. After silently dedicating today's gong ringing to world peace, I open the door to the meditation hall lobby and come face-to-face with Teja. He winks at me with a broad grin. Feeling exposed and vulnerable, I cannot hide my affection for him. After the afternoon Qigong class, Teja passed by my locker, and we both smiled and reached out to touch hands. Strong energy is flying back and forth in the silence. I decide to write Jack a "Dear Abby" letter to ask how to handle the distraction of a Vipassana crush. Forgetting that dinnertime is earlier than usual on Mondays, I take a walk through the beautiful, fern-filled woods. I nearly miss supper, because guests are arriving to eat before the weekly Monday night meditation class. My mindfulness has flown out the window.

I am experiencing the dhukka of wanting material possessions. Andrea purchased two items I requested: a silent alarm clock and an ace bandage for my sore wrist. I have been feeling too sensitive to tolerate the sound of my old clock ticking, even when I hide it under a pile of sweaters. Am I becoming like the hypersensitive "Princess and the Pea" in the fairy tale? I cannot figure out how to set the new digital clock, and I have no way to cut the bandage, because Mexican airport security officials have confiscated my nail scissors. Feeling frustrated, I arrange a "dhukka consultation" with the retreat manager. She uses the office scissors to snip the ace bandage and kindly points out that unless I remove the sticker covering the clock's face, the time will eternally read 12:38 p.m. I am too surprised by the simplicity of the solution to feel embarrassed. As I leave her office with the now-functional goods, Andrea joins me in giggling about my most recent karmic lesson. Mindfulness practice is so humbling. Just as I think I am flowing in the "zone," I knock up against my ego again.

Tonight Robert gives a dharma talk about letting go of preferences and opinions. He tells us about some of his own past experiences. After serving as a psychiatrist in the U.S. army at Fort Knox, he was challenged by Fritz Perls: "Come work with me." At the age of twenty-nine, Robert left everything behind to join Fritz in leading Gestalt therapy sessions at Esalen in California. In that adventurous atmosphere, he took Hatha yoga classes, and Ida Rolf gave him intensive bodywork. From Esalen, he traveled to India to study meditation techniques. Robert reminds us, "Letting go is a process that results in a cessation of clinging. It is a noun, not a verb. First comes letting things be. Afterwards, letting go involves relinquishing attachment to material possessions and comfortable locations." I am impressed by his openness about recently leaving his marriage and home of twenty-three years to move to Todos Santos, Mexico with his gay lover.

Robert is a dharma teacher who is courageous in thought, word and deed. Asking us to consider all our addictions that come through the sense doors, he confesses his own struggle to give up smoking. He says that we must learn to let go of ideas about who we are. I enjoy hearing Robert reminisce about letting go of leading his own workshop because all the participants had chosen to attend a competing session led by Trungpa Rinpoche. Instead of nursing a hurt ego, Robert joined the crowd in Trungpa's workshop, and that experience resulted in a new spiritual path. We never know when a disappointment might turn into an opportunity.

Robert states that although a defining myth of our times is the fall from the Garden of Eden and the assumption that each of us must prove our worth, this myth is just a concept. What a persuasive concept it has been in my life. He notes, "We tend to cling to our territory." I have to admit that on retreats I am very territorial about my zafu and my spot in the meditation hall. Robert continues, "We cling to governments and nations and institutions. We resist letting go of attachment to our spiritual practice and personal stories about our past. When the heart opens, there is room only for now, so we must let go of ideas about progress." He is right that after a blissful sit, I feel dismayed if the next one is miserable. I am definitely attached to making progress in mindfulness. Just as I start to worry about my spiritual clinging, Robert helps me lighten up by citing the Buddha: "The only addiction you can keep is mindfulness."

Randolf Stone, a spiritual mystic and energy healer, taught Robert to let go of ideas he had about doctoring and to embrace a new philosophy about healing: Awakening is a bodily process. Whatever the mind holds onto, the body holds onto also. The tightness in the body is the path—a direct, present-time expression of attachments. Recognize pain, name it, accept it, and let it go. Opening to just now without fear or desire is noble, sacred work—the only commitment that makes any sense. It is being kind to one's Self. Willingness and effort are necessary to practice letting go.

At the end of this discourse, I feel motivated to follow Robert's example. He lives what he preaches. His words about letting go inspire me to start weaning myself from my writing habit. Robert mentioned that before he could give up smoking, he had to bring sufficient mindfulness to how much he was hurting his lungs. Likewise, before releasing my dependence on writing, I try to connect fully with the pain of my right wrist and with Teja's advice to "under-do everything."

On Tuesday, March 18, in honor of the eighty-third birthday of my former therapist, Eleanor, I declare an armistice on writing. My new wristband will help remind me of my intention to rest my arm and to let go of my addiction to writing for twenty-four hours. ❦

CHAPTER SIX
OF MEN AND WAR

A t 12:30 a.m. on Wednesday, March 19, I am awakened by the nearly full moon, whose silvery light filters through the window blinds onto my pillow. I feel triumphant about surviving a whole day of strong emotions without writing about them. I simply noted each instant as it was arising. Letting go of my addiction to writing entails trusting the river of life to carry me, and noticing the beauty of life's synchronicities unfolding naturally around me. Taking a break from writing has enabled me to enter sacred space. The grace of the universe is abundant. I feel humble and awed.

From a fresh perspective, I can recapitulate yesterday's unfolding: Qigong flowed seamlessly, and my Vipassana crush was contained in the enormity of vast spaciousness. During my morning Metta practice, I included Teja among my teachers. He is just one facet of so many aspects of all creation that I love. I am falling in love with the dharma—truth as it unfolds in each moment. That is my deepest conviction and container.

During the question and answer period with teachers, a yogi (whom I will call "Tammy") dominated the session with repeated queries about how to handle panic states skillfully. At first, Anna responded that with Vipassana practice we develop a capacity to contain whatever state arises. Robert followed by stating, "At root, all of us have panic." He commented that the Buddha included even the possibility of suicide being a "skillful means" in cases of excruciating terminal illness. Unsatisfied with these responses, Tammy grew increasingly insistent. Finally Eugene intervened with a perceptive query: "What are you experiencing inside as you ask these questions?" In a tight, high-pitched voice, she answered that she felt anxious and queasy. After he asked her to breathe and to sense her seat on the zafu, Tammy started to cry and admitted, "I want to stop asking so many questions in public." The sangha sighed in collective relief; we trusted that one of the teachers would give Tammy an individual interview to provide her with necessary support.

To my surprise, Julie announced my name on the list of her interviews for the day. "Normally," I have no teacher interview on Tuesdays. Wondering why, I decided to take a walk before the 10:30 a.m. appointment. I followed a deer trail through the grass into the woods and hill up into the hills. Circling back into the forest, I encountered the gracefully spreading branches of a huge oak tree. Someone had left a tiny red star in the nook of its trunk. In thanks for the unexpected gift, I "shook hands" with one low-flung, trembling bough and slipped the red star into my pocket. Wending my way towards the Generosity Hut, I left the trail and followed my intuition, through unfamiliar territory. I came to a glade with grand, old fallen trees beside a bend in the tranquil stream. Struck by such stillness and beauty, I continued on my way. In the window of the renovated Spirit Rock bookstore, I noticed a row of statues of Kwan Yin. The female form of the Bodhisattva of Compassion has been watching over me during my spiritual emergence. I made a resolution to buy a statue of Kwan Yin to accompany me back to Mexico at the end of the retreat. She represents my guardian angel.

Within the stillness of the Generosity Hut, I bowed to the photograph of the Dalai Lama and spontaneously added the tiny red star to the offerings of acorns, crystals, and flowers on the altar. Among the photos of venerable teachers in the Theravada Buddhist lineage, I found those of Jack Kornfield and Joseph Goldstein, as youthful monks with shaved heads and robes, in the company of some of their revered dharma masters. There was a solemn photograph depicting the Venerable Mahasi Sayadaw (1904-1982), who traveled with other monks all the way from Burma to bless Jack, Joseph, Sharon Salzberg and Jaqueline Schwartz as dharma teachers, at the inauguration of the Insight Meditation Society in 1979. I felt proud to be part of such a noble lineage. How satisfying to find my name listed in the Gratitude Book, among the donors who have helped to manifest Spirit Rock as a meditation center.

I arrived right on time for my interview at the Council House. Through the glass doors, I could see Julie busy attending to a tearful yogi. With a sense of equilibrium and acceptance, I removed my shoes and socks to practice slow walking meditation on the hot asphalt driveway. Upon my arrival, two sunbathing, black lizards scurried sideways and attempted to intimidate each other with puffy chests and vigorous push-ups. Walking past me on his way to the manager's office, Jack saw me and bowed. I felt reinforced by his way of honoring my practice. Today I do not sense paternal energy from him; instead, he seems like a caring older brother.

When Julie apologized for the delay, I replied honestly, "We are moving beyond clock time." Observing in her apprentice role, Diana Winston nodded to confirm the sense of timelessness that has pervaded the retreat. Julie explained that my note requesting Jack's help with my Vipassana crush prompted him to ask her to counsel me, since he was booked solid himself. I feel touched by Jack and Julie's attentiveness to my particular needs. I have been doing my best to stay mindful in the midst of a flood of stimuli. Helping the process are the simplicity of the retreat schedule, the slow pace of everyone around me, the loving energy field, the beautiful natural surroundings, the Three Refuges, and regular Metta practice. I told Julie that I am learning to sublimate the strong energy of a Vipassana romance, noticing my body sensations and emotions as they come and go, while grounding myself with mindful breathing and barefoot walking. Julie responded, "Your true nature is emerging more and more fully. I bow to your process." Unable to acknowledge the truth of her statement with words, I burst into tears of happiness.

During the subsequent sitting, I sobbed with waves of grief for the legacy of suicide, depression, and alcoholism in my family tree. While I was crying, I sensed John Travis transmitting Metta to me from his seat near the altar. I feel compassion for my "warrior woman" spirit, continuously heading towards the light of consciousness. With enormous gratitude for all that I have learned from my parents, siblings, grandparents, and spiritual teachers, I sense my soul moving steadily towards healing karmic wounds from past generations. Like the Buddha, I have been touching the earth as each new challenge presents itself.

At lunch I sat next to Edgar, the yogi with autism, at one of the picnic tables in front of the dining hall. The "polenta puttinesci" was a gustatory marvel. Afterwards I carried a cup of tea to the brook and leaped onto a large, sunny rock in mid-stream. There I sat, contentedly watching skate bugs swirl on the water's surface and listening to the swishing sounds of rivulets on both sides of the rock. After rousing myself to ring the gong for the 2:00 sitting, I decided to retire to my room for a siesta. Moment to moment, I have been following my impulses in a wholesome, nurturing way.

I awoke from the nap in tears, remembering Robert's words: "You never know what you will be asked to let go of next. Your soul must follow the call of the mysterious unfolding of the universe." I wondered if it is time to let go of my identity as a music therapist. Maybe I should focus on becoming a meditation teacher to spread the dharma that has helped me mature spiritually. After receiving good preparation in the Community Dharma Leader training, I want to increase my knowledge and authority to lead the sangha in Mexico. More and more, my close friendships are related to meditation practice. Increasingly, my energy is going into practicing Vipassana, reading Buddhist texts, giving dharma talks, and leading weekend retreats for the Mexican sangha. My inner stream of questions went: "Should I ask Jack or Julie to train me to be a dharma teacher? Would it be a good idea for my husband and me to relocate to northern California, where Mark could pursue his interests in the Institute of Noetic Sciences and the Grof Holotropic Breathwork training? But wouldn't I miss teaching music therapy courses and leading international trainings in Guided Imagery and Music?"

Suddenly I caught myself absorbed in fantasies about future scenarios that might or might not occur. At that moment, I needed to slow down my thoughts and calm down. I decided to take a hot bath in the downstairs tub. On impulse, I checked the upstairs linen closet to see if there was a clean washcloth. There it was—a single fresh washcloth just as I had imagined. Rinsing my face and bathing myself felt soothing and refreshing. I am learning to take care of myself tenderly.

With red, puffy eyes from so much crying, I emerged into the afternoon sunlight, reassured by the sight of fellow yogis concentrating on their own activities. Gina was lolling like a lizard on a sunny bench, and Heather was sitting in solitary meditation on the back porch of Karuna dormitory, where she was nursing a serious knee injury. I joined Margot, who was walking mindfully back and forth across the patio in front of the meditation hall. How soothing and grounding it felt to sense my feet touching the stone surface of the patio. "Being walked" seemed timeless. The dinner bell reminded me that time exists. Redirecting my footsteps, I was one of the first yogis to arrive at the dining hall and to experience the joy of truly tasting moist, warm, three-berry crumb cake, bathed in melting soy ice cream.

To begin his dharma talk, entitled "The Sure Heart's Release," John Travis read a poem about the river of life, flowing between pleasant sensations on one bank and unpleasant ones on the other. Our task is to surrender our hearts to the current. In gratitude, we can recognize that all is perfect as it is, with nothing missing. John told a story about his retreat in rural Nepal, where he had repetitive dreams about a huge snake. One day, he emerged from his hut to find the local villagers attacking an eight-foot snake that had crawled out from the space beneath his sleeping quarters. Because of their fear, these Nepalese farmers killed the benevolent animal that had been eating rodents who robbed their grain supply. So often, we react fearfully against the very element that could be an ally if we would welcome it. How can we learn to befriend all life? John said, "Metta is a naturally arising state. Notice it and nourish it each time it arises, until you feel it in your bones." After the discourse, I bowed to John and thanked him for addressing my heart's present condition. His kind demeanor consoled me.

My fellow veggie washers were empathic about my bandaged wrist and spared me heavy loads. In our closing ritual, I anointed the hands of Ida, Toby, and a newcomer, Eileen, with hand cream for our chapped hands. Ida and I attempted to out-bow one another with low farewell reverences. After my evening routine of hand-washing clothes, I went to bed early.

In order to integrate yesterday's events, I have been writing to the sound of the stream outside my window for almost three hours. My new, Chinese-made, plastic alarm clock reads 3:03 a.m. Rescue Remedy is starting to have an effect, and I try to sleep for a while.

The 5:00 a.m. bell jolts me awake. My royal blue pashmina shawl is draped around my head like the Virgin Mary's robe. Maybe one reason that nuns wear the "veil," is to protect the open crown chakra. Wishing I had more protection for the top of my head, I imagine buying a comforting, hooded sweatshirt like the ones worn by my students with autism. Because they are hypersensitive to sensory stimuli, the students shield themselves with hoods. Now I feel the same impulse to cover my crown. I have been sensing energy streaming from my body, especially through my hot, tingling hands, my third eye, and the back of my heart. When I go outside, I see people's auras swirling around their shoulders and head. Sometimes my head swims with all the input. I resolve to request an extra interview with Julie today.

During the first walking period of the morning, I follow where my feet lead me to a grassy meadow with lush, moss-covered rocks. An inner message induces me to "go to the waterside." Jumping from rock to rock in a stream, I see tiny, maidenhair ferns alongside a series of pools linked by miniature cascades. Overhanging the brook are two strategically placed spider webs, side by side, slung between the twigs of a bush. The competing spiders have collapsed their legs to look streamlined and nearly invisible at the center of their fine-spun mandalas. These webs are visible only when the sunlight illuminates their artistry from a particular angle. As I search the streambed for a heart-shaped rock, I am amazed by the variety of colors, shapes, and sizes of all the stones I encounter. When I tune into any aspect of nature, a vast complexity and multiplicity of design reveals itself. Unsuccessful in my heart-rock mission, I choose three angular-looking stones to carry with me as worry beads. Clicking them together in my right hand calms me down.

I am astonished by the abundance of life in the ten feet of space that I have been exploring. Lizards are draped over one another, sunbathing above the water level of the stream. Bees are harmonizing on high and low pitches, as they hover over bushes that display brilliant purple flowers. On the path back to the Council House, I notice different kinds of ants—big, fat ones, rushing to accomplish communal tasks, and a tiny one, lugging on its back a leaf fragment larger than itself.

By the time I meet with Julie, I feel dizzy and overwhelmed with stimuli. There is so much life around me. I find my teacher busy scribbling process notes from the previous interview. What a relief to see that I am not the only one who writes during this retreat. Julie listens to my concerns about whether or not I should let go of my professional identity as a music therapist. Her response is, "That is only one of your many shifting identities." She is right. I am a writer, a CDL trainee, a meditation teacher, a wife, a friend, a pianist, and much more. There are many roles that I play. Julie suggests that it is possible to expand my identities without losing myself. When I confess that I wrote for nearly three hours in the aftermath of yesterday's hiatus, she gives me some useful advice: "Let go of judging how much writing you do. It is your creative gift. Note when it is grounding and integrative, when it is obsessive, and when it is a creative outlet."

After I describe how giddy and permeable I have been feeling, Julie counsels me: "Don't let your energy escape through the top of your head. Don't allow yourself to leave the body in order to relate to others or to the outside world. Let it all come to you. Receive what comes." While reminiscing about how her own meditation teacher Ruth Dennison used to mail her "dharma prescriptions," Julie writes me a prescription, which reads, "Dear Ginger, Come back in and feel your whole body. Keep coming back, relax, sense the breath, and feel your whole beautiful self." The note is signed "Julie." Accepting my "spiritual doctor's orders," I am so touched by her concern for my well-being that I say spontaneously, "I love you." Smiling, she acknowledges my words. After affirming my intuition that covering the head and wearing dark glasses is a good way to protect myself from sensory overload, Julie congratulates me for honoring my body's needs by taking a soothing bath yesterday. She warns me to drink plenty of water, so that I do not become dehydrated in the hot, dry weather. Armed with helpful advice, I feel balanced as I leave the interview.

At lunch, I am conscious of playing with my food, delighting in slathering tofu Ruben sandwiches with spicy mustard and tangy sauerkraut, and topping off the concoction with pungent pickles. My taste buds are thrilled with the culinary creation. It is so much fun to be sensorially alive. I notice that my toes wiggle when I am happy. How enjoyable to savor a slow, sumptuous feast.

After ringing the gong, I enter the meditation hall, where scores of meditators are already sitting in deep concentration. I pause to sense the exquisite stillness in the room. What we are doing here is radical. We are changing the energy field of collective human consciousness. During the sit, I sense Teja connecting with me from where he sits by the window across the hall. Because the charged energy currents distract me throughout the meditation period, I decide not to wait until the retreat's end to speak with him. As soon as the closing bell rings, I write a note and pin it on the teacher's bulletin board. My message reads: "The energy between us is so strong that I do not know how to handle it. It would be a relief to talk." By the end of the afternoon Qigong class, I feel more relaxed and grounded. I bow to Teja, who thanks me for the note and agrees to take a walk with me tomorrow to clear the air. A Vipassana crush can loom so large in the silence. A cool, gentle rain has started to fall. I trust that everything will turn out fine. I miss my husband and feel lucky to be happily married.

Eugene gives tonight's dharma talk about the luminous nature of mind. He tells the sangha:

*The universe is pure consciousness. Big mind is our true
nature. We study "small mind" in Vipassana practice. Freedom comes from identifying with roles, and, at the same time,
dis-identifying with them due to their impermanent nature. It
is a paradox to fully inhabit each moment, while recognizing
its impermanence. We must touch the universe deeply before
practicing letting go. Once the heart is open, letting go happens naturally.*

Has Eugene guessed that I have been confused about role identification?
Like the other dharma teachers on this retreat, he seems to be tailoring his
discourse to my particular necessities. I wonder if other yogis are feeling a
similar connection to the themes of the dharma talks. Eugene guides us
to experience the difference between the concept "hand" and the sensations of "hand." With eyes closed, I sense tingling, heat, and hardness.
Then I shift to recognizing cognitively that the site of these sensations is
my dominant, right hand. Eugene reminds us that without the concept
of "I," spaciousness occurs: "Our minds are like the sky. Freedom comes
from releasing all objects of the mind." Over the past few days, I have
had moments of this kind of spaciousness. The challenge is to cultivate a
spacious awareness in a busy and crowded world.

On Thursday, March 20, I am awake at 1:40 a.m. My goal for today is to speak
and act skillfully and wisely when I am with Teja. Eugene's discourse has
pointed to the paradox at the root of my present delusion and suffering. I am
struggling to reconcile my "small self" role of Mark's contented wife with the
expansion of my "big self" into the universal field of loving energy. I am in
love with the energetic opening and release that I feel in Qigong practice. It
reminds me of the bliss I felt learning T'ai Chi, while high on hallucinogens
in my hippy days. Performing the slow, sensuous movements in altered,
expansive states of consciousness led to experiences of ecstasy. As in the past,
I am more in love with the sensation of expansiveness in body and mind
than I am with the instructor. Sometimes I feel confused by the pull between
my expanded heart and my fearful, contracted "small self" mind.

Memories emerge about past relationships that I have had with men. So
often my sexual attraction has been connected to their spiritual pursuits.
In men who are devoted to meditation or martial arts, I have sensed an
aspect of myself that I wish to develop. Like them, I am a spiritual warrior,
committed to expanding my capacity for wisdom and compassion. Like
them, I try to inspire my students to open their hearts and minds. Teja,
a seeker who teaches with passion and dedication, is a male reflection of

what I love and respect in myself. He has activated the "COEX" system that involves my emotional relationships with men (Grof, 1993). This "system of condensed experience" reminds me of intimate relationships I have had throughout my adult life. With his regular suggestions to move with "no stress, no strain," Teja is healing the addiction to perfection and overwork that I have learned in my family. Maybe he and I knew each other in a past life. The connection seems old and familiar. I feel deeply grateful to Teja for supporting me on my spiritual path. My hope is that once we clear away some of the projections and delusions, we can develop an ongoing friendship. I wonder what I activate in his psyche. After decades of meditation and spiritual discipline, are we both mature enough to discover what lies beneath the surface of our energetic attraction? What can we learn from one another?

As I write, tears fill my eyes. It is through my gift of writing that I can follow the psyche's thread and find self-understanding. I feel profound gratitude for my soul's karmic journey and for the loving teachers who have helped to guide me. Every part of the life journey seems perfect as it has been unfolding. What a blessing to be alive in this body.

During the first sitting, as I begin doing independent Metta practice, my heart aches. Drawn to review the suffering of individual family members, friends, clients, and teachers, I grieve for the sorrows of the world. Then images of wildlife at Spirit Rock come to my mind. My compassion extends to deer, turkeys, lizards, and butterflies, and then to all life everywhere. My grief feels so deep that I cannot stop connecting to the enormous amount of suffering on the earth at this time. I start to transmit loving kindness to everyone I can think of around the globe. Focusing on people being tortured and killed in Iraq, I have images of war victims without food or water or shelter. Other images emerge of bombed out fields without vegetation or flowers. The anti-war song "Where Have All the Flowers Gone?" by Peter, Paul and Mary fills my head, and my heart is so sad that the pain feels unbearable. When the bell rings to end the sitting, I cannot stop crying. While the other yogis leave for breakfast, I rock myself back and forth in the throes of grieving. I sob until my body is limp and worn out. Feeling drained and fragile, I walk weakly to the public bathroom to wash my blotched, flushed face. By the time I reach the dining hall, almost everyone has finished breakfast. To my relief, I see Angie and Gina lingering over tea. As I slide onto a chair opposite them, their sympathetic expressions soothe me. Sharing the comfort of one another's presence, we sip tea together.

Throughout this retreat I have sensed the support of the Three Refuges. Sometimes I have felt the Buddha's spirit helping me touch the earth and stay grounded in the midst of the tempting distractions of Mara. At other times, I have appreciated the enduring value of the dharma. Each dharma talk has given me a kernel of truth to incorporate into my practice and my daily life. Today I honor each and every member of this sangha. We are all reminding one another to stay on the dharma path and to keep opening and raising our consciousness.

During yoga stretches this morning, I recognize that to attend this annual, month-long retreat is more important to me than to teach a spring semester course at the UDLA. No matter where I live, embodying and teaching the dharma have become priorities. Back in the meditation hall, Eugene leads an exquisite "One Mind" meditation, in which we are encouraged to expand our awareness into the space around us and be open to all incoming sounds. To my delight, I listen to the varied pitches of beautiful bells, gongs and chimes, resonating from time to time in the stillness. This is one of my favorite ways to practice sensing the infinite spaciousness around us. I am moved to tears by the beauty of the tones. It does not escape my notice that Eugene is crying at the end of the meditation.

With a sense of inner peace and strength, I meet Teja on the back patio of the meditation hall. After exchanging silent bows, we walk single-file through the woods to the platform that overlooks the hills. There we break silence and have a heart-to-heart talk. He tells me that as a teacher, uphold-ing the integrity of maintaining boundaries with yogis, he has not tried to figure out my role in his psyche. Teja had intended to wait until the end of the retreat to speak with me, but when he received my distressed note, he decided we should meet. Although he divulges very little about his personal life, I learn that he has been studying martial arts, including Aikido and Tai Ch'i, with Chinese masters for thirty years. As a long-time practitioner of Vipassana meditation, he has been teaching Qigong during short retreats at Spirit Rock over the past five years. This is the first time that he has taught at a month-long retreat.

The timing seems perfect for our paths to cross. With my studies of yoga, Tai Ch'i, energy healing, and music therapy, I feel ripe for embodying Qigong. Teja listens with interest as I describe how learning the "Eight Actions of Ch'i" is helping me to receive and disperse energy and emotions. He appears moved by my description of how I have used GIM and improvi-sational music therapy with people who have autism. I am not surprised to hear that Teja's mother was a classical pianist and that he himself is a com-poser and recording artist who plays keyboards in a band. Besides martial arts, music is another passion that we share. He and I agree that raising con-sciousness and spreading the dharma are urgent priorities in today's world.

Suddenly I ask, "Has war started in Iraq?" Teja stares at me in silence. Then he says, "Do you really want to know?" My reply is, "I have been dreaming about war. Images of suffering war victims filled my morning Metta practice. My body feels the weight of mourning. I noticed tears on Eugene's face as he led today's 'One Mind' meditation. My intuition is that the bombing has begun." Teja responds, "Yes, the U.S. started bombing Iraq last night." Even though I already knew the truth intuitively, I burst out crying and feel as if I have been kicked in the solar plexus. As I bend over and wail with grief, Teja lays a hand on my back. Somehow this gesture of support comforts me. He tells me about his Chinese martial arts teacher who survived the Cultural Revolution with an ancient practice called "Breathing in and Dissolving the Pain." This discipline reminds me of the way I have been "receiving" and "releasing" the breath and waves of strong emotion during meditation.

Teja and I discuss how vital it is to have a retreat at this time of world crisis and chaos. Most human beings are not yet conscious enough to abandon violence and warfare. Spirit Rock and other meditation centers around the globe provide crucial refuges, where people learn to honor all life and find peaceful means to resolve conflicts. Teja informs me that the Spirit Rock teachers have decided not to tell the yogis yet about the outbreak of war, because the safe container of the retreat would be broken, and the contamination of fear could harm meditators who are in an extremely open and vulnerable state. The teachers want to break the painful news closer to the retreat's end, when they can facilitate the necessary integration and grounding process in a skillful way. I promise Teja not to divulge my secret knowledge except in teacher interviews. My intention is to mourn privately by writing in my journal, practicing Metta, and taking walks in nature. I confess, "I got more than I bargained for in this discussion." Teja notes that there are no accidents in life. I have merely confirmed what my heart had already sensed. We bow to each other with mutual respect and return through the woods to Noble Silence.

On impulse, I break the rules once more to telephone Mark in Mexico. Hearing his voice calms me down, and it feels good to share our concerns about the war in Iraq. After our brief conversation, I am reassured that our mutual love will sustain us no matter how violent and chaotic the world becomes.

In a late morning interview with Julie, I admit my intuition about the bombing in Iraq and my phone call to Mark. She asks, "Has your attention shifted to the outside world? What is happening with your internal retreat process?" When I report new insights about my relationships with men, Julie smiles approvingly. She recommends that I make no more phone calls and that I ground myself by walking and wearing dark glasses and a hat to block out stimulation. Julie is clear that if I want to teach the dharma and guide suffering people, I must learn to sit nobly with my own sorrows. Her suggestion to contain my grief during the final days of silence on the retreat makes sense to me. I describe how the Three Refuges have been supporting my mourning process. Then I wonder aloud if I should do the Tibetan "Tonglen" practice—breathing in the suffering of the Iraqi people, and breathing out compassion for the victims of war. Julie's response is firm: "No, you are in too expanded a state. You would be overwhelmed by the enormity of pain that is occurring there. Metta practice is good for now."

I go on to describe the sensation of heavy weight on my chest, the queasiness in my belly, and the intensified pain in my left knee. My body seems to be absorbing some of the agony of people hit by the bombs. My grief is not only for the people who are being wounded and killed at this moment, but also for the animals and plants and land that is being destroyed. Our poor Mother Earth is hurting. I tell Julie that I have no intention of speaking to any yogis about the war, and that hearing Mark's voice gave me enough support that there is no need to phone him again. She understands my need to touch base with my husband at this time of world crisis. The interview ends with my promise to restrain my impulses and to practice self-containment.

I take a long, slow walk to the "skin trees," rubbing my hand along their smooth, cool, bark-less trunks. Ten deer, mothers and fawns, pass by me without accelerating their leisurely pace. The fragile beauty of wild, white iris blossoms touches my heart. The forest is full of fresh, spring blooms. On my way back, I stop in the Gratitude Hut to leave a Metta prayer "for all beings" in the pile of notes to be added to the prayer wheel. When I return "home," I take a hot bath. How soothing and refreshing it feels to soak in the water. I am learning to follow my natural instincts and to take good care of myself. Lying down on my bed, I place one hand over my heart and the other over the "hara" energy center below my navel. I feel too tired to attend the 6:30 p.m. sitting. What an emotional day it has been.

I wake up groggily after falling into a deep sleep. It is too late to attend tonight's dharma talk. I wonder which teacher is speaking and if anyone will notice my absence from the front row. My belly aches. How hard it is for me to digest the idea of war occurring outside the safe container of Spirit Rock. Feeling sluggish and heavy-limbed, I rouse myself to fulfill nightly veggie-washing responsibilities. Working silently alongside my sangha-mates calms my nerves. By now, we have learned to complete our chores as if we are performing a graceful dance. Each of us has learned the choreography, and there is no need to communicate verbally. At the end of the work period, my companions line up facing me, so that I can anoint their hands with lotion. Toby and I stay behind to have cups of chamomile tea. As she helps herself to a bowl of gluten and wheat-free "Perky's" cereal from the yogis' snack cupboard, I decide to follow her example. Sitting side by side, we chew the crisp nuggets of grain and sound like feet crunching on gravel. The "suchness" of the metal spoon and china bowl are like balm for my worries. After eating such simple food, my stomach feels more settled. As I walk out under brilliant stars, I see the Big Dipper directly above the meditation hall, as if it is protecting the sacred space inside. The constellation seems to provide a large enough container to hold all the world's joys and sorrows. ❧

CHAPTER SEVEN

BEYOND BOUNDARIES

On Friday, March 21, the first day of spring, I awaken at 2:00 a.m. The soft luminosity of a gibbous moon, emanating through the window blinds, falls across my face. My body rhythms are disrupted; I am sleepy during the day and alert at night. Because of last evening's nap, I did not sleep long tonight. I am learning to ride waves of energy as they surge through my body. What a blessing to have a single room, so that my strange hours of repose and awakening do not disturb anyone. I am aware of my lungs expanding and contracting like bellows. Breathing is such a miraculous event that I so often take for granted. Inhaling and exhaling consciously helps me deal with the sour taste of war in my mouth. I open the window to smell the scent of spring and to hear the trickling sound of the stream. How delicious it feels to be aware of my sensory impressions.

As I follow natural impulses and flow with synchronistic events, I seem to be entering sacred space and time. In Teja's words, I am "in the flow and I am the flow." Is this how to reach the bliss of peak experience and spiritual opening without the crazy edge of mania? I feel safely held here and now. With the sixteen colorful crayons that I requisitioned, I can express my shifting moods by drawing mandalas. I like the soothing sensation of giving my feet Reflexology massages with body cream. The acupressure points on the soles feel so sensitive that I feel better walking barefoot, like some of my students with autism who resisted wearing shoes. Because the roof of my mouth feels hypersensitive, I have been sucking on hard Ricola cough drops from the manager's office to help numb the prickling sensations. A turquoise-colored scarf is wrapped protectively around my vulnerable throat chakra. Inside the cocoon of my pale blue pashmina shawl, which protects the crown of my head, I feel like a "magical child," who is exploring innate, childlike playfulness and elemental sensuality. It is as if my soul were expanding through my soles and my crown. As I lie in a fetal position, a pillow is supporting the tender region of my lower back near the kidneys, in the area that Teja calls the "Gate of Life." The silvery moonlight seems to be nourishing the chakra of my third eye.

At 3:30 a.m., I begin Metta practice. It helps to steady myself by opening my eyes from time to time, whenever I feel dizzy from strong sensations or emotions. By the time I arrive for Qigong class, I feel tired from so much early morning activity. There I notice other yogis who are resorting to self-protective tactics like mine. Several people are wearing hooded sweatshirts and dark glasses. Collectively, we are becoming weirder and weirder. Does "i" come before "e," or "e" come before "i" in the word "weirder?" Spelling seems such an arbitrary exercise in a non-ordinary state of consciousness.

Because I feel chilled and shivery, I have wrapped myself in layers of clothing made with natural fibers—a silk camisole and a cotton turtleneck shirt, covered by a large tee shirt, a pashmina shawl, and a woolen cape. Yesterday I included a polar vest and a zippered jacket among the layers. I look like a multi-colored "mariposa." As I practice Qigong, I warm up and shed the outer-most covering. By the end of the half-hour class, I have unwrapped most of my cocoon, so that I am wearing only a few layers of clothes. But soon afterwards, the chill returns to my bones and I bundle myself up again like a papoose. It is comforting to use articles of clothing that I have been given by dear friends and family members. I carry the positive energy of Mark in my favorite scarf; of Leena in my lightweight, canvas sneakers; and of Mom in my rainbow-hued socks. No longer am I wearing any jewelry, because it weighs too heavily on my wrists and earlobes.

I am developing an autistic-like sensitivity at all my sense doors. Recently the sound of the vacuum cleaner has bothered my supersensitive hearing to such a degree that I avoid going inside during morning cleaning periods. I remember my student Scott, who could not tolerate listening to blow dryers in public bathrooms. Now his aversive behavior, which used to seem like an autistic eccentricity, is perfectly comprehensible. My peripheral gaze has expanded so far that I can almost see what is happening behind my back. Draping a scarf over the sides of my head provides me with "blinders" like those used to calm skittish horses. Teja has been encouraging us to use a "soft gaze and peripheral vision" in Qigong classes. He speaks of allowing energy to flow through the inside of our "hollow bones," and he recommends an exercise for the joints called "band warming" to cleanse the tendons in our hands, wrists, arms, and ankles. The more sensitive I become, the more I soak up his teachings.

While I surrender to opening up as fully as possible, I am observing minutely every detail of the process. If I did not trust that Jack and Julie know how to help me ground myself enough to leave this retreat safely, I might be frightened. This self-research is fascinating. I feel totally involved in studying unfolding aspects of the Self. It is like intensive "Authentic Movement" practice, but for the mind rather than for the body. As I allow myself to regress to a state of what Freud termed "primary process," I am trying to note whatever arises. Writing helps me stay balanced in a state of childlike innocence and openness. Rocking my self back and forth feels consoling.

On the walk to breakfast, I stop to appreciate a particularly shiny dawn. The sun's aura highlights tall, golden grass atop the hilltops. During a trip from dew-soaked meadows, turkeys have left wet, three-toed footprints across the asphalt driveway. Inside the dining hall, I observe Edgar with compassionate amusement, as he balances a tray, piled high with dishes, plates, and glasses. His awkward, jerky, noisy movements have caused most yogis to avoid him, but I like to sit next to him, parallel, but not too close for comfort. Perhaps sensing that I "know" autistic rhythms and needs, he has smiled at me on several occasions. What I am learning on this retreat is to embody those hypersensitivities and coping strategies that I used to treat in others with professional detachment. Moving beyond compassion for souls who have incarnated in autistic bodies, I am now experiencing "being autistic" within a safe container. This practical knowledge will help me connect fearlessly to people in states of regression. I catch myself leaping forward to the future. Right now I must keep my balance as I experience my own regression.

During today's first meditation, I notice rapid-fire mental acuity and steady concentration. There are moments of profound stillness and nothingness, interrupted by involuntary jerking in my torso. My nervous system seems calm and quiet. After ringing the bell to end the session, Eugene requests that all yogis respect the container of the retreat, as it metabolizes from the tight structure of the beginning to the deepening concentration of the middle. He asks us to refrain from writing notes to other yogis and to resist the temptation to plan for ending the retreat.

Anna and Eugene lead this morning's question and answer period. In response to the question, "When does karma begin?" Anna quips, "When does karma end?" Eugene answers that there is no beginning to karma, which is an imponderable mystery. He goes on to explain the difference between Metta and Karuna (compassion) practice. The latter involves phrases such as "I care about your pain and suffering. May you be free of pain and suffering." Unlike Metta prayers, which focus on transmitting loving kindness, Karuna practice emphasizes the phenomenon of suffering. After his enlightenment, the Buddha was known as the Bodhisattva of compassion. The Jakata tales document some of the thousands of lives dedicated to purifying his heart until he incarnated as the baby who became the Buddha. Listening to how long it took the Buddha to reach enlightenment, I feel less impatient with my own slow progress on the path of spiritual purification.

While I walk mindfully to the lower walking room to do some Feldenkrais stretching exercises, I notice that the chronic pain in my right shoulder has vanished. In the process of learning to trust my inner wisdom and to beginning to fly freely, my injured "wing" is healing.

How thankful I feel that Julie has been scheduling me for daily interviews. So that she would not worry about my absence last night, I left her a note to explain that I was sleeping in my room during the dharma talk. At today's meeting, she uses my note as evidence of how sleep-deprived I am: "Three hours a night is not sufficient rest." Julie writes me a "prescription" to take naps after lunch, even if it means that the retreat manager has to find a substitute to ring the 2:00 p.m. gong. To my dismay, she informs me that Jack gave an inspirational dharma talk last night about Bodhisattvas, who, upon becoming enlightened, choose not to rest in Nirvana, but to help other sentient beings reach spiritual liberation. How I regret missing one of Jack's discourses. In tears, I thank Julie for accepting me at my most vulnerable and for caring enough to correct my course when I am unbalanced. The bond of trust between us is growing stronger, as I swim in the sea of not knowing. In a boundary-less state, I value her ability to set clear limits.

Before the interview's end, Julie breaks the news that on Sunday neither she nor Jack will be at Spirit Rock. My immediate reaction is an infantile fear of abandonment. A moment later, when she asks if I would feel comfortable having an interview with John Travis during her absence, my adult self has regained control. I assure her that I like John, and that I am sure he will be a fine substitute. Julie suggests that I rely on the structure of the retreat to hold me: "no more missed dharma talks." While being firm, she is acting like a good mother, trustworthy and nurturing, with my child-like self. Bidding her farewell, I feel a pang of separation anxiety.

During the subsequent sit, my head is full of worries about both surrogate parents being gone this weekend. In my primal state, I am reliving the time when I was eighteen months old, separated from my parents, when they left me with Deedee during their belated honeymoon in Spain. By the end of the sit, I have made two resolutions: to request an interview with John, and to attend both the morning and afternoon Qigong classes that Teja will be conducting on Sunday. By seeking proximity to trusted teachers, I hope to create a tight and secure container around me.

At lunch, it takes me a while to find just the right spot to eat. Watching me move my plate from one table to another, Angie catches my eye and grins. I finally settle down on the sun-baked, back steps to the dining hall. There I peel off my socks to sense my naked feet touching the wooden steps, thus grounding myself. Once again, I am sustained by the image of the Buddha touching the earth at the moment of his illumination. How did the Buddha discover such a radical way to shed ego attachments? I have renewed respect for the Spirit Rock teachers, who enter Noble Silence repeatedly and prepare themselves to support those of us who follow in their footsteps.

Following my instincts, I take a nap right after the meal. What a relief not to keep myself awake in order to ring the 2:00 gong. I sense myself relaxing and letting go another notch. With gratitude to Julie for her latest prescription and to Andrea for finding a substitute bell-ringer, I doze off. The sound of the gong pulls me from my "Metta nap" to attend the afternoon sit. My mind is caught up in questions: "Before incarnating, does the soul choose its karmic path and manner of living? Are the people who are dying in Iraq destined to leave their bodies in this violent way? Why them and not me?"

As fear surges inside me, I feel humbled. Part of my identity has been to consider myself intrepid in my spiritual journey. Now I am over my head in tears and faint-heartedness. It helps to remember that whatever I am experiencing, the Buddha did too on his long path to enlightenment. Surely my teachers Jack and Julie have encountered moments of terror during prolonged retreats. I think of the long line of dedicated dharma practitioners who have needed to touch the earth for steadiness amidst waves of fear. As I shiver with doubt, I sense the loving presence of my student Jerry encouraging me to trust this process. What a brave soul he is to face the hypersensitivity of autism every day. How I admire him. The book that I wrote as a tribute to him and my other students with autism has an entirely new meaning to me now. The title *I Dreamed I Was Normal* seems especially apt for my present situation. I have been living in a dream or a trance. What most people term "normality" is just the relative truth of the small self. In a sea of shifting perceptions, emotions, sensations, and thoughts, I have been embodying an autistic need for predictable routines and structure. Anybody experiencing the fluctuations in sensory processing that characterize autism would cope in similar ways. It is so easy to judge as abnormal what we do not understand.

At the sound of the closing bell, I feel frightened and shaken. My worldview is changing. What used to seem certain no longer feels secure. Longing for some outer confirmation that I am not going crazy, I decide to write Teja a note asking, "Have you had times of fear?" As I head for the teacher's bulletin board, Teja approaches me with a look of concern on his face. His question, "Are you O.K.?" makes me wonder if he is reading my mind. In tears, I admit, "I feel scared." He touches the crown of his head to mine and invites me to attend the afternoon session of Qigong, starting in a few moments. Calming down a bit, I follow him upstairs to join the class. He introduces us to a practice called "dissolving," which is new to me. After we all lie face up on the floor, Teja guides us in an imagery exercise from feet to head. We imagine each body part dissolving from the quality of ice, to water, to steam, into the infinite space of our unified true nature. I allow sobs to flow through me and to pass into vast spaciousness. By the end of the class, I feel more grounded and tranquil. I am thankful for Teja's soothing presence and the perfect timing of his dissolving practice.

How fitting that John Travis is leading Karuna (compassion) practice this afternoon. While he gives instructions to begin with an image of oneself, his voice sounds so gentle and caring that I cry. I picture myself as a toddler, missing my mother and resisting Miss Jolly's administrations. I feel deep compassion for the child I have been embodying in my regressed state. In tears, I ask forgiveness for the countless times I have driven and pushed my poor body beyond its natural limits. I vow to do my best to be tender with myself, giving my body the food, rest, baths, and massages it deserves. I promise to take a bath before supper and to treat my poor, exhausted self as kindly as possible.

John suggests that we extend our Karuna practice to include a loved one who is in pain. I image my dear friend Guillermo, who is mourning his father's death and his own near death from surgery. With my heart so raw and open, it is easy to feel compassion for his suffering. John concludes the practice by guiding us to send compassion to all beings, recognizing that each one has a measure of sorrow. Afterwards I feel so moved that I approach John and bow in thanks. To my surprise, he lends me his "Pocket Buddha Reader," edited by Anne Bancroft. Gratefully, I open the little book to an excerpt from one of the Buddha's discourses: "Loving kindness is a freedom of the heart which takes in all the ways. It is luminous, shining, blazing forth. None of the ways you can use to further your practice has a sixteenth of part of the value of loving kindness. For it absorbs them all, its luminosity shining forth." On my way to Karuna dormitory for a restorative bath, I cross paths with a yogi who gazes at me with such a loving expression that I weep once more. I wish I knew her name.

As if on cue, Julie gives tonight's dharma talk on the theme of vulnerability. She quotes the Tibetan nun Pema Chodron, who refers to vulnerable moments as opportunities for awakening, "when our idea of who we are or who we think we have to be dissolves" (today's key word). So-called failures or mistakes can be viewed as valuable lessons. Julie reminisces about accepting the gift of a sabbatical for a much-needed personal retreat: "The real gift is the practice of receiving the moment—a doorway to our essential nature. It does not take a month. It only takes a moment. Receiving transforms who you think you are. On retreat, old beliefs, stories and memories are released in a purification process." I acknowledge to myself how healing it was for me to receive Teja's teachings this afternoon.

Julie tells us an archetypal "bedtime" story, the ancient Sumerian tale of Inana, the Queen of Heaven and Earth, who chooses to descend to the Underworld to face her fears and incorporate her missing parts. By entering unknown territory, the queen embraces her vulnerability. She wears a crown, a robe, and a lapis lazuli necklace, among her seven symbols of identity. (Julie reminds us how we each bring meaningful possessions to retreats for protection as we enter unknown inner terrain.) Inana's sister, who represents greed, hatred, and delusion, has been exiled to the Underworld, where she drinks dirty water and eats clay. On her own descent, Inana is stripped of all her power and possessions, one at each gate she enters. She is killed, and her body is hung from a hook on a wall. (Julie points out that on retreats, the competent part of us that handles the outside world falls away, and we are plunged into our own "underworld.") The sister mourns Inana's death. After waiting for three days for her mistress to return home, Inana's servant goes to the God of Wisdom and Nature, who bestows a gift of two tiny beings, one with food and one with water. These compassionate figures have the ability to stay present in the face of pain.

They go to the grieving sister and accompany her during her mourning. Because she is not used to being heard and seen in her vulnerability, she is grateful and offers the compassionate strangers a gift. They ask for Inana's corpse, and they resurrect her with the food and drink of life. Inana returns from the Underworld with a more complete understanding of life and death. After choosing to be initiated and taking on the powers of rebirth, nothing can surprise or overwhelm her anymore.

In conclusion, Julie connects Inana's tale to our retreat experience: "We have consciously undertaken this silent retreat as an opportunity for initiation. By staying open to whatever arises from within ourselves, we come back to life. As we learn to breathe with all aspects of ourselves, we transform from victims into Goddesses. There is only one way out—being awake, open, and vulnerable to life."

Unusual body sensations awaken me at 1:15 a.m. on Saturday, March 22. As I lie in bed, sensing energy flowing through the soles of my feet, the palms of my hands, and the top of my head, I image Jesus with a golden halo around the crown chakra and rays of light streaming from open hand and feet chakras. He is beaming radiant energy and transmitting universal love and healing prana to all sentient beings. Suddenly I understand what being a Bodhisattva is. I want to stay on this earthly plane to help others awaken. As a music therapist, I have been serving in this way without consciously connecting the work to my Buddhist practice. Now I recognize that apart from my professional mission, I tend to respond compassionately to family and friends in pain; to people suffering from autism; to my Nicaraguan godchild, who is in treatment for juvenile arthritis; and to colleagues in Bulgaria, who are struggling in the aftermath of forty years of Communist oppression.

Expressing love feels natural and healthy to me. My husband and each of my closest friends are on a similar Bodhisattva path, and I have been drawn to spiritual teachers who model lives of service to others. All the people to whom I am strongly attracted are consciously cleansing themselves to become clear transmitters of loving energy. It is through sitting with our own suffering that we create a strong enough capacity and a large enough container to carry out missions of love on this troubled planet. There is such an urgent need for awakening and facing whatever stands in the way of becoming messengers of peace and compassion. It seems like no accident that Mark and I have had the honor of spending time with His Holiness the Dalai Lama, the personification of loving kindness.

My key lesson from this retreat is to care for myself as tenderly as I tend to care for others. Now I see why it is so reassuring to start every day with

Metta practice, and to begin the prayers with myself as the focus before concentrating on other beings. With my soul's purpose ever clearer, I can be committed to helping other people in the process of awakening to their own true Buddha nature and to our shared unity with all life. If I can shine some light of awareness into the darkness of confusion, doubt, fear, and despair around me, I will be satisfied with my life. At this moment I am permeated with happiness and affirmation that the strong spiritual yearning inside me has born fruit. There is no doubt that I still have much soul work to do and parts of myself to clean and refine, but the basic foundation has been laid.

My heart is full of gratitude to my teachers, Jack, Julie, and Teja, who have been tending to my internal birth process with kindness and patience. I am joining a long line of spiritual warriors who have undergone a similar process of self-purification and initiation through sitting with their own pain and darkness. Right now I am awake to my innate Buddha nature and my Bodhisattva path. I feel unafraid to live fully or to die, because I know that death is a transformational process. My body is calm and tired, and my hand is worn out from writing. It is time to shower and to ground myself for the day.

The first sit of the morning seems exquisite, with no resistance to letting go into nothingness and stillness. Later on, when Julie leads a period of questions and answers, she speaks about how important it is to sit with the energetic effect of strong emotional states in the body, noticing the sensations and vibrations as they change and transmute. She cautions us not to resist or avoid the body's truth, so that we can learn its messages. I wonder if other yogis are absorbing her message with every fiber of their being, as I am.

In today's interview with Jack, I recount enthusiastically this past night's experience of awakening to my true Buddha nature, and I express my desire to teach the dharma in order to help others wake up to their own natural divinity. After receiving my words in a supportive way, he points out how wide open I am energetically and emotionally. His advice is to begin the process of grounding myself so that I can "go out into the marketplace to perform loving, Bodhisattva work when this retreat ends in just six days." Suddenly I feel a bit panicky at the thought of leaving the protection of my teachers and the tranquil beauty of Spirit Rock. I wonder aloud if Mark and I should relocate to the Bay area in order to be nearby Spirit Rock. Jack seems surprised that I would consider such a radical move and asks what my husband would do if we relocated. Even as I explain that Mark could lead Holotropic Breathwork workshops as a graduate from Stan Grof's training, I realize that my mind is grasping at unrealistic ways to maintain proximity to my teacher. Jack acknowledges that I am prepared to teach the dharma in Hispanic communities, but he encourages me to contemplate ways in which my life in Mexico is ideal for transmitting the dharma in Spanish. He cautions me, "Instead of trying to figure out how you will change your life after the retreat, ground the experiences and energies that are unfolding." This advice rings true. Jack goes on to recommend that I start making a transition by doing less sitting meditation and more walking, both energetically and slowly, while consciously sensing my feet touching the earth. He suggests taking baths more often and volunteering to chop vegetables in the kitchen, or any other activity that centers me and contains my energy. Like a good father, he advises me to try to sleep more regularly, and he is pleased to hear that Gina has volunteered to ring the 2:00 bell so that I can take afternoon naps. He grins with approval as I demonstrate with my hat and dark glasses how I have been protecting myself from overwhelming input. We agree that my regular Metta practice helps with the grounding process.

Even in my expanded state, I am aware that this interview is lasting far beyond the normal allotted time of fifteen minutes. Jack is providing me with a large enough container to hold my big waves of ideas and emotions. He supports Julie's opinion that it would be good for me to have an interview with John Travis tomorrow, when my regular teachers will be absent. Since Angie has just left me a note to inform me of her early departure from the retreat, I ask Jack "permission" to break silence tomorrow to bid her farewell. He nods his assent. I leave the interview feeling "well-fathered."

By now it is obvious how altered my state of consciousness is. My little warrior's body is cold and depleted, and I long for a warm bath and a nap. Thirst seems to be a constant companion, and I am sipping regularly from the water bottle I carry at all times. While I eat lunch in the quietest corner of the dining hall, I feel speedy and a bit anxious. Wearing dark glasses and facing the wall help me to reduce stimulation. Jack is right that I must slow myself down in order to negotiate the chaos of the outside world all too soon. I wonder if he thought I was crazy during today's interview. It comforts me to know that he will alert John Travis to look out for me during his absence.

As soon as I finish lunch, I luxuriate in a hot bath and then take my tired body to bed, after drawing the blinds to block out the glare of this cold, grey day. With the support of Rescue Remedy, I sleep deeply for two hours. Waking groggily, I realize that my body has warmed up after bathing and napping. On the wall facing the bed, the poster of Kwan Yin watches over me in this snug, small room, and the Goddess of Compassion seems to be protecting me in the midst of primal process. I have abandoned all identity and am following the flow of each moment. The sounds of the stream and the cawing crows outside the window calm me. I trust this process of relinquishing boundaries. When I return to "normal" space and time, this experience will serve me in my roles as teacher and therapist. No longer will I be afraid of my clients' primary process: "been there, done that!"

I decide to follow Jack's advice to cut back on sessions of sitting meditation. Even yoga class seems too confining for my expanded energy field. But I do want to attend the guided Mudita practice at 3:45. How grateful I am for the dependable structure of the retreat schedule. In the midst of swimming through swirling perceptions and boundary-less, timeless, sacred space, I have become so familiar with the retreat schedule that I can depend on predictable guidelines to help me land on solid ground.

The chakras in my feet are wide open and tingling, and I ground the soles on the mattress, with my knees raised to prop up my journal. Writing here in bed is a tool for monitoring my process, a navigational device that allows me to track my moment-to-moment sensations and feelings, so that I do not become inundated. I have been writing myself into and out of a peak experience, trusting my innate, intuitive wisdom and my foundation in spiritual practice and psychotherapy to sustain me. After decades of journaling about my inner life and noting down dreams, I have become an expert witness of my own experiences. My observing eye is strongly developed from so many years of tracking verbal and nonverbal communication of clients as they travel in sessions of Guided Imagery and Music.

Suddenly I miss playing the piano. I imagine the feel of piano keys, hard and firm beneath my sensitive fingertips. It would feel good to play my favorite Brahms Intermezzo right now. During this regressed ego state, I would appreciate having some modeling clay or a sand tray for nonverbal, creative self-expression. Reading feels like a challenging, overly cognitive task for my present level of functioning. The gong interrupts my free association and summons me to the meditation hall.

Anna leads Mudita practice with skill and humor. She starts off by explaining that the basis for the practice of "sympathetic joy" is that there is enough love for everyone to share. What the Buddha called the "near enemy" of Mudita is envy or "comparing mind." Although Anna warns us that Mudita is the most difficult Brahma Vihara to cultivate, I realize that it is not challenging for me to celebrate the happiness of the people I love. When she guides us to imagine a person or a pet that makes us smile, a friend on this retreat comes to mind. I direct the phrases "I appreciate your happiness" and "May your happiness increase" towards Dianita. Then Anna suggests that we use the phrases for a benefactor and then a "loved one." I choose Julie Wester and my husband for these categories.

Once Anna stops actively guiding us and leaves a period of silence for independent Mudita practice, I am unable to concentrate. All of a sudden, I feel anxious sitting in the spacious meditation hall with so many people. In an attempt to soothe myself, I rock my body back and forth, do reflexology on my hands and feet, and sense the firmness of the zafu beneath my seat. These coping mechanisms do little to alleviate my anxiety, and I keep checking my watch to see how much time is left in the session.

The nearby presence of Mark, the teacher-in-training, anchors me and provides some reassurance. As soon as the closing bell sounds, I approach him to request an emergency consultation. Without any hesitation, he leads me to an interview room and listens compassionately to my description of how hard it has been to sit quietly, while I am in such an open and regressed state. As I dissolve in tears, I am painfully aware that both of my teachers are away today. To my relief, Mark first refers to the Buddha's words about cultivating wholesome states of mind and then states emphatically: "At this time it is skillful NOT to sit in meditation and NOT to do slow, mindful walking." He recommends that I take long, energetic hikes in the hills to burn off excess energy and that I find ways to remember my innate sense of humor. Right away his suggestions make sense to me. I ask, "How can I handle recurring thoughts about the war in Iraq?" Mark's response is, "Right now consciously direct your attention away from thinking about the suffering of the world." Like a patient doctor, he advises me to eat well, to continue taking hot baths, and to ask the retreat manager for Valerian herbs to help me sleep better. When I confess that I have already had two showers and a bath today, we agree that I deserve the loving attention that I am giving myself after so many years of self-deprivation. I exit the interview feeling good about having asked for help and about Mark's skillful responses to my situation. It comforts me that he has the same first name as my husband.

At dinner, Margot and I sit across from each other at our favorite window seats. We grin at each other's eccentric tastes in food. I pour so much honey over a biscuit that my hands end up covered with sweet stickiness. We both enjoy the sensuality of peeling and chewing juicy mandarin oranges. What fun it is to fully engage in child's play. After eating, I run up into the hills and laugh out loud at the silly escapades of a pair of courting wild turkeys. Mark's prescription seems to be working.

Tonight John and Robert are leading a question-and-answer session in the meditation hall. One of the topics is the tendency of yogis who are on

A SILENT CURE

prolonged retreats to retrieve early memories stored in the "body-mind." The ensuing discussion makes me feel less alone in facing this phenomenon. The teachers speak about how Vipassana is a purification process that cleanses us from restricting patterns. Robert says, "The rain of dharma gradually soaks into us as we practice over time, and insights sink in along the way. Our 'true abiding' is timeless and space-less. It is 'suchness' that is always available no matter what activity we pursue. There is a presence, an 'isness' that we can relax into, to truly become who we are." His words resonate with my present experience.

Another theme is the blending of Buddhist practice with Western psychotherapy techniques. Spirit Rock has earned a reputation internationally for being "touchy-feely." John mentions that when he returned home after traditional Buddhist training in Asia, he was skeptical about the value of psychotherapy for meditators. But in the throes of marital and parenting difficulties, he found therapy sessions to be beneficial. He realized that Western culture is individualistic and characterized by issues of family wounding that are different from the typical experience in Eastern cultures. There is a valid concern, however, that healing may become a higher priority than liberation for Western meditators. Robert mentions his own training with Freud's student Wilhelm Reich, and explains that whereas Freudians see the goal of healing as "functioning as a normal neurotic," Buddhists view it as the transcending of suffering.

One yogi asks, "Does a person who commits suicide break the precepts?" In response, Robert explains that from a Buddhist perspective, suicide is usually a refusal to deal with suffering. Suicide is not "Thou shalt not behavior"—not sinful—but it avoids facing suffering. Interestingly, the Buddha approved of the suicide of a particular monk who had terminal brain illness and who was not trying to avoid suffering by dying. Admitting that a few of his psychotherapy patients have committed suicide, Robert considers their decision as "beyond my control and out of my hands." He reminds us that some Vietnamese monks practiced self-immolation to protest the Vietnam War. As they burned to death, these monks were attempting to demonstrate both the body's impermanence and the delusion of war. Their radical actions reflected an ancient Vietnamese belief that it is worthy to kill oneself in order to protest the killing of others. If I grapple honestly with the complexities of these issues, I cannot judge as right or wrong other people's decisions to terminate their lives.

Robert concludes the question-and-answer period by stating, "Transpersonalism is not yet mainstream. Healing and liberation are intertwined. The dharma is transmitted through the heart. When I was in Asia, I did not understand the language of my gurus, but I paid attention and received their words in my heart. Attention is the focused and directed aspect of awareness. There is a self-existing awareness that is part of this 'field,' and occasionally we pay attention to it." He leaves us with a parting joke: "You make up these questions, and we make up the answers. Nobody really knows!" I am touched by the blend of wit and wisdom in these dharma teachings.

Back in my room, I draw a mandala that looks like a rainbow-colored orb with all the hues blending into one another. No color appears distinct or separate. The drawing represents my present sense of being an integral part of the entire fabric of life. An image comes to me of the Qigong class performing the eight actions of Qi, while breathing in unison as one collective entity. This group practice seems to connect us to the unified field of universal energy. I feel grateful to have art materials so that I can express nonverbally experiences that are hard to convey in words.

As I prepare for bed, I note how pleasant it feels to urinate, to wash and dry my hands, and to pull on my nightgown. I feel so alive attending to every little sensation and leaving nothing out of awareness. When I snuggle under the blankets, the sound of soft rain falling on the leaves outside my window is soothing, and the sensation of my pale blue pashmina shawl around my shoulders comforts me. Before closing my eyes, I re-read the affectionate note that Alison wrote to me before I moved to my single room. It seems like ages ago, even another lifetime, when she and I were rooming together.

On Sunday March 23, I am awake at 2:00 a.m. With hopes of slowing down the nightly flood of insights and ideas, I swallow another Valerian pill to help me go back to sleep. On the little paper cup that Andrea gave me to contain the Valerian capsules is a picture of a butterfly flying above some daffodils. The symbolism makes me smile; my totem animal is the butterfly, and daffodils are the flowers associated with March, my birth month. Meaningful patterns underlie the web of our experience all the time, but we seldom notice them.

This morning I change my routine and, instead of joining the sangha in the meditation hall, I do yoga on my own. Arriving a bit late for breakfast, I feel no need to rush. I take time to enjoy hot oatmeal, crunchy almonds, ripe banana slices, succulent grapefruit wedges and steaming Bengal Spice tea, sweetened with honey. As I savor the meal, I can sense myself coming down to earth. It has been hard work to nurture my abandoned, two-year-old inner child. I have conscientiously given myself the sensory contact thatI had been missing since my toddler years.

A SILENT CURE

Today's prayer wheel message is "wise speech." How appropriate to receive this reminder just before Angie and I meet for our farewell talk. In silence she leads me to her favorite spot, which turns out to be the Gratitude Hut, one of my preferred refuges at Spirit Rock. After shedding our shoes to enter the small, round room, we sit together on a bench beneath a photograph of Ramana Maharshi at Arunachala Mountain Ashram in India, where he used to teach students by simply gazing at them with profound compassion. His fundamental meditation instruction was to inquire continually, "Who am I?" Looking at the dates inscribed beneath the smiling image, I see that this Indian sage lived from 1884 until 1949, dying the year after my birth.

Before we break silence, Angie and I take a moment to appreciate our tranquil surroundings and to gaze into each other's eyes. Although she was born in Argentina and I grew up in New York, there are amazing parallels in our lives. She is just three months older than I am, and we both had hysterectomies two years ago. Both of us teach the dharma in Spanish. When Angie was four years old, her parents left her with an unkind nanny for two months while they traveled abroad. Apart from similarities in age and personal history, however, our temperaments are very different. While I have been dealing with hyperactivity on this retreat, Angie has faced bouts of sleepiness. After reaffirming our bond as dharma sisters and our shared appreciation for the teachings and natural surroundings at Spirit Rock, we bow to one another and exchange good-bye hugs.

Walking through the meditation hall lobby, I notice a card tacked beside the coat rack and read, "For as long as space exists and sentient beings endure, may I be the living ground of love for all beings." This quotation, attributed to Shantideva, touches my heart and brings tears to my eyes. By the time John Travis welcomes me into his interview room, I have mastered my emotions. He listens with kindly attention to my retreat saga. He responds, "Now your practice is to give the little girl inside love and rest. The dharma will take care of itself until you heal. Let this beautiful, safe place hold you, and trust the container." With minimal words, John conveys compassion and deep understanding. At the close of the interview I thank him for the quiet strength of his presence, which has calmed me throughout the retreat.

On my way to lunch, I find Margot leaping up and down to unfurl the wind-blown Tibetan flags draped across the entrance to the dining hall. When I join her to complete the playful task, she smiles at me in childlike glee. After filling my plate, I retire to eat in solitude, perched on a sunny rock by the stream. By the water's edge I process the morning's interactions. After weeks of Noble Silence, so much talking and socializing has depleted my energy. In the midst of musing, I sense someone watching me. Turning around abruptly, I catch a short man with intense, dark eyes gazing at me. Embarrassed at being caught staring, he averts his eyes and then looks back to meet mine directly. We both grin in recognition. Rick, who arrived for the last two weeks of the retreat, met me years ago at a meeting for Spanish-speaking meditators. I resolve to seek him out at the retreat's end.

Back in my room, I lie in a warm patch of sunlight on the bed and wake up after a long, restorative nap. Memories emerge of Mom making me and my siblings take post-lunch naps when we were young. Resurrecting this old childhood habit feels wholesome. So many times, instead of honoring my body's urge to snooze after the mid-day meal, I have driven myself to work on a low battery. Right now I have no choice but to listen to my instinctual needs. Nothing else seems to matter. I must forgive myself for all the times when I have ignored bodily signals to rest or eat. As Jack says, "Forgiveness means giving up all hope of a better past." Although I cannot change what has passed, I want to take responsibility for caring for my inner child now. If not now, then when?

Instinctively I have replaced my bright red pashmina shawl with a pale blue one, switching from an assertive to a gentler mood. It is not time to wear hot colors. I have run out of corrector fluid. The message is clear: I do not have to correct mistakes or to try to be perfect. I want to trust my intuition. With the modeling clay that Andrea delivered, I let my fingers guide me to form a pink heart, and a yellow star. It feels fun to play and to create without any agenda.

Qigong class gives structure to my afternoon. Teja compliments us on how well we "dissolve." He mentions that Qigong means "energy work" and that the "Eight Actions of Qi" evolved from T'ai Chi martial arts exercises. I like learning the significance and history of this daily practice that has helped to sustain me throughout the retreat. Even Edgar has improved his physical coordination after weeks of daily classes. With blue ink he has written the word "IMPERMANENCE" in capital letters on his forearm, and he seems pleased by the surprised expressions of those who read his enigmatic message. On my exit from class, I pass the "flower girl" whose yogi job is to keep the meditation hall and bathrooms adorned with lovely fresh blossoms. Her joy in this task is palpable. Outside, Dianita approaches in her golf cart, which bears a sign: "Joy Riding in the Mudita Mobile." Spontaneously I hitch a ride, and we careen downhill, giggling like schoolgirls. So much playfulness is in the air.

After dinner, I join Robert Hall, who is silently admiring seven grazing deer in the dimming sunset. When he turns and smiles at me, I summon courage to ask if he has time to review some of my poems. He nods graciously, and I run inside to fetch my notebook and deliver it to him. What an honor to be taken seriously by an experienced, published poet. During the 6:30 p.m. meditation period, I walk to the platform in the woods to witness the sacred stillness of the last sunlight on the hills. Looking down at the rocky path leading to the platform, I notice that a pale green fuzz covers most of the stones. I like lichen. It seems like a natural protection and softens the hard, grey surface of the rocks. I jump down from my perch and follow a zigzagging trail through the hills towards the dining hall. As I sashay back and forth, I trust that what appears to be heading away from my destination will eventually lead me to my goal. This circuitous path reminds me of the indirect route I have taken towards spiritual awakening. My timing is perfect, and I return to the meditation hall just in time to hear Robert's dharma talk on the subject of happiness.

Robert starts off by citing the Dalai Lama: "The purpose of life is to be happy" and goes on to say that we find meaning in our lives through learning what makes us happy. Since this theme is dear to my heart, I take notes throughout Robert's discourse: Buddhist practice works towards the "inevitability of happiness"—the alleviation of suffering. We recognize that we have returned to our natural state by the absence of all desire and fear. Whereas self-concern is a symptom of our delusion, ultimate happiness is freedom from "selfing."

Robert lists a number of ways that human beings seek happiness. Some experiences of happiness depend upon receiving sensory stimulation from the outside world. They are fleeting, and we tend to cling to them. For instance, if we overeat, we regret it afterwards. It may feel pleasant to long for connection and relationship, but clinging to pleasant sensations and feelings leads to disappointment. Other kinds of happiness come from intellectual discoveries, clear thinking, and creative planning. We often lose touch with the body when we focus on ideas and imaginative thoughts, which are as impermanent as sensory pleasures. Another kind of pleasure stems from moral restraint—following the Buddha's Noble Eightfold Path by using "right speech" and "right action." This kind of happiness is more durable, as is generous giving. One of the three pillars of the dharma is generosity, and not only towards others. When we let go of desires, compulsions and plans, we show generosity towards ourselves. Pleasure is associated with falling in love, which can be a delusion and a sickness of the mind. Falling in love is usually not a solid basis for a lasting marriage, and romantic love is characterized by a possessive and sticky, clinging tendency that leads to disillusion. More lasting and satisfying pleasure is derived from intimate relationships that have a spiritual foundation and a mutual commitment to support one another's path. Although spontaneous and intellectually stimulating friendship makes us happy, the kind of happiness that arises from within each individual brings deeper contentment and peace.

All of us seek happiness, and our search can lead to an analysis of the impediments that obstruct our quest. Robert cautions that psychotherapy that consists of analyzing unhappiness can be an exercise in futility. He recommends instead the deep happiness that results from concentration (absorption) practice. When we attend to the breath in Vipassana or withdraw attention from the senses in Metta practice, we can experience joy and freedom from thoughts and obsessions. These rewards require effort, discipline, time, and commitment. "Vipassana happiness" comes from a pristine mind that sees reality clearly, a luminous mind that perceives the true nature of things.

In order to reach freedom and real happiness, we need what the Buddha called the Seven Factors of Enlightenment: "mindfulness" of the four foundations (body, feelings, mind and objects of the mind), "investigation" (wise curiosity about the life journey), "effort" (which helps to start and stay with the journey), "rapture" (which transforms vital energy into expansiveness), "tranquility" (which provides calm in the midst of rapture), "concentration" (which adds a spiritual warrior quality), and "equanimity" (which allows for balance and imperturbability). Here Robert tells a story about a fierce samauri who interrupts a meditating abbot with the challenge: "Do you know who I am? I could cut through you with my sword." The abbot replies calmly, "Do you know who I am? Your sword would pass right through me."

Robert concludes that the most profound happiness comes from opening our hearts to the truth of suffering. I jot down a line from a Sufi poem that he reads: "We break open to the place inside, which is unbreakable, while learning to sing." The dharma talk ends with a recitation of one of Robert's own poems, titled "Happiness is Free:"

> We never know when happiness will strike.
> Just like the way the heart beats and
> The lungs fill with food for life,
> Those bubbles of champagne delight
> Appear out of nowhere and
> Ripple up our grateful vertebrae
> As though they have always been there
> And those long dreary dreamlike days of
> Grey sadness never happened.

The wait is worth it.
But wouldn't it be nice if the interval
between despair and being awake
could shrink like time does when happiness
makes all the clocks useless
(Hall, 2000, p. 115). ✤

CHAPTER EIGHT

PEAK EXPERIENCE

On Monday, March 24, my clock reads 1:50 a.m. when I awaken with an insight about my own insubstantial nature. Outside my window the stars are breathtakingly beautiful and so serene that it is hard to believe that a war is going on in Iraq right now. All thoughts of the external world disappear as I sense a spaciousness opening up among the cells of my body. My breathing relaxes, and my physical being lets go of its solidity. As in "dissolving practice," I move from the quality of ice, to water, and then to steam. All solidity disperses and opens into universal emptiness. There is no fear or resistance. As the transition flows naturally, I feel a bit dizzy and light-headed, as if I am levitating. I surrender to the expansiveness around what I usually perceive as a solid sense of self on a physical plane. With temporary liberation from attachment to my corporal form, I sense how illusory are our perceptions of solidity.

On a flyer that Teja gave us in Qigong class is a quotation by Albert Einstein: "A human being is a part of the whole called by us 'Universe,' a part limited in time and space." What I am experiencing right now is a sensation of merging with the whole of existence. Although I can sense my fingers touching the pen and paper, the writing is occurring on its own. I am not doing anything. Writing is happening in spaciousness, and my mind is witnessing the phenomenon without attachment to "me" or "mine." I feel "light-bodied," like the true "light beings" we all are fundamentally. My mouth is "being smiled," and a cloud-like state of happiness and peace is billowing through the spacious openness. It is not "my" happiness, but rather a quality of energy that feels easy and liberating. As Teja says, "no stress, no strain." In this very moment I am "getting out of my own way."

Teja's dissolving practice and daily sessions of Qigong have prepared me to surrender to unfamiliar experiences. When he guided us to "dissolve" yesterday, I was in such an innocent, childlike, open state that there was no resistance to the melting process and no tangible sense of "me" to transcend—only the experience of surrendering to unity with everything. Now I perceive thoughts bubbling up about the insubstantial nature of individual existence. These memories and thoughts do not "belong" to me. They merely enter the stream of consciousness that I am attending to in this instant, and then they pass away. As a detached witness, I am aware that the wrist of the hand that is writing has painful sensations from continually recording experiences that come and go in the flow of this extraordinary retreat. The sensation of pain is not "mine," and it does not prevent the present writing from unfolding, because the intention to write is stronger than the desire to protect the "small self" or the physically solid sense of self. It seems important for my soul's evolution to be recording this expansion into nothingness while it unfolds, without getting in the way of it.

As Robert said last evening in his dharma talk, "You will know that you have returned to your natural state by the absence of all desire and fear." The thought arises, "I must find out if he was quoting someone and, if so, who." I note, "clinging, clinging." It does not really matter who was the author of that specific statement or that particular perception about the truth of reality. Each seemingly separate embodied form in the vast sea of consciousness has its own slice of the collective pool of wisdom available to all humanity. My present experience of tuning in to the universal truth underlying relative truth is as valid as any other such perception. The cloudiness that normally obscures the mind is dispersing. The clouds are parting to reveal the sun of consciousness, luminous and eternal. I am floating in that ocean of bliss.

The thought arises, "Is this an enlightenment experience?" Part of my small self is trying to make sense out of what is happening, making an effort to bridge universal and relative truths. I feel great affection for the small self I have been given, the incarnated form I am inhabiting on this earthly plane. I love the "Ginger" that contains part of universal consciousness, who embodies compassionate, honest, playful, intelligent, spiritually wise qualities. I feel no attachment to "Ginger" right now. I appreciate her essence, her particular vibration and energy field. She has worked long and hard, in a warrior woman's way, on a Heroine's Journey, to arrive at this moment of truth and to perceive clearly her inseparable connection with the totality of the universe.

During this retreat, I have been aware of moments of dizziness, as if I have been swaying at the edge of a void. In some of the Qigong classes, I have felt on the verge of fainting, surrendering individual consciousness to the spacious energy field around me. When Julie asked if I have low blood pressure," I knew that my light-headed sensations were not due to physical causes, but rather to expanding consciousness. I am awakening to a more expanded sense of how human existence fits into the universal energy field. All of my work on the physical plane with yoga, T'ai Chi, Feldenkrais, Alexander, Rolfing, Reiki, Authentic Movement, playing piano, dancing, and toning, and on the subtle energy plane with sound healing, chakra balancing, aura clearing, and Qigong practice—all these intentional disciplines have led my incarnated soul to this moment of realization of my place in the universe. I sense the underlying truth of existence and the pulsation of life connecting me to all life.

As my hand continues writing, tiredness permeates my being. The thought "it is done" comes to mind. Essential insights have been experienced fully, absorbed and recorded as best as they can be for now. There is nothing more to do. I can trust that I will not forget the essential unity of all creation. Now I can return to my little bed in the safe container of Spirit Rock. Dizzy sensations feel stronger. After so much expansion, it feels disorienting to contract into the small container of the physical body. A slight regret and sadness accompanies the integration process. The physical plane seems tighter and more constricted. And yet it is karmic unfolding that has led me to incarnate in this particular embodied form at this moment in time and space.

On this retreat, I have tasted the pleasures of being fully aware and connected to sensory experiences through each of the sense doors. Intensive meditation has heightened my sensitivity, so that my energetic field is vibrating at a high rate. While sensing my place in the collective human energy field created by so many meditators, I perceive my oneness with deer, turkeys, birds, trees, flowers, rocks, clouds, slugs, and ants. I am in touch with my infinitely loving heart and my life purpose to follow a Bodhisattva path. So it is well worthwhile to return to this embodied form. There is more dizziness now, and more acceptance of the inevitable return. Everything is impermanent. It is not possible to cling to a state of expanded awareness. My body needs to rest.

Now I sense my breath moving inward, "receiving," and outward, "releasing." The breath holds onto nothing. As my feet touch the sheets, I feel the firmness of the mattress once again. An urge to pee arises. Can I walk steadily? I will try. I am still dizzy and a bit scared of moving from the security of writing here in bed, where I have felt safe enough to let go of boundaries. I can do it. This retreat has been helping me to wean myself from writing. Deeper than an attachment to writing is my longing for truth and healing and liberation. So be it.

I feel humbled by this experience, in awe of the perennial truths I have glimpsed. A deep peace and contentment has permeated my being. Now I can truly rest in the universal energy field, trusting my place in the divine plan. How beautiful and exquisite—how perfect—is every aspect of life. I bow to the mystery of the universe. I feel honored to be here now. This entire unfolding has transpired between 1:50 and 3:30 a.m., but as Robert said in his closing poem last evening, "Happiness makes all the clocks useless." Donning my clothes, I carry my journal to the Manager's office to make copies of the latest entry for Jack and Julie and Teja. Above the photocopy machine is a sign that reads, "Feel yourself being quietly drawn by the deeper pull of what you truly love." I am in love with the dharma.

Walking back to Karuna dormitory under a starry, starry night, I appreciate the orange glow of a half moon. I feel energized and ready to do Metta practice. Yesterday I bought an indigo blue pashmina shawl at the Spirit Rock bookstore, and it feels like the perfect color to wear today. My sixth chakra feels wide open after receiving so much information through my third eye, which is traditionally associated with the color of indigo blue.

During morning Qigong class, I feel in the flow, and it feels good to do mindful, grounding yoga instead of attending the 6:00 sit. On the way to breakfast, I am touched by the beauty of the mist steaming above the tall grass and the golden aura of the early morning sun, ascending from behind the hills. With awareness of caring for my inner child and my bodily vessel, I savor the taste of delicious pancakes made of kamut. Today's prayer wheel spin brings "wise intention." I resolve to be as skillful as possible in choosing with whom and how to speak about my expansive experiences. At this moment, I barely resist an impulse to yell joyously "I am free! I have seen the light."

Angie and I bid each other a fond farewell. While I help clean her room and carry her sheets to the laundry, she reads my journal account. She and I agree that it is through facing and healing our early wounding that we integrate cut-off, blocked parts of ourselves. I will miss my dear next-door neighbor.

Instead of attending the 8:30 a.m. sit, I go on a strenuous hike to burn off some of my abundant energy. The idea of sitting in the meditation hall makes me feel anxious again. As I climb upward, I notice an intricate spider's web, dew-drenched and glistening in the sunshine. It is carefully constructed right next to the Spirit Rock sign that announces "Retreat Area, Quiet Please." The weaver of this web seems to be drawing attention to the importance of respecting the retreat's Noble Silence. I am reminded of "Charlotte's Web," the story about a clever spider spinning letters and messages to save her friend Wilber the pig. When I pause atop the octagonal deck, Margot passes by on her way down from the hills. In celebration of her being, I ring the little meditation bell that sits on the balustrade. In response, she laughs with delight and performs a little dance before departing.

Continuing my ascent, I meet Mark, the dharma teacher-in-training, on his way to the meditation hall. He grins with an approving nod for my "cutting class" and following his advice to expend excess energy. As soon as he is out of sight, I start to tone "Om" on a low pitch. The sound vibrates through my chest and torso, helping to ground me. On impulse, I look back over my shoulder at the vast expanse of hills and the spotless blue sky. Involuntarily, I exclaim "Wow!" Such natural beauty takes the breath away. As I enter the "skin tree" woods, a state of awe encompasses me. Every dewy blade of grass seems sacred. In their capes of moss and lichen, all the trees appear to bow with me to the mystery of life. Patches of purple iris are celebrating too. Each step I take feels charmed. Spontaneously, I burst into singing "Amazing Grace," and the birds around me add refrains of praise. I shake hands with the longest limb of the grandest tree. Everything I see or hear or touch seems as blessed as I am. Even poison oak has its place—at a distance. Simultaneously, I feel small and insignificant and yet empowered and full of divine energy. Overcome with rapture, I sense my feet firmly on the earth. Life is precious in all of its manifestations.

As we have planned in an exchange of notes, Teja and I meet at 9:30 a.m. for a walk to the platform in the woods. There I express gratitude for the grounding that he has provided during my periods of fear, regression and expansion on this retreat. He says that he has enjoyed teaching me Qigong, because I am like a sponge, soaking up whatever practices he offers. We have been in the flow together. He is impressed by how wide-open and full of rapture I am in the aftermath of so many insights. After affirming our mutual appreciation, we return separately to the main hall.

During the hour-long wait for my interview with Julie, I feel too restless to be still. I walk to the Spirit Rock gift store, and return laden down with Buddhist paraphernalia — an ironic burst of consumption for a practitioner of nonattachment. It seems important to have small wooden statues of the Buddha and of Kwan Yin to accompany me home. When a retreat manager passes by on a golf cart, I hitch a ride with my loot, door-to-door to Karuna dormitory. On our ride uphill, I confide, "I am bringing the Buddha back to Mexico with me." It does not surprise me to hear that he used to live in Oaxaca and wants to retire in Mexico. We exchange farewells in Spanish.

Julie is delayed, and I shed shoes and socks to pace barefoot back and forth on the hot asphalt in front of the Council House. It feels like an effort to stay grounded. Just as Julie signals me that she is ready, Mark arrives and receives my permission to observe the interview. After reading them the account of my "awakening," I cry from relief at being able to share the experience after such a long morning. Both listeners are visibly moved, and Julie affirms that I am staying in touch with my feelings and caring for myself through whatever unfolds. But she expresses concern about my sleep deprivation and my breaking retreat rules about teacher-student relationships to meet privately with Teja. When I explain that he has helped me ground expansive energy, she relaxes.

Then Julie gives me a "prescription" to take a post-lunch nap and counsels me to "put breathing on your 'to-do' list." It is clear that I must focus on taking good care of my body. Before the interview's end, I read aloud my poem "Skater's Waltz," which I have copied onto a greeting card to give to her. She is close to tears as I finish. I mention that my Mexican address is written on the back of the card, in case she wants to send me any dharma prescriptions. Julie grins in assent. I hug her and Mark goodbye and say, "It's been good to have another Mark nearby." As I leave, I wonder if they think that I am in a crisis state. Because of my past history with hypo-manic episodes, I must prove to myself and to my teachers that I am capable of bringing myself down to earth after a peak experience.

At least the teachers know that I have been in a regressed state and are looking out for my wellbeing. During Jack's absence, I have been reaching out to substitute father figures—John for an extra interview, Mark for a crisis consultation, and Robert for a poetry review. Now that Jack is back "on campus," I feel more relaxed.

At lunch, I feel very vulnerable. I carry my meal outside to the back steps of the dining hall, where I sit near Dianita, whose presence transmits comfort. Before eating in slow motion, I shed my shoes and socks to sense my feet touching the sun-baked wooden step. When I finish the meal, I set down my plate and close my eyes to bask in the sun. It feels like too great an effort to wait in line to wash my dishes. To my surprise, I hear a scraping sound and open my eyes to catch Margot adding my plate to hers. Did she read my mind and come to the rescue? As she pantomimes dish washing, I nod gratefully and escape the public eye to take a hot bath. How delicious to be able to crawl into bed for an afternoon siesta. Once I wake up, I find it calming to write and catch up on recent experiences. So much emotion has been rising and passing away.

Before dinnertime, I decide to take a brisk walk and expend excess energy so that I will be able to sleep tonight. Even though the weather is mild outside, I pile on layers of clothing to combat the deep chill that permeates my body. It is obvious how much weight I have lost during the past few weeks. My pants nearly slide down over my hipbones. Intuitively I replace the bright, indigo-colored shawl with my old, soothing, baby blue one. Fear surges through me sporadically. Will I be able to slow down and land on the earth by the retreat's end? Do I have the strength to emerge into a world at war? Repeatedly I pull myself back to caring for myself in this very moment. Everything else is beyond my control. I must remember to keep drinking water and to follow Julie's prescription: "breathe."

Suddenly I recall that today is Monday—the day of the week that we dine early, at 5:00. It is two hours later back home in Cholula, Mexico, where my friend John should be leading the University sangha in my stead. What gratitude I feel towards him for serving as my substitute while I am on retreat. In my vulnerable state, I cannot imagine leading anything or anyone. While visualizing the members of the UDLA sangha, I send them all Metta. Then I think of my husband preparing to fly to Guadalajara tomorrow morning for another Holotropic Breathwork training week with Stan Grof. I trust that Mark will phone me at the end of the week on my birthday. That thought gives me solace. Gradually more and more thoughts are surfacing about home and the world outside of the retreat.

Before heading for the dining hall, I check the teachers' bulletin board and find a message from Jack: "Dear Ginger, I loved reading about how you tracked your opening last night. Be careful not to call it 'an enlightenment experience,' which solidifies it and you with it. Let all things come and go, and be grounded. Otherwise the energy can verge on becoming too 'high.' I know you realize the importance of stillness and calm as well. Metta, Jack." As I pocket the note, I sense Jack's words steadying me and giving me courage. This process of coming down from an expanded state is difficult. It hurts and feels tight and constricting. Munching crumbly rice crackers slathered with sticky peanut butter gives me a welcome change of focus. I have enough playful energy to confiscate Margot's empty plates and take my turn as dishwasher for both of our dishes. She bows in thanks.

Anna is giving tonight's dharma talk on the theme of "Seasons of the Heart." A vase of lovely, fresh, purple irises and yellow roses sits on the altar near her seat. She begins by commenting that whereas here at Spirit Rock spring has sprung and the red clover is starting to bloom, in South Africa summer is turning to autumn. Around the globe, people are cycling through different seasons simultaneously. Anna makes the analogy that on retreat each person experiences the same gamut of emotions again and again. But while I may be sobbing in a "wet season," the yogi next to me may be entering an arid period of boredom. At varying times, each of us repeats emotional cycles that are as "impersonal" and beyond our control as the seasons of the year.

Years ago, when Anna undertook an eleven-month retreat at the Insight Meditation Society, she passed through four seasons of emotions. Autumn was a time of loss, letting go, impermanence, stripping away illusions, and facing the truth of suffering; winter represented a period of hibernation, withdrawal, and plunging into unknown territory. In wintertime she felt stuck, hit impasses, and had doubts because it appeared that nothing was happening, yet this dark season was when "the seeds of spring lay dormant." For her, spring held the promise of new beginnings and directions, inspiration, creativity, and renewed faith and devotion. Springtime was associated with falling in love, sensing a connection with all life, and affirming a belief in the self. Finally, summer was filled with abundance, generosity, service, and manifesting ideas in the world. It was in summertime that Anna saw the fruition of her practice and discovered that "giving and receiving are the same." (At this moment I seem to be blossoming in springtime.) As if reading my mind, Anna cautions, "You don't get spring without autumn. By letting go of illusion, we learn to forgive and to live with greater kindness to ourselves and others." All of us must pass through periods of renunciation. She quotes Suzuki Roshi: "Renunciation does not consist in giving up the things of this world, but in accepting that they go away."

No matter what emotional season has arrived, we can notice that many of our self-definitions are based on fleeting states. The Buddha referred to mindfulness as "wise attention" and taught that unwise attention creates a fixed sense of self. As Anna points out, "None of these inner seasons are 'me' or 'mine.' Seasons move through time, and we learn to respect the timing of our own unfolding instead of forcing progress." She continues, "Nobody is always angry or never angry. Notice when you are angry and when you are not." During Vipassana practice we can stop at any moment and discover that it is possible to face the truth of each emotion directly, without shame or blame. All emotional states are impermanent and pass away like clouds, but we tend to resist difficult feelings and to be uncomfortable sitting with them. While the Buddha was a model of patient endurance and clear intention or resoluteness, Anna notes, "We live in an impatient world. Effort is the perseverance to wait and be still." (Her words relate to my struggle to stop so much inner and outer activity.) The dharma talk concludes with the idea that we can practice being open to all of the interdependent seasons.

Exhaustion hits me as I leave the meditation hall. My eyelids feel too heavy to open. How thankful I am that there is very little kale to rinse during my yogi job, so that the veggie-washing team finishes earlier than usual. Fully sensing the weight of my body, I drag myself uphill to bed.

March 25 dawns before I awake. At last I am beginning to catch up on sleep. While dressing, I reflect upon the uniqueness of each person's "flavor," rhythm, or style. Particular friends or loved ones come to mind through auditory, visual, and even kinesthetic channels. Sometimes I recall the peculiar resonance of their voices; other times I envision them in their distinctive, favorite clothing; and still other times I sense the contact of them hugging or touching me. I imagine my parents in their youth, visualizing my father as a young soldier or my mother as a beautiful girl with long, jet-black hair and green eyes.

Here on retreat I have names for each person with whom I feel strongly connected in the silence. Because she is the most elegantly attired yogi, in her silken, Japanese-styled outfits and exquisitely hand-woven sweaters, Gina is "Fashion Queen." In my mind's eye, I image her lolling on benches, basking in the sunshine, and lounging around sipping tea long after other yogis have left the dining hall. Dianita is "Forever-Young," with her habit of plaiting her straight, blond hair in two pigtails, one tied with a bright pink ribbon and the other with a royal blue one. Margot has the nickname "Play Pal" because she has been my kindred spirit in moments of childlike delight and nonverbal glee. Edgar's dark, intelligent eyes signal that there is more to him than his awkward, autistic body indicates. For that reason I have dubbed him "Secret Sage." Inwardly I hear the sigh of pleasure that he expresses each time he prepares to eat from his heavily laden tray of food. "Theresa-of the-Thousand-Shoes," who lives across the hall from me, has a dreamy smile that touches my heart. Ida, with her zany sense of humor and her wardrobe of orange-hued shirts and pants, has earned the sobriquet "Star Veggie Washer." I feel great affection for each of the sangha members, most of whose names I do not know. From the upper walking hall, where I have been doing yoga, I watch the stream of meditators leaving the building to descend the hill for breakfast, and I send Metta to each precious person.

I wonder if any of the yogis has a nickname for me. Have they noticed my propensity for wearing intense turquoise colors under my fiery red cape? Do my fellow meditators know that I am addicted to using lip balm and eye drops, that I like the sensation of combing my hair, washing laundry by hand, and massaging my hands with lotion? I now consciously enjoy these previously unconscious habits and recognize them as comforting behaviors. I can admit my eccentricities, without worrying about how others might view them. It is refreshing to observe myself affectionately, without self-judgment or criticism.

My butterfly self is coming down for a landing. Now I can sense the soles of my feet open and firmly planted on the ground. What a relief it is to surrender to the reality of returning to earth instead of resisting the landing process. Somehow my psyche knows that it is time to complete this stage of the journey. I am weaning myself from using corrector fluid when I write. Witnessing the Freudian slips that reveal themselves in my unconscious "mistakes" is amusing. My attachment to perfection is loosening. Can I flow with the inevitable changes that are associated with ending this retreat?

Today the regular schedule posted on the bulletin board has been revised: this afternoon we will begin "talking practice" to prepare us gradually for re-entering the world outside Spirit Rock. Suddenly I feel sad at the thought of speaking with the yogis around me, and it is obvious by the upset facial expressions of other yogis gathered around the bulletin board that my sentiments are shared. I want to treasure the last precious moments of silent communication with my fellow travelers on our extraordinary spiritual voyage. We seem like soul mates at a heartwarming reunion, and we are reluctant to return to our separate states and nations. Years ago my nonverbal student Jarrod typed, "I am here to teach people to love beyond appearances." Now I know in my "hollow bones" that, no matter where they live or how they look or what capacities they have, all people are connected through their divine essence. It gives me joy to watch each yogi's unique and quirky manner of self-expression. Everyone represents a glint on the infinitely faceted diamond of existence.

What a miracle love is. My soul is being nourished by receiving and expressing love without any need to talk. This retreat has been a mystery school that is teaching us to act more lovingly towards all manifestations of life. I feel indelibly imprinted with Spirit Rock. How can I part from this healing place? Right now I am rubbing with my left thumb the smooth surface of a solid, heavy chunk of greenish rock that attracted me enough to pocket it. Every stone has its unique quality of energy. As I am becoming attuned to "rock language," the challenge of practicing right intention, right effort, and right speech with a human partner seems daunting. I want to remember not to overdo speaking. As Teja says, "use the seventy percent principle when expending energy, so that you can be fully present for what is happening." I am glad that he and I have already practiced breaking silence in a skillful way, and that afterwards I have had a restorative respite from talking.

Right after breakfast, I spin the prayer wheel, which stops precisely between two inscriptions: "wise speech" and "wise intention." How perfect for today. Then I set off for a walk in the hills. Spectacular filigree clouds branch like Indra's net across the azure morning sky. Ahead of me I see a yogi transfixed by the sight of three deer walking right in front of her. When I enter the forest of Manzanita trees, I touch the smooth trunk of every tree I pass. Three peacefully feeding turkeys ignore me and, for once, maintain silence. As I "shake hands" with the long, loose bough of my favorite, wide-spreading tree, I notice delicate, silvery threads, spun by a resident spider, sparkling in the sunlight. This is another blessed day.

Despite my fear of sitting in the meditation hall after two days of "expanded abstinence," I enter the big room with a clear intention to do Metta practice during the 8:30 a.m. sit. Thinking of the Buddha consciously repelling Mara's forces of greed, hatred, and delusion, I maintain my dignified posture even though waves of anxiety surge through me. It helps me to sense the nonverbal support of Mark on my left, Teja directly across the hall, and Jack and Julie, who are sitting in their usual spots among the other teachers. Anna rings the bell just as I finish sending Metta to my loved ones and to "all beings everywhere."

Mark announces that today is his final day on this retreat. He thanks us yogis who permitted him to witness interviews when we felt extremely vulnerable, and he assures us that sharing our experiences will empower him to teach the dharma more wisely. Before Mark departs, I plan to give him a copy of Thich Nhat Hanh's little book *Be Free Where You Are* as a thank-you gift. I have inscribed the title page: "Dear Mark, Muchas gracias for your kind and supportive presence at my left elbow in the meditation hall. Your gentle advice has helped me to ground my expansive energy, reminding me of my husband Mark's soothing influence on my soul. With Metta, Ginger." May my small token of appreciation please this sensitive student teacher.

Anna asks if there are any questions from yogis who have not yet spoken in the hall. One man responds that his mind has been full of obsessive thoughts about his need to speak publicly on this twenty-fifth day of the retreat. He admits that he has counted forty-one times of noting "thinking, thinking," and thirty-one times of rehearsing the question he wants to ask. Before addressing the content of his query, Anna reassures him, "We can all relate to your crazy thinking." I find it reassuring to know that I am not the only one with a head full of too many thoughts. Before adjourning the session, Anna reminds us that at 2:15 p.m. we will make the transition to practicing wise speaking and listening.

On my way outside, I visit the Metta community altar at the back of the hall and feel moved by the sweetness of the notes and prayers left for beloved family members, friends, and pets. Because I have just been using Metta to quell fears, I am well aware of the power of this practice of loving kindness. One quotation on the altar reads, "People have many views of the moon, but, from the moon's perspective, it is always full." Right now my heart is full to the brim with gratitude.

To my surprise, I learn that Julie has scheduled an extra interview for me this morning. She is happy to hear that I am coming back to earth, and she gives me feedback about the written account of my spiritual opening. Her opinion is that the most important aspect of that experience is my newfound capacity to stay with the process of expansion and contraction, without fearful dissociation. When I ask about the possibility of her mentoring me to become a dharma teacher, Julie replies that she is not mentoring any yogis now because her focus is on raising her daughter. Instead, she suggests that I apply for the next Dedicated Practitioner Program (DPP) offered by Spirit Rock teachers. All of a sudden I am painfully aware that Julie has seen me at my most regressed moments on this retreat, and that she has not witnessed the mature, competent side of me. I remind her that I let my ego dissolve because I wanted to understand the most wounded and vulnerable parts of myself. Julie and I agree that my heightened self-awareness will benefit not only my own life but also the lives of everyone in my family, as well as my psychotherapy practice. I solemnly dedicate the merit of my conscious inner work on this retreat to the wellbeing of my godchild Ashley and my six nieces and nephews. The interview ends with this positive intention.

Although I missed the first guided session of equanimity practice yesterday, I opt to join other yogis in the meditation hall and to listen to Anna's instructions. It is clear that I need to re-establish an inner balance. She recites, "All beings are the heirs of their karma. Their happiness and unhappiness depend on their actions, not on my wishes for them. May I accept things as they are. I wish you happiness but cannot keep you from suffering." This prayer of equanimity helps me contemplate the horror of the war in Iraq without overwhelming grief for the countless people who are wounded and dying there. I have trouble accepting that in the United States, where I was born and raised, our leaders continue to initiate violence in distant lands. The decision to bomb Iraq seems like sowing the seeds of bad karma. In a more personal context, equanimity practice is useful when I question why some of my friends are suffering from serious illnesses like multiple sclerosis and cancer, and why others are burdened by depression. On a societal level, if I reflect upon how many millions of people do not have adequate food or shelter or health care, I can feel guilty about my own good fortune. By developing equanimity, I can find more productive ways than self-recrimination to address problems that affect my friends and society at large. It is reassuring to feel the support of the Spirit Rock sangha and to recall my membership in organizations like the Buddhist Peace Fellowship. When I remember my connection to the web of life, I know that I am not alone in bearing the world's pain.

During the last lunch before we break silence, I treasure the stillness in the dining hall. But there is a nervous energy in the air, as if the entire sangha is gearing up for a different way of interacting. It feels good to take my meal outside, where I sit on a large, level rock and eat in solitude. I concentrate on nourishing myself and on calming myself down. After washing my dishes, I take a siesta to conserve my energy for speaking this afternoon.✤

CHAPTER NINE
BREAKING SILENCE

A t precisely 2:15 p.m., Eugene addresses all of
us yogis in the meditation hall: "This is our
opportunity for mindful speech and sangha practice. Notice your mixture of fear and excitement about
starting to speak. The retreat is continuing, but the form
is expanding to include the person on the next cushion.
Stay in your body and trust it as you speak. Attention to
the body is more important than what you say. Speech
can come from the heart instead of the head. There is
no need to perform for your partner."

When Eugene instructs us to pick partners, I turn towards the row behind me and reach out to take Theresa's hand. Her sweet smile sets me at ease. Our assignment is to take turns talking about our retreat experience for two minutes apiece. My partner tells me that she has been here for six weeks and that she has been drawn to my smile. She does not seem ready to say anything more. As we look at each other in silence, I relax with the thought that we must be "smile sisters." When it is my turn, I convey how much I have enjoyed living across the hall from her and her great collection of shoes and boots. My comment makes her smile again. Even though we have exchanged very few words, we sense a heart-to-heart connection.

My next speaking partner is the man who has been on the cushion to my right. His name turns out to be "Mark," so I have been sitting in between two Marks during this retreat. This particular Mark has been here for two months, watching the gradual transition from winter to spring. Today he is excited about an iris that has just bloomed in front of the dining hall. Because I, too, was touched by witnessing the unfolding of that beautiful plant, I nod in understanding. After he tells me that he entered the retreat on the day after his fiftieth birthday, Mark is amused to hear that I will be leaving the retreat on my fifty-fifth birthday. Before ending our brief conversation, we wish each other a "happy birthday."

As we all regroup and sit facing the teachers again, Jack reminds us, "The personality is not yours. It's karmically impersonal—what you have been dealt. Be gentle to yourself as the personality kicks in again during verbal interaction. We have been blessedly free of our personalities in the silence." His words resonate with what we have just been experiencing as we practiced speaking in dyads. I had just been wondering if my partners considered my verbal expressions superficial.

Jack switches to a serious mode and begins to speak about war. He reminisces about his Peace Corps experiences in 1968 inside Cambodian refugee camps. At one point, some visiting Quakers criticized Jack for sitting on his cushion at Ajahn Chah's monastery, while they were working hard for peace in a warring country. But he viewed the monastery as a sanctuary during the Vietnam war. Within the monastery walls, his lost watch was honorably returned, whereas outside the gates, people were stealing and pillaging. Jack quotes Ajahn Chah: "Wars come and go. We need to create places of compassion and honesty in times of war."

Then Jack gives the sangha what he calls the "Reader's Digest" version of world news. He tells us that the United States has been at war in Iraq for five days. As yogis around me gasp in shock and start sobbing, I relive my own horrified reaction to intuiting days ago that the bombing had begun. Jack continues to report the awful facts:

> *On Monday, March 17, George Bush gave Saddam Hussein forty-eight hours to leave Iraq or the bombing would start. Now two hundred and fifty thousand American and British soldiers are headed towards Baghdad, where government buildings have been bombed. About fifty invading soldiers have been killed or captured, and about four hundred Iraqi soldiers have died. So far there has been a low number of civilian casualties—one hundred and fifty—because the whole world is watching what is happening. The Iraqi army is resisting more than was expected. It is hard to tell who the Iraqis hate more, Saddam or George Bush. Greed, hatred, and delusion are very deep, and they cause deep suffering. Anti-war demonstrations are occurring worldwide. Eleven million people protested around the globe in February, and two million British citizens protested Tony Blair's support of Bush's war plans. Last Sunday, 250,000 protesters marched from Times Square to Washington Square in New York City. The United States and Britain could not convince other countries on the United Nations Security Council to join them in going to war. Turkey refused a bribe of thirty million dollars and would not allow U.S. forces on its soil.*

At this point, many yogis are crying and looking nauseous. Jack tells us that he has been attending war protests in San Francisco, a center for the peace movement in the United States. He says that he feels relieved to return to this retreat, where yogis are facing the forces of fear, hatred, and delusion. Jack quotes from the "Dhammapada," an anthology of verses attributed to the Buddha: "It is an ancient and eternal law that hatred never ceases by hatred." Then he asks us to count off by sixes, dividing the yogis into six groups, each to be guided by one of the teachers.

I feel fortunate to end up in group number three, led by Jack himself in the lower walking room. A dozen of us huddle in a tearful circle on the floor. He gives each of us a chance to speak about our feelings and to ask questions about the war. My fellow yogis are amazed that I knew when the bombing started. I feel especially connected to Dori, who says, "The world needs the beauty of Spirit Rock to balance the ugliness of war," and to Gina, who is worried about her husband, alone in a cabin right now. I tell her how much it helped me to phone Mark, and she resolves to call her husband's mobile phone today. Gina tells me that she has enjoyed serving as my substitute as bell-ringer. I thank her and propose that, tomorrow at the appointed hour, both of us ring the gong together in honor of world peace. After an hour of giving one another comfort, Jack invites us to exchange hugs and to congregate with the other small groups in the meditation hall. There Teja leads the entire community of teachers and yogis in grounding, heart-centered Qigong exercises. Then we all sit still with eyes closed, listening to the sound of people crying around the room. The sangha feels like a spacious, compassionate container for each individual's grieving. We go back into Noble Silence for the rest of the evening.

At dinner, Teja announces that he and Robert Hall will be leading a "listening meditation" this evening in the Community Center hall, for anyone who would like to attend. Margot and I are among the first to arrive, and we sit on the floor in the front row, closest to the teachers. After a group of about thirty yogis has assembled, Robert shows us a copy of a C.D. called "Mysteries," which he recorded in Teja's music studio. On the recording, Robert reads some of his own poetry, while Teja improvises on guitar and synthesizer, matching each verse with appropriate rhythms, melodies, and harmonies. Robert suggests that we lie down in a relaxed posture with closed eyes and "listen in the middle of the words and the music, not trying to catch the sense of every phrase." The poems are devotional tributes to God, creation, and the dharma.

Before the first selection has finished, I am dissolved in tears. Teja's music is exquisite and seems divinely inspired. During playful verses accompanied by Blues-style riffs, I laugh and hold hands with Margot, while during solemn sections, I cry and sense my heart wide open and tender. As a musician and music therapist, I have a refined musical ear in ordinary circumstances, but this listening experience seems extraordinarily powerful in the aftermath of a month of so much silence. My neurological system feels highly sensitive to any stimuli. At the end of this creative contemplation, I hug Teja in gratitude and then join the cue of yogis who are congratulating Robert. Before I have a chance to tell him how deeply his poetry touched me, Robert returns my poetry notebook, saying, "Your poems reflect the beauty in you." He has enclosed an appreciative note about my "poetic prose vignettes." Not trusting myself to speak articulately, I bow to him silently.

When the two teachers leave the hall, I surrender to wrenching sobs. My heart is overwhelmed by Robert's kind words, Teja's musical talent, and the beauty of their co-creation. As Margot hugs me, I joke, " I can't emote any more today." She quips, "Never say never!" I start giggling through my tears, and Gina approaches to give me a sympathetic hug. Without saying a word, she appears to understand my mixed-up emotions. Gina's quiet composure reminds me that we are supposed to be maintaining silence this evening. I stop talking and recognize how grateful I am to be with loving dharma friends, while Iraq is being bombed.

Jack gives tonight's dharma talk on the theme of war. As usual, he sets the stage before addressing the sangha. After spreading books and papers around him, he perches atop two zafus and adjusts his special lamp above the lectern, so that he can read from a distance, without having to wear his spectacles. Before starting his discourse, Jack asks us how we are handling the news of the bombing in Iraq. Several yogis report emotions that range from numbness to sorrow and anger.

Jack comments that when we hear terrible news, the nervous system receives a shock and then adjusts to the circumstances. He wonders if it might be better not to adjust to war and injustice. His daughter Caroline, who has been organizing peace demonstrations at her high school, wept when the war began and felt that her efforts had failed. Jack reminds us that, even in defeat, we must continue trying to do what is right. He tells us about a protest group of twenty-five women who dress in pink and call themselves "Code Pink" or "Code Human." This past week they sang a gospel song for peace and marched in Washington D.C. towards the White House. Security guards prevented them from advancing, but an African American policeman, who was moved by the gospel music, allowed the women to pass to the White House gates. There they protested nonviolently until federal troops arrived and arrested them.

Jack states, "Ordinary people look at results. The wise look at conditions. Greed, hatred, and delusion are conditions for war." He describes the approach of Dr. A. T. Ariyaratne, known as "the Gandhi of Sri Lanka," who has proposed a five-hundred-year peace plan to broker peace in his country's seventeen-year civil war. The rationale is that because it took five hundred years to build the conditions for conflict, it will take the same amount of time to undo them.

War is indeed a "failure of human imagination." Jack tells us about an innovative organization called the Nonviolent Peace Force. In the Hague in 1999, ten thousand people from international peace groups met to create a standing peace army. They have raised funds to send representatives to various hot spots around the world, where they introduce conflict resolution tactics to both sides. Just as daring and imaginative is Maha Ghosananda, the Supreme Cambodian Buddhist Patriarch, who, during the reign of the Khmer Rouge, sang peace songs and led nonviolent marches throughout the countryside, despite facing gunfire from the regime's soldiers. When he built a temple in the center of a refugee camp, twenty-five thousand worshippers came for the inauguration, even though they had been threatened with death if they attended. Together with Ghosananda, they chanted the words: "Hatred never ceases by hatred, but only by love." Somehow, acknowledging this universal truth protected them.

Jack tells the sangha that when the Buddha learned that an army was on its way to invade territory where he was teaching, he sat calmly in the path of the aggressors. Touched by the Buddha's commitment to peaceful resistance, the invading king turned back with his soldiers. Later on, the warrior king changed his mind and invaded anyway. But a Bodhisattva is "committed to compassion and awakening no matter what happens."

On a lighter note, Jack gives us a brief account of the Oscars, which were awarded a few nights ago. I feel encouraged to hear that during the ceremonies, Dustin Hoffman spoke about peace, and Susan Sarandon flashed a peace sign. When he accepted the award for best documentary film director, Michael Moore proclaimed, "Our president won in a fictitious election and started a war for fictitious reasons. Shame on you, George Bush." At least the international community will know that the United States is strongly divided about the war in Iraq.

Jack advises us not to forget "the one who knows." In Carlos Castenada's books, the indigenous sage Don Juan knows that life is short, and he keeps death as an advisor. "The one who knows" sees life pass by with equanimity. An example of such a person is the Colorado woman who created a "salt monument" that contains just the right amount of salt crystals to represent each of the six billion people on the earth. Each day she carefully removes 200,000 crystals to symbolize that day's deaths and adds another 200,000 crystals to represent that day's births. Another "one who knows" is a Chinese prisoner named Wu, who was forced by soldiers in the Cultural Revolution to sit on a stool for ten hours a day without moving a muscle. For eleven years he refused to sign a false confession and sustained himself by visualizing the faces of his loved ones. When he was finally released, Wu stated, "I could not let them down." Jack observes that none of us can resist all by ourselves: "We do not exist alone. We are all in it together."

Jack asks, "If you had only a few days left in your life, who would you call, what would you say, and why do you wait to do so?" He cautions us not to run around trying to fix the world, but instead to listen to our

Bodhisattva nature within: "Remember the innate goodness and spaciousness in your heart." Across the room from where I am sitting, Jack points out a temporary "peace altar," where he invites us to place prayers and objects that symbolize peace. Above this altar, in a solemn ritual, he hangs a large thangka that depicts the Buddha. In closing, Jack leads us in a Metta chant for all beings everywhere.

I leave the meditation hall with a sense of deep appreciation for Jack's uplifting dharma talk, and for the skillful orchestration of periods of discussion and of silent integration. The sangha has been masterfully contained and guided. I value the way the teachers have helped us to process unpleasant world events in our bodies, minds, and hearts. Yet right now, my nervous system feels on sensory overload. There are so many paradoxes to balance in my sensitive state. I will be sad but relieved when the retreat ends. I cannot maintain such intense emotions very long. I long to share with my husband all that has happened here. It feels like a lifetime since I left Mexico on February 28.

On Wednesday, March 26, I wake up at 2:30 a.m. with too many thoughts in my head to sleep. I feel scared by the enormous challenge of entering the chaotic, warring world outside of Spirit Rock in a mere two days. Fortunately, I have arranged to visit friends in nearby Sebastapol, California for the first two days following the retreat, so that I can postpone dealing with Mexico City's crowded airport. Kacey and Andy's home has become my regular "safe house" for emerging from Noble Silence. Both of these friends are meditators who know from their own experience how vulnerable yogis tend to feel during the re-entry process.

Yesterday in Jack's small group discussion about the Iraq war, one woman reminisced about attending a Spirit Rock retreat at the time of the 9/11 terrorist attacks on New York City's World Trade Center. After she left the safe cocoon of the retreat, an armed security guard searched her at the San Francisco airport. He appeared more afraid than she was, because she had the benefit of coming from a sane, serene refuge. Ironically, I feel lucky to be returning to the "relative sanity" of Mexico, a third-world country that is neither rich nor powerful enough to start a war. Jack has informed us that so far no countries other than the United States, Britain and Iraq are actively engaged in this war. But that could change. I am sure that my Jewish friends are worried that Saddam Hussein could send bombs towards Israel in a desperate, parting gesture.

The karmic consequences of initiating this war have yet to unfold. Metta prayers are urgently needed. I believe in the power and positive energy of prayer. How reassuring it is for me to know that millions of people around the globe are praying for peace at this moment. It soothes me to remember the monastic communities around the world, where monks and nuns are practicing Metta. I can visualize His Holiness the Dalai Lama and Thich Nhat Hanh praying for peace. They know first-hand the importance of liberating their own minds before working to liberate the world around them. President Bush must realize that his decisions and actions are being scrutinized by an international collective jury. May the public eye restrain him from reacting from instinctual fear of terrorism or from hatred of Saddam Hussein, who thwarted prior attempts by Bush's father to encourage revolt in Iraq. Right now many people are consciously creating a huge container of awareness to hold this war. Can I trust the durability of this container?

Even if the world as we know it comes to an end, I am determined not to stop working towards my own awakening and that of other sentient beings. The only thing that makes sense now is to love my own incarnated self and the manifested forms of all life. To me, Spirit Rock symbolizes paradise on this earthly plane—a sanctuary for human beings who are sufficiently awake to practice being kind, considerate, thoughtful, gentle, courteous, restrained, responsible, tolerant, and honest, in community with one another. What we are creating together on this retreat is radical and vital—a new consciousness and a paradigm for living in harmony with all creation.

I have been yearning to do something good to counterbalance the hatred in the world. Maybe I could join the International Peace Brigade that sends volunteers to do conflict resolution in countries on the brink of war. Despite my expansive state, I acknowledge that, in addition to fantasizing about traveling the globe on peace missions, I have been imagining Julie mentoring me to teach the dharma in Hispanic communities, Anna incorporating my Guided Imagery and Music techniques into her Creative Vipassana retreats, as well as Teja and me co-leading workshops that combine Qigong, music therapy and Vipassana meditation. My imagination has been running wild, without limits. It is time to ground myself in this very moment.

Last evening, as I listened to Robert and Teja's exquisite C.D., I recognized that I have been following my soul's purpose as a music therapist for thirty-five years. My unique gifts in this lifetime have to do with music, imagery, and subtle energy healing. That is one reason why Teja and I have resonated so strongly in each other's presence. It is not only that we both love the discipline of Qigong practice, but we also share a fascination with divinely inspired music, and with "Spanda," or the vibration of the spheres, the sound of creation that underlies silence and that indicates the sacred motion of life in the universe. Yes, music therapy is my true path. It is my main avenue to the dharma.

Throughout this retreat, I have been grieving about shedding my old identity as a music therapist. I grabbed onto the idea that I should be shifting my focus to teach the dharma, because there is such urgency, in our war-torn world, for awakening. But, as I am writing, with my worn-out hand, I realize that the best way for me to spread the dharma is through following my calling in music and psychotherapy. Offering GIM workshops and trainings in Spanish for Mexicans is my particular way of doing international peace work. I can share common goals and purposes with the International Peace Brigade, while developing and expressing my own unique talents. My heart feels full of happiness, because I already have the training I need to teach what I want to teach. The impulse to improve myself by changing my career has disappeared. I am fine as I am. It is now 4:20 a.m., and this period of reflection is done. Pulling my red woolen cape over my pajamas, I walk to the manager's office to photocopy my latest journal notes and then hike over to the lobby to tack them on the bulletin board for Jack. With this mission accomplished, I rest before the first bell of the day.

As dawn breaks, I hear a songbird producing trills and arpeggios, a riot of joyous sounds, outside my window. Just listening to its high-pitched song energizes me. Spontaneously, I start toning along with the bird. It feels invigorating to produce harmonics with my voice. The little songbird is as much of a sound healer as I am.

Breakfast is a fun, nonverbal dance. By chance, I meet Margot at the toaster, where we exchange glances of mock dismay at burning some toast. Then she shows up in the far corner of the room to prepare her tea at precisely the same time as I do, so we have to slide past one another. I sit beside her at a corner table, and when she leaves to fetch more toast, I carefully arrange three almonds in a cloverleaf design at the center of her empty plate. Upon her return, she reacts to my creation with such a funny expression that we both suppress giggles of amusement. To avoid laughing out loud, I leave to wash my dishes, and then, still grinning at our shared silliness, I hurry out of the dining room.

Today's prayer wheel spin brings me the message "wise effort." As I set off for a walk in the rain-drenched hills, I resolve to do a better job of balancing bursts of activity with rest periods. My body is begging for more sleep. But for now I delight in watching mist streaming off the treetops and the sunshine chasing away lingering clouds. Whenever I pass a yogi on the path, we exchange bows to honor the Buddha nature within each other.

My peripheral vision seems to have a wider range than usual; in the "skin tree" forest, I have a newfound capacity to observe a broad swath of trees, ferns, mosses, and lichens all at once. Suddenly I remember to look at my watch. I have barely enough time to run to the meditation hall for the 8:30 a.m. sit.

Among other stragglers, I slide onto my zafu at the last moment. My face is red and perspiring, and I feel breathless. Gradually, as I practice Metta, I let go of bodily tension and sense energy descending from my head to deep in the belly. What a relief to be able to ground myself before the bell announces the end of the meditation. Afterwards, there is an open discussion period. Ida thanks the teachers for their skillful, loving way of breaking the news about war to the sangha: "Here I don't feel 'Swiss,' but part of a global family that includes compassionate and caring Americans." I wish that other "foreigners" had Ida's forgiving attitude towards Americans. One person worries about the negative effects of reading newspapers and watching television, when we are feeling so vulnerable. Jack recommends that after the retreat we limit ourselves to fifteen minutes of world news per day and that we use a "seed intention," such as "Watching the news, I feel compassion for all those suffering in war." He quotes Thich Nhat Hanh: "Be careful about what you bring into the living room of your mind." A female yogi complains that ever since she learned about the bombing, she has been experiencing strong physical symptoms. Jack guides her to be conscious of the basic elements in her bodily sensations and to report them aloud. She closes her eyes and utters words such as "hard," "warm," "heat," etc. His advice is to "give each sensation space to happen mindfully. Maybe these sensations will intensify, or maybe they will lessen. Name each change as it occurs, and note any accompanying emotional states as they arise and fall. This is your mindfulness practice for now." As my teacher addresses my companion, I am jotting down every word to facilitate my own awareness. At the end of the open forum, he counsels the sangha: "Today try to be peaceful with whatever arises. Don't push yourselves. It is time for integration. Use Metta and equanimity practice wisely."

As if sensing my struggle to stay earthbound, Jack seeks me out in the lobby. After reading the copy of my journal notes, he is aware that my mind is still very active. He recommends that instead of doing Vipassana meditation, I should focus on Metta. Once he hears that I am already doing so, he suggests that I take hot baths to soothe my nervous system and naps to catch up on rest. His fatherly caring touches me.

But before following his instructions, I keep an appointment with Anna to discuss possibilities for incorporating Guided Imagery and Music into the weeklong "creativity retreats" that she leads each September at Spirit Rock. While I explain the Bonny Method, she listens carefully, and then we draw parallels between this form of music therapy and the archetypal primary process involved in spontaneous painting. As a visual artist, Anna shares my fascination about the psyche's capacity to generate healing imagery. It feels good to sense that my professional ego is still functioning. Over the past weeks I have been in such a childlike condition that I had forgotten how much I like to interact as a competent adult.

I descend the hill for a delicious Mexican meal that includes corn tortillas, guacamole, and black beans. Are the cooks preparing my taste buds for returning home to Mexico? Joining other yogis on the back steps of the dining hall, I savor every mouthful, and we eat in companionable silence. Our skin absorbs the pleasant heat of the noonday sun. Lazily, I think about how this is ideal weather for lizards; those little creatures have much to teach me about how to relax and be still. Interrupting my thoughts, Gina comes outside, carrying her lunch. She is the person I most associate with lizard-like sunbathing. I catch her eye to pantomime: "You ring gong; I sleep." She smiles and nods in assent. Once I am assured that she will continue to act as my substitute bell ringer, I head for my dormitory to take a siesta. Downing two Valerian capsules with water dosed with four drops of Rescue Remedy, I surrender to deep sleep in the warm sunshine streaming across my bed.

The sound of the gong awakens me. Priding myself on how forcefully and punctually I have fulfilled the bell-ringing job, I note with some satisfaction that Gina is striking the gong weakly and a bit behind schedule. It is interesting to notice when my ego shows up. It is returning from being on holiday. Groggily, I prepare for a 2:30 p.m. interview with Jack. In the hallway, I notice all Theresa's shoes packed in a huge plastic bag. Near her door I leave a note: "Dear Theresa, please don't leave without giving me a farewell hug. Your amiga from across the hall, Ginger."

When I arrive at Jack's office, he is still speaking with the yogi scheduled before me. I turn around to wait on the patio and find my way blocked by three fat, wild turkeys with unfurled tail feathers. Eying me belligerently, the big birds huff and gaggle their way across the pavement, before flouncing off towards the hills. Jack comes outside to find me, and together we watch the end of the turkey parade. In the interview, my teacher is happy to hear that I have just had a nap and that I am landing from the heights of an expanded state. We speak about my Vipassana crush on Teja. I praise Teja for his ethical behavior towards me, which has helped me to take responsibility for my projections and to understand more clearly my pattern of relationships with men throughout my life.

Jack and I recall the ten-day retreat at I.M.S. years ago, when I was able to bring myself down from a hypo-manic state without medication. Because of that experience, I could let go of my self-definition as a manic person. During this retreat, I have been releasing more primal patterns and ways of identifying myself. Jack listens while I review how it has felt to enact a one-and-a-half-year-old child, lying in bed in a fetal position, bathing myself tenderly, and creating little animal figures out of play dough. Then I laugh and report how my ego has been surfacing again. Nodding, Jack says, "You need your ego now. It's healthy to have one in international airports." To further strengthen my ego, he gives me an assignment to walk to the Woodacre Deli for lunch tomorrow. The idea of leaving the secure confines of Spirit Rock fills me with dismay. But when Jack insists that it is time for me to practice facing the noisier, outer world, I know that he is right. If I cannot deal with the sparsely populated hamlet of Woodacre, how will I cope with Mexico City, with its twenty-three million inhabitants?

In spite of the fact that it is "against the rules" for yogis to record their experiences in a journal, I ask if he will read what I have written on this retreat and give me some feedback. Assuring me that he is a rapid reader, Jack promises to do so. He likes my proposals that Anna and I collaborate during a retreat incorporating the arts, and that the Spirit Rock gift shop sell copies of my book *I Dreamed I Was Normal*. I could not ask for a more supportive father figure. At this point, Jack seems to be consciously reinforcing my mature, adult tendencies. Before leaving the room, I ask for a hug, and it feels good to be hugged by my spiritual guide.

At 3:45 p.m. the entire sangha meets in the meditation hall to hear Jack and John talk about mindful speech. First, Jack jokes about "mindful shopping practice" for anyone who wishes to buy tape recordings of dharma talks at the Spirit Rock bookstore. I am impressed that the Dharma Seed recording company works on a donation basis to disseminate Buddhist teachings, without charging a specific price for cassettes and compact disks. "Dana," which is the Pali word for "generosity," is an integral part of every retreat that I have attended. Spirit Rock teachers and staff receive no direct payment for teaching or managing the retreat, and the cooks are dedicated volunteers. Jack reminds us that it is our financial support that sustains Spirit Rock and ensures that dharma teachings continue in the Western hemisphere. Dana offerings from yogis are placed in separate boxes for teachers and for staff. The money in each box is pooled and split evenly among the recipients. During this retreat, the manager and six cooks have served us. Today I am feeling particularly generous, because Andrea, the teachers, and the cooks have all shown me extra support and kindness throughout the past month.

To prepare us for a two-hour period of practicing verbal communication, John lists what he calls "the fundamentals for mindful speech:"

1. Keep your mind in the body.
2. Come from the heart while you are speaking.
3. The five Buddhist aspects to wise and skillful speech are to be truthful, helpful, kind, timely, and positive.
4. Use periods of silence wisely, and pause for integration.
5. Trust your own need for boundaries.

At this point, Jack invites the four "people of color" to meet together. I feel sad that among scores of Caucasians on this retreat, there are only two African American women, one Hispanic man, and one Asian American woman. I am aware of several Spirit Rock teachers who have been making a concerted effort to reach out to people of color by offering scholarships and holding an annual retreat that addresses their particular concerns. The topic of diversity has been central to the Community Dharma Leader trainings, and extended retreats are gradually becoming accessible for others besides wealthy, white yogis. But I am acutely aware that the yogis on this retreat are far from representative of the general population of the United States, much less the population of California.

The rest of us meet in groups of six and wander off to converse in places other than the meditation and dining halls. These two areas are reserved for silence and provide much-needed refuges for those of us who feel overwhelmed after a short period of speaking. In my group is Heather, who suffered a serious knee injury in the second week of her two-month retreat. She has been practicing sitting still and caring for herself tenderly. Like me, she intuited that the war had started. Theresa came to Spirit Rock after another retreat at Thich Nhat Hanh's meditation community of Plum Village in France. For six weeks here, she has been doing Metta concentration practice. No wonder she radiates sweetness. Her daily routine has been to meditate all day until 2:00 a.m. — the time that I have been waking up to start my practice. Theresa is about to enter another retreat tomorrow afternoon with her Tibetan teacher. In comparison, my four weeks in silence seem like a warm-up period. Catching my competitive tendency, I note to myself, "comparing, comparing." I remember that on this spiritual path all seekers have their own unique rhythm of practice. Cheryl comments that she feels nourished by a month of introspection, Keith talks about riding waves of grief, and I give a brief summary of my regression experience. Susan speaks about her departure from New York City four weeks ago, when panicking people were buying duct tape in a futile attempt to protect themselves from terrorists. On this retreat she has re-established her equilibrium.

At this juncture, I excuse myself from the group, because I am starting to feel nauseous from the sensory overload of listening and speaking to so many people at once. Sitting in a quiet corner of the lobby, I concentrate on writing checks and then place my donations in the dana boxes for teachers and staff. My cognitive mind in not yet functioning well, and it is hard to do simple rational tasks like calculating finances. Before supper, I visit the peace altar in the meditation hall. How moving it is to read different prayers inscribed on rocks, leaves, and whitened bones. In the midst of wild iris blossoms, crucifixes, rosaries, "malas," and icons of the Buddha and Saint Francis of Assisi, is a slip of paper displaying lyrics to John Lennon's song "Imagine."

By the time I reach the dining hall, I feel exhausted and tearful from absorbing so much stimuli. I find a secluded spot to sip my soup in peace. Instead of attending the 6:30 p.m. sit, I take a solitary walk in the hills. As I watch the last pale colors of the day highlighting wispy clouds on the horizon, I sing out loud "Thank You For This Day." Following my intuition and tending to my needs from moment to moment restores my depleted energy.

Eugene gives this evening's dharma talk on the theme of sangha. He begins by asking the assembled yogis, "How many of you have felt that you did not belong on this retreat?" I am amazed to see that everyone is joining me in raising a hand. Eugene continues, "We feel as if we do not know how to be adults. We have an existential angst about lacking enough training or degrees to belong, so we wander around looking for refuge." His next question to the sangha is, "How many of you live where you were born?" Only two yogis raise their hands. Nodding to indicate that he is not surprised by this meager response, he says, "Most people leave home to search for a sense of belonging. We are all refugees."

According to the Buddha, the third kind of "dukkha," or ordinary human suffering, is feeling separate. Eugene defines "refuge" as "shelter or protection" and "to entrust, commit, or turn one's course." He reminds us that on retreat we hand ourselves over to the care of the dharma: "You are in the hands of the Buddha, and they are good hands. Take refuge in the dharma. It is a receptive and an active commitment." Because the dharma goes against the stream, yogis turn away from conventional society. Referring to his religious background, Eugene states, "Turning back to God is considered one of the holiest things a Jew can do. When we come to the dharma, we are returning to the truth and to awakening."

Of the Buddha's three refuges, Eugene emphasizes sangha, which means community, connectedness, unity, and belonging. He gives some historical background: in the time of the Buddha there were four original sanghas, with two separate ones for monastic men and women, plus one for lay men and another for lay women. Later on, Mahayana Buddhists broadened the definition of sangha, allowing lay people to take Bodhisattva vows. Eugene says that here at Spirit Rock "we commit to a sangha of awakening together. We do not take refuge in our personalities, but rather in our nobility, goodness, and our living expression of the Buddha." He explicates the word "community," which stems from the root "communis," or "ready to be of service." Together on retreat we create "an energy field of goodness."

The sangha that Eugene leads near his home has a "sister sangha" in South Africa, where people are devastated by AIDS. Funds flow from his community in California to the Buddhist retreat center across the ocean: "The Bodhisattva path implies unity." He tells us, "We practice not only for ourselves, but for every sentient being. We can bring goodness to the world at this time of war, ignorance, greed, and delusion." When Ananda, the Buddha's cousin and attendant, asked him if sangha is half of the holy path, the Buddha replied, "Not so. It is the whole path."

In his early teens, Eugene attended Beatnik parties and relished his separateness from the "squares." Then he became a "hippy," separate from the "straights." As a musician, he kept aloof from commercial musicians, and as a beginning meditator he was attached to the idea of "us" and "them." But he has learned over time that on a profound level "there is no 'us and them.' There is only 'us,' even if we don't like all of 'us.' The universal sangha includes all beings." Eugene cites Groucho Marx, who quipped, "I never wanted to join a club that would take me as a member." A more serious citation by Rumi follows: "You can't distinguish whose radiance is whose when you focus on the light." In closing, Eugene advises us, "Simply enjoy your life with people and don't be separated by 'isms.'" He announces that tonight we will have a "vigil sitting" for peace, with yogis taking turns spelling one another throughout the night.

Margot is close behind me as we leave the meditation hall. I signal to her and write a quick note inviting her to accompany me to the Woodacre Deli tomorrow for a silent lunch, "to try out my ego in the outside world." She nods in agreement and points to the lobby as our meeting place. What a relief to know that I will have an ally when I venture beyond the Spirit Rock gates. I walk out into the cold, windy night and gaze at brilliant stars that seem to be shining with extra strength, contributing light to our peace vigil.

After so much intense emotion and so little sleep, I have a stuffy nose and a scratchy throat. Stopping in the manager's office, I purchase some Oscillococcinum, a homeopathic remedy for colds. Just before the 10:00 p.m. "bathing curfew" starts, I take a rejuvenating shower under very hot water. Curling up in my snug little bed, I feel safe and comfortable. Before I join the peace vigil, I need to rest.✿

CHAPTER TEN

CLOSING MOMENTS

O n March 27, I wake up at 2:30 a.m. with a sense that on an energetic level I am a spirit of light whose every breath is coming from a higher source: I receive loving energy on inhalations and disperse loving energy on exhalations. My body seems so transitory. Nevertheless, I must take care of it. Before heading for the meditation hall, I bundle up in layers of warm clothing. At this hour, there are only two yogis sitting in front of the altar with its eight peace candles. One person is a young man with a beard, who starts a series of slow prostrations. He is a spiritual warrior, among the small group of retreatants who are following ten precepts, including one that prohibits eating food after noontime each day. Although I respect his fierce discipline, I recognize my own physical limitations and have no wish to emulate him. Settling on my zafu, I start Metta practice for all beings. When I stop and look around, several more yogis have joined the vigil.

It is 4:45 a.m. by the time I leave the building. Myriads of bright stars and a sliver of an orange-golden crescent moon shine above me. In the stillness, I think, "All is well. All is as it should be." Suddenly I hear the sound of munching near where I have stopped to star gaze. As my eyes grow accustomed to the darkness, I realize that I am standing face-to-face with a deer. We stare into each other's eyes for a prolonged moment, and then the deer turns and trots away. What an unexpected gift.

After a long, hot shower, I walk to the upper walking room for Qigong class. The morning star guides my steps as I send Metta to Mark at our agreed-upon daily 5:30 a. m. tune-in time. The Qigong exercises send vibrations humming through my body. Ever since I decided to focus on centering myself, I have been maintaining a respectful distance from Teja. The energy between us feels strongly charged, and I need to calm myself down. It has been a hard discipline to restrain my impulse to write to him or to approach him at the end of Qigong class. There are only a couple more hours before we can drop our official roles, and it will be easier to talk as friends instead of as teacher and yogi. On my way to breakfast, I pass Rick. He bows and asks to speak with me before he leaves the retreat today, when he will join a peace demonstration in San Francisco. We agree to meet at the dining hall at 8:00 a.m., as soon as he finishes his yogi job as a breakfast pot washer.

Today the prayer wheel stops mid-way between "wise intention" and "wise speech." No surprise. Rick and I hike up to the hills, where we have an extraordinary discussion. He is fascinated by my account of regressing to repair the wounds of separation from my parents fifty-three years ago. At a very early age, he, too, was separated from his mother and wants to explore on a cellular level how that trauma still affects him. What has seemed like my unique regression process may be a more common experience than I thought. As psychotherapists, Rick and I share the "wounded healer" tendency to help others in pain. On different sides of the border, we both work in Spanish with Mexican clients. Before we return to Noble Silence, he encourages me to write about my process on this retreat as a way to benefit others with pre-verbal trauma.

As Rick and I descend from the hills, we pass Teja walking uphill with a pretty blond yogi, who, like me, has attended every Qigong class. I feel adolescent pangs of jealousy and quickly remind myself that I am a happily married woman. Exhausted from talking so intensely with Rick, I retire to my bedroom for a nap. It is clear that my most important task is to follow a deep instinctual sense of what is wise for me in the here and now. Before I face the stimulation of another afternoon of mindful speaking practice,

I should sleep. I am aware of the spaciousness and freedom for choice in each moment as it unfolds. There is no need to plan ahead, the way I am accustomed to doing. I can trust that I will know intuitively what decision to make in each minute. My sage inner impulses are what Jack calls "the one who knows" or "the heart of wisdom."

I awaken from my siesta just in time to meet Margot for our lunch date. She proves to be the ideal partner for my first foray outside the sanctuary of Spirit Rock. As a long-time meditator, she knows a shortcut to the Woodacre Deli. Happily, I allow her to lead me on a grassy path, over a fence, and into a tunnel that serves as an underpass beneath Sir Francis Drake Boulevard. I am thankful that Margot is sparing me from dealing with highway traffic. The floor of the tunnel is soaked from recent rainfall. We enjoy the sensation of sloshing through mud and springing across puddles. Margot guides me past a riding school, with stables, paddocks, and inquisitive horses, who approach to let us stroke their silky chins. This seems like magical territory. I love the smells and sounds of this horsy realm, full of snorts and whinnies. Posted near the paddocks is a sign that reads: "You have two choices: #1. Ride at your own risk, and #2. Don't ride." This message seems like a metaphor for life.

Concentrating on completing our mission, Margot heads across the country lane that divides the riding school from the Woodacre post office. Our destination is close at hand, but we have not yet reached our goal. Even though I know that the few cars passing us must be driving slowly on this narrow, back road, I perceive them to be zooming along at a startlingly rapid rate. The noise and speed disconcert me so much that I am tempted to turn back. Undeterred by these obstacles, Margot presses on, and reluctantly I follow her into the deli. The screen door bangs loudly behind us.

Staring at the glass display case, Margot and I burst out laughing at the huge selection of delicious foods. We have become used to the simplicity of Spirit Rock's buffets, with labels identifying all the ingredients in each dish. Now we are nonplussed by the surfeit of choices. Barely controlling my giggles, I ask a friendly Hispanic employee to give me small containers of grilled tofu, roasted potatoes, and marinated artichoke hearts. My taste buds desire strong and contrasting flavors. Margot fetches a bag of organic potato chips, which we munch contentedly until her turkey sandwich is ready. Like a genie, she finds a half-chocolate, half-vanilla cookie, which looks like a yin-yang symbol, for us to share for dessert. Since she is here at my invitation, I insist on treating Margot to lunch. Dealing with dollars and making change are further challenges for my still-inwardly-directed mind.

On our way outside to sit at a picnic table, we see Rick reading the daily newspaper. Margot and I recoil at seeing the headlines about the war in Iraq. After introducing my two friends, I tell Rick that I cannot imagine reading world news in my present hypersensitive condition. Grinning, he admits that as a political activist, he habitually reads the daily news. He reminds me that he plans to do civil disobedience tomorrow in San Francisco, where he may be arrested. Margot and I express admiration for his dedication to enter the chaos of an anti-war protest directly after being on retreat for two weeks. There is a bond of solidarity among the three of us —a Canadian who lives in Vancouver, a Puerto Rican residing in California, and a New Yorker with a Mexican visa.

After wishing Rick good luck, Margot and I resume silence, and I thoroughly enjoy every morsel of my lunch. On our way "home" to Spirit Rock, we rinse off our muddy shoes in a puddle and pick yellow wildflowers to wear in our hair. We arrive outside the meditation hall just in time for me to ring the 2:00 bell, loudly and repeatedly, to proclaim peace in this corner of the world.

Dianita invites me to attend a Buddhist Peace Fellowship circle in the upper walking room. I join about fifteen yogis to hear her describe how she and other committed meditators sit silently on their zafus as a form of protest at peace rallies. Inspired by her example, I volunteer to start a BPF chapter in Mexico. Then, pleading sensory overload, I retire from the group for another rest period. I need quiet time to integrate all the thoughts provoked by speaking.

In the evening, the entire sangha gathers in the meditation hall for the teachers' closing words. Jack starts off by asking if we are all "buzzing" from so much talking. Most of us nod affirmatively. He extols "the beautiful work we have done together to transform our hearts" and says that "we have each touched moments of freedom authentically." Jack recalls the twin pillars that protect the dharma in Asia: *dana* (generosity and service) and *sila* (morality or ethics). His advice is to "be generous to yourself as well as to others" and "follow the practice of non-harming." He asks, "How would it be if we stopped killing people, let alone animals?" If we truly incorporate reverence for life, we will refrain from stealing and from misusing sexuality. Besides reviewing the five precepts that we honored on the first day of the retreat, Jack cautions that upon returning home, we will face scores of e-mails and closets stuffed with clothes. He suggests, "Simplify and shed." From past experience, I know that he is right. I will need to pace myself carefully and catch up gradually with all the business that has accumulated over the past month. I can practice Feng Shui and give away excessive material possessions.

To my dismay, Jack announces that he and Julie will both be leaving Spirit Rock early tomorrow morning. I wonder if I am ready to wean myself from my surrogate parents. Julie is eager to be with her young daughter, and Jack plans to join a group of two hundred clergy in an act of civil disobedience — blocking the entrance to the federal building in San Francisco and waiting to be arrested. After all the yogis applaud his courage, Jack teases the other teachers for making him promise not to go to jail until the retreat's end.

Taking her turn to bid us farewell, Anna's recommendation is "Forgive yourself ahead of time for mistakes that will occur." She jokes about an apocryphal interchange between a spiritual master and a yogi: When the student asks, "What is the secret of life?" the teacher replies, "good judgment." To the question, "How do I develop good judgment?" the master answers, "experience." The student persists, "How do I get experience?" The response is "bad judgment." After our appreciative laughter dies down, Anna continues more seriously: "Cultivate the intention to be open, mindful and compassionate in your daily lives. Remember the intention that brings you to practice." She urges us to rely on the sangha to help us remember wise intentions.

Julie's parting words are typically simple and sweet: "I invite you to look in the mirror at your own eyes. Take a snapshot in your mind's eye of how open and present you are in this beautiful state." She mentions that continuity in practice requires sitting with joys and sorrows and with cycles of expansion and contraction. In closing, she cites Rumi's poem called "Bird Wings:"

> *Your hand opens and closes.*
> *Your deepest presence is in*
> *Every small contracting and expanding,*
> *The two as beautifully balanced and coordinated*
> *As bird wings.*

Eugene receives the microphone from Julie and thanks us for our sincerity, effort, and goodness. He states, "Retreats do not really end, because the dharma continues. Let go of this retreat. On retreats we receive extra support for good intentions, and we can 'pretend' that our whole life is the dharma. But you can pretend the same in your daily life, and create a structure to support your practice. Attend a sitting group, and, in the safety of the sangha, speak the truth about your practice." I envision weaving the dharma more fully into my home life: in addition to a regular morning routine of Metta prayers and yoga, I can incorporate Qigong and take time to set a wise intention for each day. Although I receive sustenance from leading the

UDLA sangha each week, I could benefit from initiating a sutta discussion group to deepen my understanding of the Buddha's teachings. Eugene concludes his homily with, "Meditation is like the in-breath. Expressing yourself in sangha is like the out-breath. Live the dharma. Have fun."

Robert takes his turn at the microphone and asserts, "We are transitioning from a sane to an insane environment. Of all the thousands of words we teachers have spoken, you will probably recall only a few of those words. What has happened to you on this retreat is your own inner experience —not our words." He warns, "Outside, when people ask how your retreat was, be selective about who you talk to and what you say. Don't proselytize. Be a Buddha instead of a Buddhist." While I am often tempted to preach to friends about the benefits of meditation, I know that it is the way I live my life that most impacts others. Robert cites the Dalai Lama: "Don't teach Buddhism. Teach kindness."

Finally, John Travis adds some characteristically brief and pithy words of advice: "Take care of your vulnerability. Don't over-talk and drain your energy. On the way home, you can do walking meditation in airports and meditate on airplanes. Respect the work you have done here." He cautions, "Outside, there is a big drama about the Iraq war. Consciously choose what to attend to and when to drop out of the drama." In my own experience, I know that John is right: "Happiness," he remarks, "depends on our capacity to stop and pull back from life's dramas." In my childhood I developed a habit of ricocheting from one personal drama to another. Now I am recognizing the satisfaction of restraining myself and resting. Over the years I have learned that after a month of sitting in silence, there is a process of integration that continues to unfold. If I plunge into many activities right away, I will not be able to absorb fully the lessons from this retreat. I do not want to miss any step of the inner journey.

After each teacher has had a chance to speak, Jack describes a "Parvana" ritual held in Asian temples and monasteries at the end of retreats. The abbots and teachers step out of their roles and bow to the students, indicating the basic humanity that connects everyone in the sangha. Following this tradition, our teachers descend from the dais and kneel on the floor. Jack states on behalf of them all, "If in any way, intentionally or unintentionally, in thought, word, or deed, we have harmed you, we ask your forgiveness." The teachers then perform three prostrations. Although I have witnessed such ceremonies in the past, I am moved to tears by their humble gesture. When I look around the room, nobody's eyes are dry. How could we not forgive the human failings of such dedicated dharma teachers?

On March 28, my fifty-fifth birthday, I wake up at 2:00 a.m. with memories from a year ago, when I was recovering from a hysterectomy at my parents' home in New York. Before I flew home to Mexico, my parents held a dinner party in my honor. In front of the guests, Mom stood up to toast me, her beloved namesake, "little Virginia." I received her tender words gratefully and without surprise. My mother has always been able to express verbally how much she loves me. Then, to my amazement, my father rose to his feet and proposed a toast "to my daughter, Ginger, whose dedicated work with autistic children and successful book about music therapy make me proud. Ginny and I had the pleasure of visiting Ginger and Mark at the beautiful campus of the university where they teach in Mexico. We were impressed by the good work they do with students and by the close friendships they have formed." As Dad raised his glass to me in salute and the guests joined him in toasting me, I sat stunned. He is just beginning to understand the importance of voicing appreciation for his children. Probably he has no idea how meaningful that toast was for me. I will never forget his generous tribute, which was a turning point in our relationship.

As I arise to shower and to pack my suitcase, I think how perfect it is that this retreat is ending on my birthday. Ready to start a new year of life, I feel cleansed and clear about my priorities. After thoroughly cleaning my precious, single bedroom, I bow to the image of Kwan Yin on the wall. This figure of compassion has guarded me well. Before the morning sit, I walk from Karuna dormitory to Upekkha, where I began the retreat a month ago. I want to bid farewell to Dianita, who has been staying down the hall from the double room that I had shared with Alison. Dianita is in the midst of packing, but she has a surprise for me. Remembering that turquoise is my favorite color, she lends me her Buddhist Peace Fellowship tee shirt "until we meet again." I know what a sacrifice my friend is making to part from the emblem of the institution where she has been working so devotedly. In thanks, I promise to wear the shirt as protective armor on my plane ride home. I tell her that the bright color will help me to publicize the new Mexican chapter of the Buddhist Peace Fellowship. Without knowing when Dianita and I will be together again, I resolve to take good care of our "collective shirt."

John Travis leads the closing ritual in the meditation hall. He speaks about the lineage of Buddhist practice that extends twenty-six hundred years into the past and then observes that, "our sangha is expanding to contain all life and the whole world." He refers to Chris Brown, who has written about communal loyalty among geese, whose "V" formation gives an aerial lift to those in the rear. If the leader tires, he drops back into the ranks, and another goose slips into his place at the fulcrum of the "V." Whenever a goose is sick or falls from the sky, two geese accompany their weaker companion until he heals or dies, and they catch up later with their flock. John cites Chris Brown's comment that if we had as much sense as geese, we would help each other. In our sangha, I have witnessed many instances of kindness among yogis and teachers. May we all continue such compassionate action in our daily lives.

A protection cord ceremony follows. As he, Eugene and Anna distribute red-colored strings to all the yogis, John mentions that he owns a box containing thirty-four protection cords from various retreats he has attended over the past decades. He quotes Trungpa Rinpoche: "We need protection most of all from ourselves." Initiating a call and response chant in Pali, John leads us in honoring the Three Refuges: the Buddha, dharma, and sangha. I like the custom of chanting these refuges at the start and the close of every retreat. We all follow instructions to tie one knot in the center of the cord, and then we join John in reciting the five precepts "to keep the mind cool and stable." He declares, "The precepts of non-harming provide us with self-protecting lights along the spiritual path to prevent us from falling into precipices on either side." Once we have made a commitment to do our best to uphold the five precepts, each person ties a second knot in the protection cord.

When it is time to pair up and to tie the cord around a partner's neck or wrist, I turn to Heather, who is sitting beside me. She conveys her familiarity with the ritual by asking, "Would you like it tied tightly, or loosely enough to remove when you shower?" While I opt for looseness, she requests that I tie her cord as tightly as possible without strangling her. We bow to one another, affirming our bond as soul sisters. As soon as everyone is wearing their protection cords, Anna states, "We are all in Bodhisattva training, with just enough pleasure to keep us encouraged and just enough pain to keep us challenged." She reads us some passages by the spiritual devotee Shanti Deva: "There is no difference between us and others. So let us make others happy. Let battling with weapons become playing with flowers, and may all people think of benefiting others."

John resumes leadership and initiates a beautiful Metta practice. With our eyes open, we scan the faces of everybody around us in the meditation hall. Everyone looks trusting and innocent. Meanwhile, John prays, "May we send Metta to everyone in this sangha, to the Indra's net of all people and to all beings everywhere, to those in fear and those in war—those who experience it and those who perpetuate it. May those in power awaken and those who are victimized by power be free from harm. May we listen to the earth and learn to live in harmony with nature, so that all beings may live peacefully for countless generations. May all beings, seen and unseen, known and unknown, have joy and equanimity." These words of love fill my heart to the brim. Finally, Eugene brings the retreat to a close with the statement, "May we offer the merit of our practice for the benefit of all beings."

Recalling that I plan to visit friends near his hometown, Teja approaches to offer me a ride to Petaluma. Before I accept, I express concern that he has acted seductively towards me and other female yogis. At first he is taken aback by my words, but I explain how much his physical touch, his eye contact and his playful notes have affected me during the retreat. I have done my best to take responsibility for my projections and to face my own patterns in relationships with men. But yesterday, when I passed Teja walking with another woman from the Qigong class, I realized that I was not the only yogi with a Vipassana crush on him. I admit that I felt jealous. Teja assures me that his intentions have been pure and reminds me that this is the first time he has taught at a Vipassana retreat. He is not used to Qigong students being in such sensitive and vulnerable states. With appreciation for my honesty, he promises to contemplate ways to be more discrete in future retreats. I feel relieved that he could receive my difficult message so openly, and I thank him for all that he has taught me. It is clear that we both value the dharma more than the ego's pride.

Before our drive to Petaluma, Teja and I go separate ways to bid farewell to various friends. Margot and I hug goodbye, and she is interested to hear that I felt autistic during my most regressed moments on the retreat. While Edgar passes by, hauling his luggage, he overhears our conversation. Awkwardly, he approaches to comment, "I am intrigued by what you are saying." Margot excuses herself to catch a ride to the airport and leaves me and Edgar on our own, face to face for the first time since we encountered one another. He admits that he has some of the symptoms I have been describing. I take the risk of telling him, "You may have a high-functioning form of autism called Asperger's syndrome." Edgar stares at me a moment before inquiring, "What are the characteristics?" I describe difficulties with assessing appropriate timing for speaking, perceiving customary physical distance between people, expressing feelings, and coordinating body movements. Edgar responds, "That is exactly what I experience." I ask if he has had trouble establishing intimate relationships and allowing people to touch him physically. He nods affirmatively. My next question refers to whether he has hypersensitive sense perception and telepathic abilities. Again he nods. Edgar asks for one of my business cards and confesses, "I have had problems justifying to special education administrators my need for disability payments. Because my handicap is so subtle, they have been skeptical about my inability to hold a job. It would help to have a label like 'Asperger's' to give credibility to my need for a monthly stipend." I write "Asperger's syndrome" on the back of my card and suggest that Edgar consult the Internet for more data about this kind of autism. After expressing gratitude, he agrees to write me for information about books by Temple Grandin, a successful university professor with a Ph.D., who writes honestly about her own Asperger's syndrome. Without warning, Edgar brusquely ends our conversation to run off and catch a ride home.

As I watch the clumsiness of his gait and the blundering way he is hauling his bags, my eyes are misty. If this retreat has been a challenge for me, with relatively intact perceptual and expressive abilities, how difficult it must have been for a man with the disabilities of Asperger's syndrome. I admire Edgar's valiant efforts to better himself and to pursue his spiritual inclinations. It seems like no accident that he and I have met, and that, because of my many years of work with students who have Asperger's, I could offer him an explanation for why he has been struggling so hard with tasks that seem easy for those around him. Somehow, it feels right that Edgar is the last person I speak to before passing through the gates to leave the retreat area of Spirit Rock. I see Teja waving to me from his car, and roll my suitcase to join him for the half-hour drive northward. Without any need for verbal interaction, we maintain silence as the car moves slowly down the driveway towards the outside world. ❦

CHAPTER ELEVEN

AFTERTHOUGHTS

With the sensitivity of long-time meditators, my friends in Sebastapol welcome me warmly and usher me to their guestroom, which has been made comfortable for my re-entry process. I am delighted to hear that, as a birthday present, a masseuse will be arriving this afternoon to give my tired body a relaxing massage. Understanding my need to be alone for a while, my friends keep their two rambunctious sons occupied in another part of the house. Despite their tender care and the quiet surroundings, it is still an effort to wean myself from the Spirit Rock sangha and the retreat schedule. I feel breakable.

But I am starting to have a kind of aerial perspective about the past month. In an overview, I can see various roles I played with yogis, teachers and staff at Spirit Rock. Each person was like a piece in a karmic puzzle, teaching me life lessons from disparate angles. We all brought our own personal histories to the retreat, and, in that safe and spacious setting, I had an opportunity to interact in ways that helped expand my awareness and heal wounds from the past. Before the retreat, I had been primed with years of meditation, psychotherapy, dream analysis, bodywork, creative arts exploration, and spiritual discipline. None of that preparation was wasted. During my regression to a pre-verbal period, I accessed all the resources I had gained over the past fifty-five years.

The process of withdrawing projections is beginning. Now that I am away from Jack and Julie, I can let go of my childlike dependence on them. It is no longer necessary for them to play the roles of my nurturing parents. During yesterday's drive together, Teja and I started a transition from the roles of teacher and student to those of friends with many common interests. Somehow he seemed shorter in stature, and his voice sounded less resonant and authoritative than when we were at Spirit Rock. As my ego rebounds, I feel more self-sufficient and better able to imagine resuming my respon-sibilities as wife, professor, and psychotherapist.

Mark phones from Mexico to wish me a happy birthday, and I reconnect with how much I love my husband. I am eager to see him in two days. Then my mother calls from New York, just after I unwrap a lovely green shawl that she sent as a birthday gift. Thanking her from three thousand miles away, I feel grateful for her ongoing generosity to me. When I was born, Mom was twenty-one years old and married for just a year. At the time, she was madly in love with my father, and neither of them had any idea that I could be traumatized by their absence during the summer after my first birthday. When Mom asks about the retreat, I know that it will take me months to digest the regression experience, and that it would not be wise to broach that subject now. My response is simple: I learned a great deal about myself in the month of silence.

After hanging up the phone, I know that there is nothing to forgive. My mother raised me in the best way she knew, with the level of consciousness she had then. How could I have done any better as a young, inexperienced mother in the era of the late forties? That was the epoch of the post-World War II baby boom, when best-selling author Dr. Benjamin Spock was advis-ing new mothers not to cuddle, breast-feed, or over-protect their babies. I have never had children of my own, and I cannot presume to judge my mother's childrearing practices of so long ago. She has been attentive and loving to me in countless ways, and to that I owe my basic faith in the goodness of people.

My friends and I decide to drive to Muir Woods for a hike on Sunday, the day before I return to Mexico. Walking slowly amidst the majestic, ancient trees, I sense my feet on the earth. These trees have witnessed far more than I will in my lifetime. I feel humbled in their presence. These splendid natural surroundings provide me with a healthy transition time between Spirit Rock and the Mexico City airport.

Back home in Cholula, Mark and I are delighted to be in each other's presence again. Over long meals, we start to share what has transpired in our lives during the four weeks we have been apart. The evening after my homecoming, he accompanies me as I resume leadership of the UDLA sangha. When I arrive at the meditation room, my substitute sangha leader, John, and the rest of the group are already assembled. They applaud enthusiastically to welcome me back, and several people ask eager questions about my month of silence. Thanking them for their animated greeting, I suggest that before discussing the retreat, we sit in silence. As we settle into our familiar practice, I feel thankful for this Mexican sangha, my local spiritual home. After the sit, I decide not to give a dharma talk as I usually do. Instead, I review some highlights from dharma talks that I heard at Spirit Rock. A professor questions me about what it is like to be on retreat for a month. Most of the members of this sangha have never maintained silence for longer than two days, on the weekend retreats that I lead at the end of each semester. Because I have not had time to integrate my own personal retreat experience, I describe the general tendency, in prolonged periods of silence, for the senses to become more sensitive, the mind more concentrated, and the perceptual field more open; with intensive practice, meditators tend to develop wisdom and compassion and to have moments of profound insight into themselves and into universal truths that underlie daily existence. My response seems to satisfy the sangha.

In the weeks that follow the retreat, I notice how openhearted I am. Friends and music therapy clients tell me that they feel touched by the compassionate way I listen to them. Often their stories about difficult or sad circumstances move me deeply. I follow through on one of the resolutions that I made at Spirit Rock—to acquire a puppy. Although Mark and I have fantasized for years about owning a dog, I have to persuade him that we can fit a pet into our busy lives at the university. It is clear to me that attending to the needs of a small, furry, four-footed animal will be healthy for us cerebral academics. On April Fool's Day, we drive to a local pet store, where I hold a tiny, eight-week-old, miniature Schnauzer against my heart.

Turning to my husband, I declare, "She's our dog." Over the years, Mark has learned to trust my intuition. We carry our puppy home and abruptly enter a new phase of our relationship. Suddenly we empathize with friends who are parenting children. Instead of following our regular daily routines, we must adapt to the vocal and physical demands of a very active and messy new family member.

Mark and I call our dog "Marisol," a common enough given name in Mexico, but one that has special significance for us. In the process of choosing a name, we broke the word down into the Spanish terms for "sea and sun" (*mar y sol*), implying psychological depth and spiritual transcendence — with the added connotations of the English "soul." The symbolism hints at elements that love for this sentient being contributes to our lives. Marisol continues to remind us that the heart and the body are priorities, and, for me, she will always be associated with lessons that I learned on the retreat in 2003.

Honoring my vow to take better care of myself, I make appointments to have a massage and to receive a subtle energy treatment to balance my chakras. My neurological system is still overcharged and hypersensitive. Because I have not yet resumed my normal sleep patterns, I wake up sporadically throughout the night. Even daily yoga and Qigong practice are not suffi-cient to calm down my abundant energy. When my "sanación energética" teacher, Loly, checks my chakra system with a pendulum, she detects that my upper chakras are vibrating strongly, but that the lower ones are barely active. This means that while my heart, throat, third eye and crown chakras are working overtime, the root, sex, and will chakras are underemployed. No wonder it seems challenging to stay connected to my body and to man-age daily tasks. Loly perceives my aura as imbalanced and reports that I am wide open energetically on the "astral" and "celestial" planes.

Of the seven main layers of the aura, my fourth and sixth, by Loly's analysis, are very expanded. In the auric field around the physical body, the first three planes are called "etheric," "emotional," and "mental." As the psychic and former physicist Barbara Brennan writes, "On the physical level, con-sciousness takes the form of instinct, automatic reflexes and the automatic functioning of internal organs" (Brennan, 1988, p. 138). She explains that consciousness is expressed at the etheric level in terms of sensations like physical pleasure and pain, at the emotional level as basic primal emotions and reactions, and at the mental level as rational thinking. Next comes the astral layer, which bridges the physical and spiritual planes, and is charac-terized by strong emotions that stem from identifying with all humanity. It is on this level that my aura is especially expanded. At the fifth layer, known as the "etheric template," consciousness expresses itself in altruism. On the "celestial level," it is expressed as higher feelings, such as universal love for all life; in the aftermath of my retreat, this sixth layer is also disproportionately extended. The seventh "ketheric level" is characterized by higher concepts of integrated knowing or belief systems (Brennan, 1988, p. 139).

Loly describes to me her psychic perception of my expanded capacity to sense a loving connection with all life. Recalling the enormous grief I felt during the retreat for those who are suffering in the Iraq war, I am not surprised by her assessment of my aura. We both agree that in order to negotiate everyday life, I must contract my energy field and focus on more mundane concerns. Directing me to lie face up on her massage table, Loly gives me a Reiki treatment and then uses her hands to sweep the highly charged energy around my head downward to ground it in the earth. With another subtle energy technique, she diminishes the expansiveness of the fourth and sixth dimensions of my auric field. After the treatment, Loly gives me a bottle of sandalwood oil to rub onto my breastbone each morning, further aiding my grounding process.

Gradually I find my footing in regular routines around the home and reestablish connections with family, friends, and therapy clients. But after a month at Spirit Rock, my awareness has shifted. The theme of peace has become part of my consciousness. Sensing the ghastly bombing in Iraq affected me on a cellular level while I was on retreat. Now I feel strongly committed to participate in causes for peace. When I tell the members of the UDLA sangha about the Buddhist Peace Fellowship, they seem pleased that I am starting a Mexican chapter. I phone two buddies from the retreat, Gina and Rick, to reaffirm our common interest in planning a conference on peace that might be hosted by Yale University. We decide to invite several like-minded friends to participate in monthly conference calls and to share ideas about nonviolent ways to resolve conflicts. I realize that if we do nothing more than establish an ongoing dialogue about practicing peaceful co-existence, I will be fanning in myself a flame of consciousness that was lit at Spirit Rock.

During *Semana Santa* (Holy Week), Mark and I travel to a beach on the Caribbean coast of Mexico to relax and catch up with one another. The lazy, holiday pace is restorative for both of us. We walk on the sun-baked sand, snorkel in the turquoise-hued ocean, and eat succulent local fruits and home-baked bread. Even though we have time to read some books, we focus on our sensuous side. After over a month of celibacy, it feels delicious to make love. I begin to sleep more deeply and to gain back some of the weight I lost on the retreat.

By the time we return home, I am ready to concentrate on writing reflections about my retreat experience. Somehow my old, out-dated computer does not seem adequate for such a project. Mark helps me purchase a new laptop computer, and I begin the process of analyzing what happened to me at Spirit Rock. Via the Internet, I order several books about preverbal trauma, and, as soon as they arrive in the mail, I read them cover-to-cover. Now I have a compelling reason to become informed about trauma that occurs shortly after birth.

Judith Herman's book *Trauma and Recovery* immediately helps me recognize the tame nature of my own preverbal trauma. As I read about people who have suffered kidnappings, torture, and repeated sexual and physical abuse, I acknowledge that my early period of separation from loving parents is a relatively insignificant event. In comparison to the cases cited by Herman, I feel extremely fortunate. My tendency to write compulsively and other neurotic attempts to control my experiences are mild symptoms in the aftermath of feeling abandoned.

Nevertheless, I can relate to the author's description of the aftereffects of trauma: "Traumatic memories lack verbal narrative and context; rather, they are encoded in the form of vivid sensations and images" (Herman, 1992, p. 38). She continues, "These unusual features of traumatic memory may be based on alterations in the central nervous system. A wide array of animal experiments show that when high levels of adrenaline and other stress hormones are circulating, memory traces are deeply imprinted. The same traumatic engraving of memory may occur in human beings" (Herman, p. 39). Herman's observations about similarities between animal and human physiological responses to trauma echo those of Peter Levine, whose theories I discussed in the prologue. At Spirit Rock, when I was reliving the experience of parental abandonment, I shivered with cold and had fleeting images of my nurse's bony fingers prodding me, and then of finding refuge in my grandmother's warm lap, where I rested my head on her ample bosom.

Herman cites Bessel van der Kolk, a psychiatrist who suggests that "in states of high sympathetic nervous system arousal, the linguistic coding of memory is inactivated, and the central nervous system reverts to the sensory and iconic forms of memory that predominate in early life" (Herman, p. 39). On the retreat I could not articulate verbally why I felt compelled to bathe myself in hot water and to play on the floor with children's molding clay and crayons. Luckily, my teachers encouraged me to follow my body's instincts and to care intuitively for my primal needs.

Psychiatrist Mardi Horowitz speculates that unassimilated traumatic experiences are stored in a special kind of "active memory" that has an "intrinsic tendency to repeat the representation of contents," so that the trauma can be resolved only when the survivor develops a new mental "schema for understanding what happened" (Horowitz, 1986, pp. 93-94). At Spirit Rock, I was driven to reenact past events, and I emerged from the regression with more comprehension about what happened when I was a year-and-a-half old. Long ago, Freud recognized and referred to this phenomenon as the "repetition compulsion" (Freud, 1922), and Herman is one of the current theorists who conceive of reenactments as "spontaneous attempts to integrate the traumatic event" (Herman, p. 41).

I am struck by the numerous parallels between Herman's theories about recovery from trauma and my experiences during the 2003 retreat. She comments that trauma-related symptoms that have faded over time can recur years after the event, usually prompted by reminders of the original trauma (Herman, p. 48). In my own case, I began to regress on a retreat characterized by an aloneness that echoed the period of early abandonment. I am aware that the weekend when both Julie and Jack were away from Spirit Rock was the period when my anxiety, insomnia, and obsessive writing were most acute. Decades after the fact, I transferred feelings I had about my parent's prolonged absence to the short separation from these teachers, who, for the moment, played the roles of surrogate mother and father in my psyche. During Julie and Jack's days off, I sought out sympathetic, substitute caretakers such as Teja and John. I was just as resourceful at finding nurturing replacements on the retreat as I had been as a toddler, obtaining comfort from my grandmother.

According to Herman, there are three distinct stages of recovery for people who have been traumatized. The first stage entails the establishment of safety; the second consists of remembrance and mourning; and the third involves reconnection with ordinary life (Herman p. 155). Within the context of a healing relationship, the therapist creates an environment of safety and acts as an ally who helps the patient develop insight into the trauma (Herman, p. 135). Ideally the therapist provides clear goals, rules, and boundaries for the relationship (Herman, p. 145). In my situation, I could not have asked for more insightful and caring allies than Jack and Julie. They emphasized that I was to take full responsibility for my recovery. The clear parameters of the retreat setting and the predictable daily schedule served to contain my fragile state.

Once solid groundwork for a trusting relationship has been laid, the second stage of recovery can begin. One way to work through mourning and remembrance is simply to have the patient tell the story of what happened. Herman notes that retelling a shocking event to an empathic listener can transform the way a traumatic memory is processed (Herman, p. 183). Regarding his work with combat veterans, therapist Terrence Keane comments that the "*physioneurosis* induced by terror can apparently be reversed through the use of words" (presentation at Harvard Medical School conference on Psychological Trauma, Boston, MA, June, 1990). Ironically, words were my salvation during the "silent" retreat. My journal was a constant companion, and Jack and Julie scheduled extra interviews, encouraging me to talk about whatever preverbal memories were emerging. This process allowed me to make sense of uncomfortable physiological symptoms that were occurring, so that they could dissipate naturally.

Herman has noticed that after numerous repetitions, the trauma story gradually generates less intense feeling, and the traumatic memory starts to fade, just as more normal memories do; thus the survivor realizes that the trauma is not the most important or interesting aspect of her life's journey (Herman, p. 195). At Spirit Rock, the more I talked with my teachers and wrote about memories of feeling abandoned, the less oppressive the weight of the preverbal experiences became. Then I could shift my focus to more current, adult concerns.

Regarding the second stage of recovery, Herman observes that it has a scary, timeless quality: "The reconstruction of the trauma requires immersion in a past experience of frozen time; the descent into mourning feels like a surrender to tears that are endless" (Herman, p. 195). In the midst of mourning, people often ask how long the painful process will last. Skillful therapists have no fixed answers to this question, but they assure their patients that the process cannot be bypassed or hurried, and that it will not continue forever. At Spirit Rock, when I was grieving the absence of my parents and longing for the comfort of my grandmother's hugs, I felt as if my tears would never stop flowing. I worried that I might not be able to pull myself together by the end of the retreat. Although my childlike regression lasted less than a week in real time, I lost a normal sense of the passage of hours and days. While I was floating in warm baths, time seemed magically stuck in the past.

During this second stage of healing, trauma therapists often help their patients find soothing images to counteract feelings of being unlovable. As Herman says, "One positive memory of a caring, comforting person may be a lifeline during the descent into mourning. The patient's own capacity to feel compassion for animals and children, even at a distance, may be the fragile beginning of compassion for herself" (Herman, p. 194). During my regression, I held onto the comforting image of my grandmother, who had given me hope and solace when my parents were away. In my case, this image arose spontaneously and helped me find compassion for myself. On long walks around Spirit Rock, I felt love for the small animals whose paths I crossed. Their innocence reminded me of my own vulnerability when I was a toddler. As I resonated with deer and birds, my heart was touched, and I could respond more compassionately to my own needs.

The third stage of recovery, reconnection with daily life, leads to active engagement in the world. Herman notes that prior to this stage, survivors of trauma might consider ordinary life boring, but now they grow bored with playing the role of victim and can appreciate ordinary life (Herman, p. 203). Many survivors must wean themselves from a habitual need for intensity, so that they can find contentment in mundane circumstances. At Spirit Rock I reached a point when I no longer wanted to feel like a victim of circumstances beyond my control. As I became tired of the drama of sleepless nights and writing long reminiscences in my journal, I felt motivated to talk to my teachers about my goals as an adult. Once I left the retreat, I was delighted to take walks around home with my husband and to chop vegetables for meals. Ordinary colors and textures and smells caught my attention in ways that they had not before the retreat. I felt grateful for simple pleasures that beforehand I had taken for granted.

Mark Epstein, who has written several books about psychotherapy from a Buddhist perspective, provides a different framework for understanding my retreat process. He discusses the meditative practice of *bare attention,* which involves opening to both internal and external sensory experience in a way that "does not often survive our childhoods" (Epstein, 1995, p. 117). Epstein explains that most children learn to react to their parents' needs and thus lose a connection to their true self; in this process, a child constructs a false self and a narcissistic character that becomes cut off from spontaneous feelings. By observing the reactive self and noting what arises in each moment, practitioners of bare attention differentiate habitual reactions from core experiences. Eventually they recover a state of unconditioned receptivity, which "bears an important resemblance to the feeling engendered by an optimally attentive parent" (Epstein, 1995, p. 117). Epstein quotes the child psychoanalyst Donald Winnicott, who claims that only in this "state of not having to react" can the self "begin to be" (Winnicott, 1958, pp. 183-184).

Bare attention has an element of impersonality that frees the meditator from identifying with what is occurring. The practice leads to a state that Epstein posits is similar to Winnicott's "transitional space," a period between infantile dependence and the capacity to tolerate being alone, which allows the child a feeling of solace when the parents are away (Epstein, 1995, p. 122). Bare attention also has a quality of constancy that enables a meditator to accept experiences that formerly provoked emotional disruptions (Epstein, 1995, p. 123). Like the toddler who holds a teddy bear to help her tolerate separations from her parents until she no longer needs the transitional object, the meditator becomes comfortable using bare attention and then relinquishes this tool to settle into "choiceless awareness" (Epstein, 1995, p. 123).

At Spirit Rock, it was through practicing Vipassana and bare attention that I entered into a sensitive and childlike state and gained access to previously blocked sensorial memories. In this condition, I paid attention to kinesthetic sensations and emotional moods as they came and went, and I felt no need to react to or judge them. To borrow Epstein's metaphor, I was literally coming to my senses (Epstein, 1995, p. 144). There seemed to be no distance between myself and what I was perceiving, so that I could enjoy directly the sounds of birdcalls, the sight of raindrops, and the touch of sun-baked stones, without the customary, rational filters. Because I was no longer differentiating the "sound" from the "hearer" or the "sight" from the "seer," I could receive moments of 'hearing" and "seeing" as a merging of inner and outer worlds. As I regained a nourishing sense of immediacy, I could practice parenting myself instead of longing for external sustenance.

Epstein, however, cautions meditators not to use bare attention as a psychotherapy practice. Meditation can dissolve defensiveness and strengthen the ego, thereby promoting successful psychotherapy; but it alone does not solve emotional difficulties (Epstein, 1995, p. 135). For me, weathering my regression at Spirit Rock was aided by my years of intensive psychotherapy. With a series of skilled therapists, I had examined my family relationships and my early development until I had reached an adequate understanding about the formation and tendencies of my character. Through engaging in sessions of free association, I had developed a trustworthy observing ego, which served me well as I let go of my adult self during the retreat. But instead of simply following the common tendency of meditators to identify with the detached, observing self that is noting pain, I was also able to take personal responsibility for contributing to my own pain (Epstein, 1995, p. 137). Psychotherapy sessions had given me a capacity to view my parents as distinct persons with their own positive attributes and imperfections. I could move beyond blaming them for enjoying a delayed honeymoon without their firstborn baby.

Whatever traumatic events may have transpired, "it is the individual's mind that perpetuates the suffering, and that can be trained to change" (Epstein,

2001, p. 71). Both psychotherapy and meditation can aid mental development and promote a more balanced outlook on life. In the collection of verses called the *Dhammapada*, the Buddha taught this principle centuries ago: "We are what we think, having become what we thought." We can transform who we are by transforming how we think, but such change comes only with a disciplined mind. A related passage of the *Dhammapada* states the point:

> No hate can hurt, no foe can harm,
> As hurts and harms a mind ill disciplined.
>
> Neither father, mother, nor relative can help
> As helps a mind that is well disciplined
> (Dhammapada, trans. P. Lal, p. 50).

What Epstein considers truly therapeutic for most patients is not so much the re-construction of their past in order to explain their suffering, but the direct experience, in the therapist's presence, of the emotions, emotional thoughts, and their physical residue that have remained (Epstein, 1995, p. 192). From a parallel perspective as a meditation teacher, Charlotte Joko Beck describes the essence of Zen as learning how to "melt frozen blockage of the emotion-thought" (Beck, 1989, p.71). At Spirit Rock, I discovered that this kind of "melting" can occur just as readily during a prolonged Vipassana retreat as it does in a therapist's office. When I sensed my boundaries dissolving, I felt grateful for my formation as a music psychotherapist, because it gave me a context for what was occurring.

Like Mark Epstein, I argue that the combination of psychotherapy and meditation provides us with a promising path for self-knowledge. With Vipassana practice, I learned to detach my mind from problems instead of analyzing them. After years of focusing on my neurotic habits in therapy, it was a relief to be exposed to the Buddhist message that "there is more to the mind than just neurosis" (Epstein, 2005, p. 6). On retreat, I discovered the capacity for wisdom and compassion that I share with all human beings.

Therapeutic relationships are healing when patients trust the therapist neither to intrude nor to abandon them, but dedicated meditation practice heals by fostering an internal awareness that does not depend on interpersonal relationship (Epstein, 2005, p. 215). In psychotherapy, patients investigate early childhood experience not only to uncover unconscious drives, but also to understand the origins of reactive patterns that hide their true selves (Epstein, 2005, p. 214). Meditation, on the other hand, by training the mind to restrain its tendency to interfere or abandon, is, in Epstein's words, "an effort at re-parenting" (Epstein, 2005, p. 214). The meditator learns to be patient and accepting instead of avoiding what is unpleasant or grasping at what is pleasant. As Epstein says, "No longer struggling to find certainty in an endlessly shifting reality, a person grounded in her own awareness is free to discover and declare herself afresh as life unfolds" (Epstein, 2005, p.215). The two approaches can be complementary. At Spirit Rock I relied on groundwork from decades of psychotherapy and years of Vipassana practice as I stretched my consciousness and worked through blockages to freedom. Although the dharma teachers provided me with vital support, I had to take responsibility for learning to parent myself. In the process, I faced some of my neurotic habits, accepting them as a part of myself, and I emerged from the retreat with a capacity to live in a more authentic, spontaneous way.

In the midst of judging myself for being addicted to writing, I had a glimpse of what the Buddha experienced when he was at the point of starvation as an ascetic monk. After reflecting upon how much penance he had endured over the course of six years, he wondered if there might be another way to enlightenment. Suddenly he recalled a childhood incident when he was sitting comfortably in the shade of a rose-apple tree, "with happiness and pleasure born of seclusion." The Buddha realized that, with his ascetic efforts, he had lost a connection with the happiness of simply being. His childhood memory led him to the recognition that just being was the way to enlightenment. He wondered why people tend to be afraid of such pleasure. Then the Buddha had a crucial insight that there is pleasure in simply sensing and accepting reality. It is a pleasure not dependent on the gratification of desire. Following this reasoning, it makes no sense to avoid reality by either punishing oneself or grasping at pleasure. Happiness stems from relaxing into one's own being and opening to the world as it truly is (Epstein, 2005, p. 115). On retreat, I resonated with the Buddha's revolutionary discovery by finding an inner capacity for joyful experience in pure sensation. Joy came to me in the form of feeling vibrantly alive and grateful for each precious moment.

By following the Buddha's instructions about the value of self-reflection, I practiced viewing with kindness and gentleness the various traits that make up what I call "myself." For a period of time, I let myself fall into pieces, and I learned how to treasure each fragment. In his book *Going to Pieces Without Falling Apart*, Epstein refers to the Tibetan Buddhist tradition, which views moments of not knowing as opportunities for illumination (Epstein, 1998, p. 46). Great trust is required to let go, to relax the mind's vigilance, and to overcome the fear that imprisons us in what "we imagine is sanity" (Epstein, 1998, p. 47). According to Buddhist philosophy, the true nature of mind can shine only when we let down our defenses and flow naturally with life.

Before entering the retreat in 2003, I had adopted the prevalent view of Western psychologists that the self is an entity that must be developed and improved en route to separation and individuation (Epstein, 1998, p. 85). When my ego started to dissolve, I feared "going crazy" and initially resisted the inevitable melting process that was transpiring. But it was only through surrendering to the unknown that I could shake off the shackles of old habits and attitudes, accepting my unique way of unfolding in the universe. Now I find it reassuring to read Epstein's reminder that adults often drop their ego boundaries in pursuits such as creative work, listening to music, playing sports, and making love: "Rather than indicating a regression to infantile mental life, these experiences are expressive of a hidden capacity of the psyche that is available to us in all walks of life" (Epstein, 1998, p. 84). In the aftermath of the retreat, I am more apt to let myself enjoy such ordinary experiences of ego dissolution.

The ongoing practice of meditation seems to have trained my mind to open more easily to joyous activities and encounters. During the retreat, I was able to be more generous towards myself, less of a perfectionist. I no longer had to hold all the pieces of my life tightly together. As Epstein says about his own retreat experience, "my awareness was now stronger than my neurosis" (Epstein, 1998, p. 181).

Recent research seems to support the idea that meditation can actually change the neurology of the mind. Richard J. Davidson, a psychology professor who heads the Waisman Laboratory for Brain Imaging and Behavior at the University of Wisconsin at Madison, has been studying the brain wave patterns of long-term Tibetan Buddhist practitioners of meditation, comparing these patterns with those of a control group. His study, titled "Long-term meditators self-induce high-amplitude gamma synchrony during mental practice," was published in the *Proceedings of the National Academy of Sciences* of 2004. Davidson's research shows evidence that sustained meditation causes positive neural changes that influence cognitive and emotional patterns; in fact, eight monks with intensive "mental training" (from 10, 000 to 50, 000 hours of practice) demonstrated higher levels of compassion and calmness than ten "healthy student volunteers" (Smith, 2005, p. B10). Whether or not it produces neurological benefits, I am convinced that dedicated meditation practice has led to a healthier outlook and increased happiness in my own life.

Looking at my retreat experience from another angle, I am grateful for the expertise of my dharma teachers in supervising my descent into unfamiliar inner territory. As I review my evolving relationship with them, I am reminded of four stages of supervision outlined by Benedikte B. Scheiby, an analytic music therapy supervisor at Beth Abraham Hospital in New York City. Although he intends his schema to be applied to the formation of competent music therapists, I find his stages relevant in describing the relationship between a dharma teacher and relatively inexperienced meditators. Scheiby calls the first stage "tuning in and getting to know one another" (Scheiby, 2001, p. 322). In this introductory period, the supervisor seems like a parent or authority who gives didactic instruction and support, and the supervisee often experiences and expects a certain amount of dependency on the supervisor (Scheiby, 2001, p. 322). This description seems to fit particularly my relationship with Julie, whom I had met only in passing before the retreat. At Spirit Rock, she had very little time to interact with my adult side and did not know my background in psychotherapy before I plunged into a regressive state. Julie's manner of handling my lack of ego boundaries was to listen supportively and to give me clear instructions about how to take good care of myself. At this stage, I felt as dependent on her counsel as I did on Jack's more familiar way of helping me notice when my perceptions were distorted.

Scheiby's second stage of supervision is "working on improvement of skills and personal growth" (Scheiby, 2001, p. 322). At this point, issues of transference and countertransference, resistance, projection, and resonance arise between the supervisor and supervisee, and the supervisee is "given permission" to make mistakes and to learn from them (Scheiby, 2001, p. 322). During what I now consider the second period of the month-long retreat, I transferred behaviors and feelings, which had originally surfaced in relationship with my father and mother, onto my interactions with Jack and Julie. Because I felt an empathic resonance with both of my teachers, I was able to examine with them my attempts to be a "perfect daughter" and my impulsive "bad girl" side that lead me to break silence with Teja, upon whom I projected the role of a heroic spiritual warrior.

The third stage of supervision entails establishing identity and personal style and beginning the process of separation (Scheiby, 2001, p. 322). At this juncture, the supervisor facilitates the development of confidence in the supervisee, so that she can integrate her own inner authority. Any conflicts or transference and countertransference issues that arise between supervisor and supervisee are identified and addressed, and the supervisor takes a more challenging stance, while evaluating the progress and areas of need in the supervisee's work (Scheiby, 2001, pp. 322- 323). During what could be seen as the third period of my retreat, Jack and Julie encouraged me to work independently in my own room instead of attending communal sits in the meditation hall. I trusted my instincts, taking frequent soothing baths and to request art materials for the creative expression of my inner child. Jack began to challenge me to start preparing for the end of the retreat, and he gave me the assignment to walk to the Woodacre Deli for lunch. With that mission accomplished, I felt more confident about handling adult tasks in the world outside Spirit Rock.

Scheiby's fourth stage of supervision involves consolidating identity and style, as well as dealing with termination (Scheiby, 2001, p. 233). While being evaluated, the supervisee may act like a rebellious adolescent, rejecting the ideas and values of the supervisor, and power clashes may occur; at the same time, the supervisor supports the supervisee's autonomy and the development of an "internal supervisor," and the two parties relate increasingly as peers rather than as supervisor and supervisee (Scheiby, 2001, p. 323). It was at this juncture, close to the termination of the retreat, that I objected to Julie's implication that I was not ready to be a dharma teacher. As my ego regained control, I was weighing my career options and trying to decide how much of my time to devote to studying and teaching Buddhist philosophy. In retrospect, I recognize that Julie had witnessed primarily my childlike disintegration; unlike Jack, she had not glimpsed my more grown-up, competent characteristics. But at that moment, I was irritated by her dismissal of the hopes I was sharing about expanding my role as a Community Dharma Leader. Before the retreat's end, listening to Teja's inspirational musical accompaniment for Robert's poetry reminded me of my commitment and skill as a music therapist. I wanted to show Julie that I could relate to her as a professional adult. By the time I presented her with a card that contained a farewell poem, she and I were relating as peers, and she promised to read my journal notes about the retreat.

During this fourth stage, my relationship with Jack also went through a transformation. As I began to integrate the spiritual opening that had transpired, I entered into mature discussions with him about the implications in daily life of such expansive experiences. Returning to my rational self, I realized how much time Jack was spending on anti-war protests away from Spirit Rock, and I conferred with him about what might be the most skillful way for me to deal with my aversion to the invasion of Iraq by the United States. Before I left Spirit Rock, I resonated with my teacher's passionate efforts to promote peace, and I felt compassion for his limited power to effect the positive global changes that he visualizes. By then, I no longer viewed Jack as my ideal father figure, able to solve problems in my life and our society. During our farewell hug, I felt a mutual fondness and respect, and I sensed his trust that I would transmit the lessons of the retreat to my sangha in Mexico.

Philosopher and psychologist Ken Wilber sheds some light on the kind of expansive state that I entered near the end of the retreat. His book *Grace and Grit* describes the dying process of his wife Treya, who ended her life with an experience of mystical union. Wilber makes a distinction between the states of infantile fusion and mystical unity, and he explains that whereas infants are incapable of differentiating between subject and object, mystics not only are well aware of these conventional distinctions but also are aware of the "larger background identity that unites them" (Wilber, 2000, p. 187). While infantile fusion consists of merging at only a physical or sensorimotor level, a mystical union occurs at all levels of existence, including physical, biological, mental and spiritual (Wilber, 200, p. 187). Infants experience what Wilber terms "global undifferentiation" and cannot integrate what is not yet differentiated, but mystics bring things together into a higher integration (Wilber, 2000, p. 187). Wilber has coined the term *pre/trans fallacy* to refer to the common confusion between early developmental stages that are mostly "prepersonal" (because a separate and individuated personal ego has not yet evolved) and the highest "transpersonal" or "transegoic" stages that transcend the "personal" or "egoic" middle stage of growth (Wilber, 2000, p. 188). He warns that confusing prepersonal and transpersonal states leads either to inflating the infantile state into a mystical union that it does not possess or to denying all genuine mysticism by asserting that it is merely a regression to "infantile narcissism and oceanic adualism" (Wilber, 2000, p. 188). In retrospect, I believe that on the retreat I had some transpersonal experiences that evolved while I was integrating pre-verbal traumatic material.

Wilber asserts that meditation, unlike psychoanalysis, is not fundamentally an uncovering technique aimed at viewing one's shadow by clearing away veils of repression; instead, its primary goal is to suspend the ego's mental activity so that transpersonal awareness can develop, and eventually the observing Self or "Witness" can function unimpeded (Wilber, 2000, p. 195). Once the ego relaxes, a meditator can "rest as the Witness beyond the ego," simply observing whatever arises and falls away (Wilber, 2000, p. 196). But many meditators become proficient at bypassing the "repression barrier" and witnessing their neurosis without eliminating it (Wilber, 2000, p. 196). Occasionally, as the ego lets go, blockages to repression relax too, and the meditator must deal with the eruption of shadow material such as grief and anger (Wilber, 200, p. 196). In my case, this is precisely what transpired during my second week at Spirit Rock, when I had to face a dark part of my past that had been repressed for over five decades.

Like Epstein, Wilber claims that meditation and psychotherapy can work in a complementary fashion, but Wilber's argument is different—that the two approaches address different levels on the map he calls "the spectrum of consciousness." Meditation helps psychotherapy by revealing a "witnessing consciousness" that can view problems from a higher, more objective perspective; psychotherapy helps meditation by liberating consciousness from its repressions and complexes in the lower shadow realms (Wilber, 2000, p. 197). This theory helps explain why I sensed the benefits of *both* psychotherapy and meditation in my struggle to integrate what had occurred during the preverbal epoch in my life. At some points I regressed to prepersonal, infantile states, and at others I expanded into transpersonal, mystical experiences. My ego was suspended for days at a time, and I ricocheted between a babyish, undifferentiated sensorimotor world and a transegoic opening to a higher awareness. Just before the retreat ended, I was able to return to a personal, egoic level, but with less fear and greater understanding about other levels of consciousness.

Psychiatrist and Christian spiritual director Gerald G. May has yet another point of view about what constitutes a transpersonal "unitive" experience, which he considers a recognition of an essential truth that normally goes unnoticed (May, 1982, p. 37). He sees such experiences as a form of "infused" contemplation, which comes only by divine grace, unlike "acquired" contemplation, which stems partly from intention and personal effort (May, 1982, p. 37). Although I had been methodically practicing Vipassana meditation for weeks beforehand, when my spiritual opening occurred, it felt like an unexpected and effortless blessing.

May maintains that a full unity experience has two essential characteristics: "*all* self-definition is suspended and...awareness is clear and *wide open*, excluding nothing" (May, 1982, p. 37). In my case, I had a sense of myself rising above my body, dissolving, and expanding to be part of everything around me. Because the impression of an observing self never dropped away completely, May would not deem my process a true unity experience. Throughout my expansion, I was aware of my hand writing each observation as it was unfolding. May claims that in a genuine unity experience there is "*no* sense of self" and no blocking of perception nor focusing of attention on anything in particular (May, 1982, p. 37). Even if I cannot define my non-ordinary state of consciousness as a full-fledged unity experience, it provided me with a more encompassing view of how my life is interwoven with all creation. I suspended any sense of separation from the intricate mystery of divine order, and I was suffused with feelings of love and gratitude. Everything, including my particular being, which now seemed inextricably interconnected with its surroundings, felt imbued with holiness.

I agree with May that the importance of sublime experiences lies "not so much in their precise nature but in one's response to them," and that they can best be evaluated in relation to their fruits (May, 1982, p. 42). If an experience is divinely inspired, its benefits should become manifest in daily living; thus there is no need to pay special attention to particular spiritual phenomena. At Spirit Rock, Jack helped me to move beyond my interest in the drama and excitement of my expansive state and to stay open to the "mysterious wonder of the very existence of that phenomenon" (May, 1982, p. 43). He did not accept my description of what had transpired as "an enlightenment experience," and rightly observed that such a label freezes what could be an ongoing learning process. Once I let go of attempting to categorize my experience, I could be attentive to whatever life lessons could be gleaned from having been in transpersonal realms.

May warns about the danger of becoming fascinated with transcendent "experience-for-the-sake-of-experience," even at more advanced levels of spiritual practice (May, 1982, p. 47). Seekers who are not alert may become seduced by psychic or out-of-body experiences or by states of very high energy, thus developing "spiritual inflation" and considering themselves as "chosen" or "special." At several moments on the retreat, my body was surging with excess energy, and I had difficulty grounding myself; when my teachers suggested that I practice in my room instead of the meditation hall, I was tempted to think of myself as "especially sensitive." But, with Julie's soothing support and Jack's reasonable feedback, I was able to bring myself down to earth. In the final week of the retreat, I noticed that several other meditators—perhaps having experiences similar to mine—were doing self-retreats without following the regular schedule of sitting and walking periods. It was clear that I wasn't so special after all. By that time, I was tired of processing out-of-body insights, and I felt relieved to be "ordinary" once again, enjoying simple daily chores and encounters.

The process of spiritual awakening and growth is often associated with periods of extraordinary sexual passion, stemming from accessing a deeper capacity for love and from liberating energy that has been trapped in psychological blocks or attachments (May, 1982, p. 136). When enormous loving energy is surfacing, one tends to direct passionate emotions towards a person instead of riding the energetic surges alone (May, 1982, p. 136). A longing for spiritual unity may be displaced onto a relationship with a person as a substitute. What the psychologist Erich Fromm called the "fusion" of erotic experience can seem more enticing and less threatening than the transcendent "union" of spirituality, which demands greater self-sacrifice (May, 1982, p. 137). Although unaccustomed sexual urges may lead to feelings of guilt, denial, or repression, the loving energy associated with spiritual openings should be honored, while being channeled appropriately (May, 1982, p. 137). Human beings are sexual in essence and it is unproductive to deny or repress this dimension of living; an integration of sexuality is a crucial part of one's overall spiritual growth (May, 1982, p. 138). Sexual feelings can support spiritual growth if they are treated as "specifically channeled expressions of basic spiritual energy" (May, 1982, p. 142).

When I was at Spirit Rock, I focused some of my spiritual passion onto Teja, whose Qigong classes helped me channel extra psychic and physical energy. Even in the midst of my crush on him, I recognized that many of Teja's qualities that seemed so attractive were characteristics that I like in myself. He was reflecting aspects of my own self that I was not yet ready to integrate. I am thankful that Teja treated my open state with kindness and respect, without taking advantage of my childlike vulnerability. I could express my expansive sexual energy within a safe container. It was healing for me to converse with a man who was neither afraid of strong sexual vibrations in a relationship nor at the mercy of them. Because Teja did not exploit me when I was expressing passionate feelings, I could redirect my emotions to my own spiritual quest, and I could leave the retreat guilt-free. Back home, I could enjoy freer sexual energy in connection with deep love for my husband.

As I review these theories about trauma, psychotherapy from a Buddhist perspective, supervisory relationships, neurological changes via meditation, transpersonal psychology, spiritual direction, and sexuality, I realize that each one has illuminated a dimension of my process at Spirit Rock. During the retreat of 2003, intensive meditation evoked the unexpected opportunity to work through preverbal trauma in the midst of transpersonal states of consciousness. Since that time, I have read about related topics with a new level of understanding. Although Herman, Epstein, Davidson, Scheiby, Wilber, and May might seem to be addressing a wide range of disparate subjects, each author clarifies an aspect of my spiritual quest. I recognize that every step of my journey on the retreat had its history and followed a proper sequence. I was well prepared beforehand, with my background in psychotherapy, prior attendance at prolonged meditation retreats, and familiarity with non-ordinary states of consciousness in GIM sessions. Once on retreat, I navigated inner terrain with valuable support: skillful supervision from advanced dharma teachers, Teja's inspiring presence, and the safe container of Spirit Rock. My integration process has far outlasted the end of the month-long retreat. I am still reaping the benefits of the inner work that began there. ❧

EPILOGUE

T hroughout the year following the retreat of 2003, I detected a difference in the way I was handling daily life. I felt a new level of inner strength and confidence and a refreshing sense of trust in the universe. My habitual, restless impatience with slow-moving people and events seldom surfaced. My husband noticed that I listened to him more carefully and interrupted his comments less frequently. I was less resistant to taking good care of myself, napping when I felt tired and eating a more healthy diet with more regular meals. It was as if a missing piece had been restored within myself, so that I could flow more easily with whatever each day was offering me.

But the true test of the dependability and durability of these changes occurred when I returned to Spirit Rock Meditation Center for another month-long retreat, in March of 2004. When I arrived at the familiar gates, a surge of nervousness passed through my body. Questions and doubts besieged me. Would I fall to pieces again? Was my newfound inner security and tranquility just a temporary phenomenon? How could I face Teja after he had witnessed my vulnerability the previous year? Would Jack and Julie and the other teachers expect me to undergo another regression? I breathed deeply and resolved to trust my capacity to handle whatever experiences the retreat would provide.

As I arranged my belongings in the single room that had been assigned to me, I felt grateful for starting out in a private space. It seemed appropriate that I was returning to Upekkha (equanimity) dormitory. The name inspired me to try to act accordingly. With a mixture of hesitation and excitement, I took my seat in the meditation hall to hear the opening dharma talk. How satisfying to realize that I had not even considered bringing my journal and pen to write notes. I could listen with fuller attention, and with faith that the most pertinent teachings would be integrated into my life.

On the way out of the hall, Teja passed by and nodded at me with a friendly wink. My body contracted, and I turned away, deflecting his greeting. Images of our interactions from the prior retreat flashed through my mind. In Noble Silence it seemed impossible to convey to Teja how much I had processed since the last time he had seen me. Would he always consider me childlike and fragile? Even if we had been in circumstances where speaking was permitted, the task of reconstructing our friendship seemed too challenging to accomplish.

On the following day, I awoke feeling too anxious about encountering Teja to attend his pre-dawn Qigong class. Then the universe provided me with a perfect opportunity to move beyond any embarrassing memories about the previous year. I happened to enter the meditation hall lobby just as Teja was descending the stairs, after teaching in the upper walking meditation room. There was no way to avoid meeting face to face. Nobody else was around, and I bowed to him with a smile. He grinned and returned my bow. It was so simple. In that moment the tension dissipated, and I could relax and let go of the past, forgiving myself for having shown him my vulnerabilities. When I joined the next Qigong class, I noticed that the strong energetic charge I had felt with Teja in 2003 had dissipated. Exhaling with relief, I could focus on the art of Qigong rather than reacting to this particular teacher.

During the first week of sitting, I noted tightness in a band across my upper back at the level of the heart. It felt like a turtle shell protecting what my holistic healing teachers call the "heart's will center." Staying with the unpleasant sensation, hour after hour, I gained insight into how much I had been protecting myself from receiving love. An expert at *giving* love, I felt exposed and fragile when other people expressed their love for me. In such circumstances, I would lose my usual sense of being in control of emotional interactions. Sitting with this truth evoked tears. Weeping, I recognized that everyone who lives long enough to experience old age ends up like small, dependent children, needing to accept help. It seemed like a blessing to still have time to practice letting myself be loved and nurtured. During the previous retreat, Jack, Julie, and Teja taught me that it was fine to ask for support. It took me a year to realize that it was natural to have received their compassionate attention and assistance. There was no reason for me to feel any regrets. I could not expect to be always on the giving end of counseling. As I sat with these insights, an image surfaced of my dear friend Leena, tenderly nursing her deaf, senile, ninety-one-year-old father and giving his "little boy self" whatever he needed. I resolved to give my parents that same kind of loving attention, if necessary, and prayed that they would be able to receive my care. One of their legacies to me has been self-sufficiency. At Spirit Rock I was learning to let go of being in charge.

Aware of how much slower my mind and my pace was than the previous year, I was determined to practice patience as mindfully as possible. During most of the walking meditation periods, I paced slowly back and forth atop the wooden platform on the hillside behind the meditation hall. Around the forest platform, a whole world opened up to me. I felt content and joyous, sensing my bare feet on the rough boards, watching squirrels leap from tree to tree, and perceiving rainbow glints of sunlight on count-less cobwebs in the long, dewy grass. I delighted in observing ants parade in single file across my path and listening to wild turkeys "laugh" hysterically in the distance. In contrast to my tendency on the prior retreat, I did not try to filter or freeze my experiences by recording them in poetry. It felt good to let myself be touched by each fleeting sensory impression. I was learning how to fall into the unknown of the present moment and how to receive the unfamiliar pleasure of contentment.

Another lesson was swallowing my pride and facing bouts of fear. I con-fronted fears of the void, of being tiny in the vastness of the universe, of obsessive thoughts, and of going crazy. Unlike the year before, my tempo did not accelerate, and I did not dissociate or fall apart as waves of fright passed through me. This time I felt strong enough to stay present with what-ever scary thought was arising and to admit that there are times when I am frightened, just like everyone else. It helped me to see how I had habitually sped up my pace to avoid feeling scared. What a relief it was to care gently for the fearful, childlike side of myself. I recognized that this open and vulnerable side also enables me to experience wonder and delight. Little by little, I began to trust my capacity to hold a fuller range of emotions, while staying grounded. My practice was to pay close attention to my sensations: feet touching the boards of the platform, hands vibrating with energy, hair ruffling in light puffs of wind, skin absorbing warm sunlight, and the breath, breathing itself, in and out.

As I met my fears more honestly, my heart opened with compassion for all who suffer from trepidation. I set a clear intention to follow the truth of each moment, no matter how uncomfortable. It felt as if I were laying a foundation for being more fully present and patient in whatever I do. There seemed to be fewer impulses to run away from difficult emotions or to scatter my energy. One benefit of practicing self-restraint was enjoying the process of waiting for life to unfold. I was learning how to hold more paradoxes within myself, without needing to act quickly. My reward for cultivating calm and stillness inside was a new sense of aliveness and vibrancy.

My dream life was active on this retreat, and in the final week of silence the following dream affected me profoundly:

> *Mark and I visit my parent's home on Long Island. I try on one of my mother's cotton dresses, and I am surprised by how well it fits me. But in one pocket, I find a slimy, blackened wad of food that Mom had saved from a meal years ago. I wonder how she could have forgotten to clean out her pockets. I discard the rotten food and wash my hands. Then Mom informs me that she has just discovered termites on the walls of the bedroom I had used as a child. When I enter my old bedroom, I see thousands of termites swarming across the wooden beams of the ceiling. I realize that the structure of my childhood home is being eaten away. What had seemed like such solid support is now disintegrating. I am glad that my husband is with me to help with termite damage control. Mark and I go to an amusement park with his mother and his young niece. After the four of us ride a chairlift to a mountaintop to enjoy the view and then return to the base station, I feel ready to leave. But the little girl wants to ride to the top of the mountain again. Mark's mother says, "Let her enjoy herself as a child."*

A SILENT CURE

> *The young girl senses that she has permission to board the chairlift a second time. I watch her ascend, with her bare feet dangling from the aerial chair. Mark and I both attend to his mother's words. I long for private time alone with my husband so that we can catch up with each other.*

Relating this dream imagery to my daily life, I realized that I had been attending meditation retreats in order to "clean out my pockets" and to deal with undigested "meals" of past experiences. In Noble Silence I have been learning to face the impermanence of structures that used to seem solid and dependable. My inner child wanted to return to Spirit Rock for a "second ascent to the mountaintop," revisiting territory and mastering lessons that I had explored on the previous retreat. This time my bare feet were prepared to sense the ground beneath me. As I was letting go of past structures and reconnecting with childlike joy, I trusted that my husband was supporting my inner journey.

On the first day of spring another significant dream followed:

> *I am practicing for my wedding ceremony. I prepare each step with care, even trying on a rose-hued wedding gown, a soft, silky garment that hugs my body. A salesman tells me that at the end of the bridal ritual I will be awarded a taffeta dress that is valued at $10,000. I am not excited about receiving the extravagant dress. Instead, I am simply enjoying the process of practicing to be married. I realize that there is no groom. Marrying myself to life is the goal.*

The evening before this dream, I had climbed a hill to watch the sun go down. The sunset was slow to unfold, and, when it did, rosy streaks spread softly near the horizon. The colors were not dramatic or spectacular, but I found them exquisite. With reverence for the sacredness of this nightly event, I watched each subtle shift in hue until the first star appeared. This gentle, graceful unfolding seemed to be a metaphor for my own process on this retreat: leaving behind the drama and angst of the prior one, I was gradually grounding myself and preparing for a new stage of life in which my husband and I would be renovating an eighteenth-century adobe home in Cholula, Mexico.

In the closing interviews with my teachers, Jack and Julie each found a way to acknowledge my developing spiritual maturity. They shared my satisfaction with the emptiness of my journal and the fullness of my moment-to-moment connection with life. Because she had known me for such a brief time before the retreat of 2003, Julie was particularly impressed by the contrast between the volatile and explosive nature of our previous month together and the tranquility and self-containment of this one. It seemed as if I had earned my stay in Equanimity dormitory.

As the time approached to break silence, I felt nervous about emerging into the wide world outside of Spirit Rock. For weeks, the small, sturdy forest platform had been my classroom for educating myself to pause, wait, and receive life's mystery. On the final day of silence, I ventured forth on a strenuous hike up a steep, winding path to the summit of the highest hill overlooking the meditation center. This was the first time that I had climbed to this lookout point, and I congratulated myself on staying grounded all the way to the top. On the ascent, my shoes and socks were soaked in the tall, dewy grass; my leg muscles cramped with the strain of climbing; and I pulled on and off my jacket to adapt to unpredictable gusts of wind and periods of sunshine. The reward for my exertions was a stunning aerial view of Spirit Rock in one direction and of the distant, sapphire waters of San Pablo Bay in the other. Panting and trembling, I felt joyfully alive. Metaphorically, the hike represented my experiences on the entire retreat: while staying earthbound, I had been practicing pushing myself beyond previous limits, meeting moments of discomfort and pleasure with acceptance, and opening to whatever life offers.

At the end of this month of silence, I reflected upon the ways in which I felt freer and the ways in which I was still not liberated. I identified aspects of myself that I had not yet learned to treat with compassion, such as my habitual impatience and my tendency to plan more projects than I can accomplish. With gratitude, I remembered the nonverbal support of the Spirit Rock sangha. All of my fellow yogis had been trying their best to become conscious of obstacles to freedom. I felt ready to speak mindfully with other yogis, rehearsing for our interpersonal relationships at home. It seemed clear that those of us who take the time to meditate are doing personal and universal work simultaneously. We are exploring both psychological and spiritual realms.

Before descending from the summit, I prayed that I might bring back the wisdom of this retreat to my daily life, taking good care of myself, consciously tasting nourishing food, taking naps and resting sufficiently, pausing to sense touch points in my feet and hands, and settling into my life as it is. My hope was that I could forgive myself for any human imperfections and remember that life is perfect, with its ten thousand joys and ten thousand sorrows.

On these two prolonged meditation retreats, I had revisited and healed the wounds of preverbal trauma, and I had integrated previously disowned dimensions of myself. It was time to return home and to be of service to those suffering from unhealed wounds. With a mixture of confidence and humility, I could visualize transmitting some of my learning to the sangha that I lead in Mexico, to my music therapy students, and above all to my family and friends.

Beyond my personal circle, I envisioned the universal impact of dedicated meditation practice. In a world that is torn by greed, injustice, and power struggles, the consciousness that we yogis gained in Noble Silence could make a beneficial difference. I had faith that each of the eighty meditators leaving this retreat would shine a light of awareness on many other people. Our ongoing practice would add to the positive energy generated by nuns and monks and yogis in sanghas at all corners of the globe. The recognition that the whole of life is inextricably intertwined, an insight that we share with mystics from every religious tradition, would have a positive affect on interactions around the world. The peace that we had cultivated within ourselves, I remain convinced, would contribute to global harmony. So be it. ❧

BIBLIOGRAPHY

Beck, C. J. (1989). Everyday Zen: Love and work, ed. Steve Smith. San Francisco: Harper SanFrancisco.

Bhikkhu, T. (1998). Dhammapada: A translation. Barre, MA: Dhamma Dana Publications.

Brennan, B. (1988). Hands of light: A guide to healing through the human energy field. NY: Bantum Books.

Edwards, L. (2002). Body-oriented hypnotherapy: Releasing preverbal trauma. *The Australian Journal of Clinical Hypnotherapy and Hypnosis, 23* (1), 31-44.

Epstein, M. (2001). Going on being: Buddhism and the way of change. NY: Random House, Inc.

_____ (1998). Going to pieces without falling apart: A Buddhist perspective on wholeness. NY: Random House, Inc.

_____ (1995). Thoughts without a thinker. NY: BasicBooks.

Freud, S. (1922). "Beyond the pleasure principle," in *Standard Edition*, vol. 18. London: Hogarth Press, 1955.

Goldstein, J. (2002). One dharma. San Francisco: HarperCollins Publishers, Inc.

Grof, S. (1993). The holotropic mind. San Francisco: HarperCollins Publishers, Inc.

Hall, R. (2000). Out of nowhere: Poems from the inward journey. Healdsburg, CA: Running Wolf Press.

Herman, J. (1992). Trauma and recovery. NY: Basic Books.

Horowitz, M. (1986). Stress response syndromes. Northvale, NJ: Jason Aronson.

Kamenetz, R. (1994). The Jew in the lotus. NY: HarperCollins Publishers, Inc.

Lal, P., trans. (1967). "Mind," in the Dhammapada. NY: Farrar, Strauss & Giroux.

Levine, P. (1997). Waking the tiger. Berkeley, CA: North Atlantic Books.

Palmer, H. (1988). Enneagram: Understanding yourself and the others in your life. NY: HarperCollins Publishers, Inc.

Redpath, W. (1995). Trauma energetics: A study of hold energy systems. Barberry Press.

Rowan, J. (June, 1988). "Primal integration: Historical context and development in Britain," *Aesthema: International Primal Association Journal.*

Scheiby, B. B. (2001). "Forming an identity as a music psychotherapist through analytical music therapy supervisions," in Music therapy supervision, ed. Michelle Forinash, Gilsum, NH: Barcelona Publishers.

Siegel, D. (1999). The developing mind: Toward a neurobiology of interpersonal experience. NY: The Guilford Press.

Smith, L. E. (December 16, 2005). "In the lab with the Dalai Lama," *The Chronicle of Higher Education.*

Wilber, K. (2000). Grace and grit: Spirituality and healing in the life and death of Treya Killam Wilber. Boston, Shambhala Publications, Inc.

Winnicott, D. W. (1958). Birth memories, birth trauma, and anxiety," in Collected Papers: Through pediatrics to psycho-analysis. NY: Basic Books, pp.183-184.